The Story of Narrative Preaching

The Story of Narrative Preaching

Experience and Exposition
A Narrative

Mike Graves

CASCADE *Books* · Eugene, Oregon

Cascade Books
An Imprint of Wipf and Stock Publishers
199 W. 8th Ave., Suite 3
Eugene, OR 97401

www.wipfandstock.com

ISBN 13: 978-1-62032-873-6

Cataloguing-in-Publication Data

Graves, Mike.

    The story of narrative preaching : experience and exposition : a narrative / Mike Graves.

    x + 234 p. ; 23 cm. Includes bibliographical references.

    ISBN 13: 978-1-62032-873-6

    1. Narrative preaching. 2. Storytelling—Religious aspects—Christianity. I. Title.

BV4235.S76 G38 2015

Manufactured in the U.S.A.   02/26/2015

For Cassandra and Brock, and all the others—
my students, my teachers, my muses.

"Preaching should have of all things
the very closest relationship to existing."

—Søren Kierkegaard

Contents

Acknowledgments

For some reason this book took me longer than any of my others to write, and it's on *short* stories of all things. Don't ask me why; I can't explain it. What I can explain is how grateful I am to all who helped me on the journey. John Holbert got me started on the journey, although he probably doesn't know it. Back when he was teaching at the Perkins School of Theology in Dallas he wrote an exploratory article on preaching and short stories, a topic I don't think he ever came back to, and yet one from which I could not get away. Thanks, John.

After that, there was the invitation from Tom Long, whose homiletical fingerprints seem to be on everything I do. He asked me how I planned to spend my next sabbatical, and then graciously invited me to spend it at the Candler School of Theology in Atlanta. He, along with the staff, faculty colleagues, and the students, especially Samantha Lewis, were supportive beyond words. Sabbaticals are a gift, and this one was graciously granted by the board of trustees at the Saint Paul School of Theology, where I am privileged to serve with wonderful faculty colleagues and a gifted staff. Of course, I learned narrative preaching from Fred Craddock and Gene Lowry. Didn't we all?

Along the way there was a reading group with pastors who met to talk about the preaching values to be found in short stories, many of who served as cheerleaders to me, especially Robert Fugarino, Marcus McFaul, and Joanna Harader. My students were always an inspiration, partly because of the work they did but also the questions they asked. They kept me honest and practical. Two student assistants went the extra mile, and without them I don't think this work would have ever come to completion: Trista Sondker Nicholson and Michelle Byerly.

As always, nothing I do ever gets done without the support of my two best friends: David May and Lynn Horak. Lastly, I am forever grateful to my wife, Carol, who hesitated only briefly when I brought up a sabbatical in Atlanta while she kept things running on the home front in Kansas City. You are a gift of God.

Author's Note

All stories are true, which is not to say that all stories are factual. The events and characters in this story are part factual, part fictional. They are, however, completely true.

CHAPTER ONE

It Happened in Israel

It happened in Israel. Preachers are always saying that, right? Not in so many words, no; but in one way or another, yes. Maybe it's while telling the story of prophets pleading on behalf of God, or each spring describing Jesus riding into Jerusalem on a donkey. The Bible is chock-full of stories that happened in Israel, and so naturally preachers tell lots of stories that in one way or another begin, "It happened in Israel." Well, that's where this one begins as well.

My New Testament colleague and I led a ten-day trip to the Holy Land late last May. David had been many times before, including an extended stay one summer at an archaeological dig in Banias, also known as Caesarea Philippi at another point in its history. He wasn't exactly Indiana Jones, but he knew his way around. Me, this was my first trip, so I was more than a little nervous—not about the ongoing Middle East tension but about co-leading when I'd never been to Israel before. David told me to relax. He reminded me we had an excellent guide lined up, a Palestinian Christian, also by the name of David, and I had my colleague's experience to rely upon. "Besides," he kept telling me, "your job is preparing the sermons for our evening devotionals." We had talked about this numerous times and had agreed I would lead the devotional time at the end of each day—prayer, Scripture reading, brief sermon, and communion. Looking at the itinerary ahead of time, I had chosen the Scriptures for each day of the trip, jotted down some sermon ideas, and had planned on ad-libbing depending on what happened each day.

What I had never anticipated in the Holy Land, and if you've never been, there's just no way to plan for it, were the stark juxtapositions between the ancient and modern. They should warn you on the plane about the juxtapositions you will encounter. Shortly after reviewing safety procedures and how disabling smoke detectors is a felony, they should tell you about the juxtapositions. The contrast between ancient and modern is palpable, whether it be the architecture (Wailing Wall and Marriott Hotels), the clothing (tunics and Nikes), or any number of cultural customs too numerous to name. When you are in the Holy Land, you feel like any minute King David might issue an edict, and post it on the wall of his Facebook page no less, assuming the Wi-Fi is up and running.

On the third day of the trip two juxtapositions occurred. The first was seeing one of those wells so famously described in Scripture, like where Jacob first fell in love with Rachel, and where much later Jesus encountered the woman from Samaria. It's hard to conjure up images of these wells if you've never seen one firsthand. They look nothing like the kind where Timmy falls in and Lassie comes to the rescue, oaken bucket on a rope and pulley, pitched roof overhead. Nope, not even close. Jacob's well, or most any well in Israel for that matter, is a hole in the ground with a stone over it. You feel like you've stepped back in time. Only not exactly, because next to all these ancient wells there is usually a bucket like you'd find at Walmart, the brightly colored plastic ones kids use while digging on a beach in Florida. The ancient and modern side by side. That was the first juxtaposition.

The second juxtaposition happened later that afternoon. Tuesday evening I was going to preach from John 4, Jesus meeting the Samaritan woman at that well. The sermon was pretty much ready, inspired in part by a sermon I'd heard Gene Lowry preach years ago. But earlier that day a book fell out of my backpack while I was looking for my digital camera. A friend had given me a collection of short stories to read on the plane, even if I'd chosen to sleep on the cross-Atlantic flight instead. She said it was the kind of book I'd love, stories that preachers would find interesting. Those were her words, "stories that preachers would find interesting."

Of course I find stories interesting—I'm a preacher—and different kinds of stories, too. I like the stories my granddad used to tell about his childhood in Canada. I like the ones my friends and I told around campfires when we were kids, trying to scare each other. Even as an adult, I still like fables from different cultures. I love a good novel, even if I usually only get around to novels during the summer. I wish I could say I like the illustrations preachers tell, and some of them I do; but far too often the stories preachers tell are as weak as chicken broth compared to chicken soup. Don't even get me started on *Chicken Soup for the Preacher's Soul* or whatever volumes are out there. So often, preacher's illustrations don't measure up. The idea that this was a book of "stories that preachers would find interesting" didn't really excite me. So that day in Israel I flipped it open to the table of contents with a healthy dose of cynicism. The name Alice Walker caught my eye, the author of the novel *The Color Purple*. Only this was a short story called "The Welcome Table." My cynicism melted in minutes.

Words cannot describe what happened to me on that sunny afternoon in Israel as I read Walker's story. I took the book and went across the street, where I sat outside a little café called Hillel, named after one of Israel's great rabbis who even influenced Jesus. I ate falafel but devoured Alice Walker's story. Other than the Gospel stories, I had never read anything quite so powerful and so brief at the same time. Dynamite in small packages, right?

Then it happened, right there in Israel. Walker's story, it seemed to me, was a modern-day woman at the well story. Not exactly, of course. Nothing is ever exactly the same, but this short story was definitely in the same spirit as John's story. So I decided to retell the two stories as part of my evening sermon. I would put them together like the plastic bucket next to an ancient well. If I had had the time, I would have typed out the sermon at a nearby Internet café, but I reconstructed it later and preached a similar version in the States. On that spring day in Israel, the sermon went something like this:

> Did you hear John's opening lines, "He left Judea and started back to Galilee. But he had to go through Samaria"? It doesn't sound like much on the surface, certainly not Pulitzer Prize material, but it is a masterful opening.
>
> After the last couple of days, our Mediterranean geography is greatly improved, so I probably don't have to remind you that Judah is in the south, Galilee in the north, and back then Samaria was right between them. Of course Jesus had to go through Samaria. I mean, back home in the Midwest if you want to drive from Iowa to Arkansas, chances are good you'll pass through Missouri.
>
> Only Jesus didn't *have to* go through Samaria. Some Jewish travelers did, but many went around. As you well know, Samaritans were considered the lowlifes of society by the Jews. The rabbis said, "Better to eat the flesh of swine than to eat Samaritan bread." So when John says Jesus "had to," he's not talking geography, but theology. Jesus had to because there was someone there, someone looking for water. Here's the story.
>
> Jesus and his disciples journeyed until they came upon a sleepy little town called Sychar. (That's not on our itinerary, in case you're wondering.) It was not exactly a tourist spot, although it was the place where Jacob's well was located, and travelers were always looking for water. Jesus sat down at the well, when a woman from the village came out to draw water. Jesus

then struck up a conversation, asking for a drink. The woman was shocked that a Jewish man would even speak to her.

And so was John. Did you notice? John practically sticks his head out of the curtain and interrupts the story. He does. There in parentheses, John tells his readers, "Jews do not share things in common with Samaritans," only I think he's screaming it: "Jews Do Not Share Things In Common With Samaritans!" John seems to say, "Can you believe this?"

Not only is she a Samaritan. She's a she, and the first century was a man's world. One rabbi claimed, "Better to bury the Torah than entrust it to a woman." You saw the movie *Yentl*, didn't you? Not only is she a Samaritan and a she, this woman has been married five times. But before you jump to conclusions, may I remind you that women could not file for divorce in this ancient culture. This woman has been abandoned five times. That's why she draws water at noon, not morning or evening with the other women. She has been shunned. And Jesus strikes up a conversation about water.

I really like what John has done here in how he tells the story, and the best way I know to get at that is through an analogy with da Vinci's famous Mona Lisa. As a friend of mine who teaches art history once showed me, you have to look in the background. Da Vinci was enamored with the Alps, only they are in the background of his painting. Those glorious mountains pale in comparison to Mona Lisa.

That's what John does here, and what we see in the background is Nicodemus. Get it? In chapter three we have the story of this man—a Jewish man, with a distinguished name and religious credentials. But he fades into the background here as we behold this nameless Samaritan woman who has suffered much.

And Jesus seeks her out. Nicodemus sought Jesus, but Jesus sought this woman. He *had to* go through Samaria. Not because he wanted a drink from Jacob's well. No, because he wanted to give her a drink. He calls it living water, not the wet stuff in her bucket but the kind of drink that satisfies so you never thirst again.

You know what kind of drink she wants, don't you? Same kind we do when life is hard and we feel isolated and lonely. Same kind of drink we need at the graveside of a loved one, driving home after yet another funeral. Or waiting for the results of that biopsy. Or after discovering you have just been laid off. Same kind of drink that brought us to Jesus in the first place. It's the water of life, real life. Anybody here feeling parched?

The disciples were shocked when they found Jesus talking with this woman, but I imagine John's readers were even more shocked. Do you know why? Because they had heard this story before. And so have you. You know, the story about Jacob meeting Rachel at this very well, and marrying her. It is a common theme in biblical stories. As sure as "Once upon a time" alerts us to fairy tales, stories of a man meeting a woman at a well signaled betrothal. Courtship. Marriage. Get it? Jesus comes in an intimate yet appropriate way to this lonely woman, offering her living water. And what a powerful story!

It reminds me of a story Alice Walker tells, called "The Welcome Table." Walker is best known for her novel *The Color Purple*, which is how I first learned about her. But I've just discovered this short story by her, and "The Welcome Table" is equally powerful. It's the story of a woman, nameless and black, whom Walker describes as "the color of poor gray Georgia earth, beaten by king cotton and the extreme weather."

On this particular fine Sunday morning she starts off to worship at the big white church down the road, a church that is white in many ways. The good religious folks are shocked when she appears. The reverend kindly reminds her this is not her church, as if one could choose the wrong church. The young usher tries as well to persuade her to leave, but she has come to worship God. Finally, the respectable ladies have had enough, and their husbands hurl the poor woman out onto the porch.

She is speechless. Only moments ago she was worshiping God. Then something happens. Listen to how Walker describes it: "She started to grin, toothlessly, with short giggles of joy, jumping about and slapping her hands on her knees. And soon it became apparent why she was so happy. For coming down the highway at a firm though leisurely pace was Jesus." As he approaches, he says, "Follow me," and without hesitation, she joins him there on the road, although she has no idea where they are headed. She hums. She sings. She tells Jesus all about her troubles. He smiles. Listens and smiles, and the two of them walk on until the ground beneath their feet gives way to clouds and she is truly home! Never alone! Never hungry! Never thirsty!

What a powerful story! Although the title seems odd, "The Welcome Table." There's no table in the story, not a single mention of a table. For that matter, there's no table in this Gospel story either. Or maybe there is in both stories. Maybe everywhere Jesus goes there is a table. Maybe everywhere that people know pain and great thirst, there is a table with water on it, and wine and bread. And at this table Jesus smiles. Smiles and listens. Amen.

We sat there in silence for a minute or two, and then had communion. I did something similar the next day, and every day after that. I was hooked. One evening I paired Jesus' temptation story with Stephen King's "The Man in the Black Suit." Yes, that Stephen King, only this is such a departure from his norm. I paired Peggy Payne's "The Pure in Heart" with the burning bush in Exodus. You get the idea.

The people loved the sermons, or maybe it was the rush that comes from traveling through Israel, but these experiments in narrative juxtaposition were powerful, especially for me as the preacher. I couldn't wait to read another story each day, to pair it with a text, and share it with our group. I figured out fairly quickly that not every short story out there will preach, but a lot of them do.

On the plane ride home, a day that never seems to end, I devoured several more short stories. After finishing "A Father's Story" by Andre Dubus, a story that defies explanation, I told David, "These things are modern narrative sermons. Not all of them, but many of them for sure. They are powerful beyond description." He looked up from the book he was reading and smiled. I remembered how Fred Craddock compared narrative sermons to short stories, calling them cousins. I closed the book and my eyes, and began to think about the course I would be teaching the following spring semester, an elective on narrative preaching. I said, "David, sorry to keep interrupting. But what do you think about a course on narrative preaching that uses modern short stories paired with biblical stories?"

He said, "Dr. Freeman, I think if the idea excites you, it has a better chance of exciting your students. And we all know how important that is. That's what I think."

Even if he had thrown water on the flames of my little Pentecost, I'm pretty sure I would have plunged ahead anyway. So that's what happened, and as I said, it happened in Israel. Even on that flight I knew that one of the first things I would do in that class would be to pass out copies of Walker's short story. Turns out, I passed out several short stories that semester. I thought these stories might be just the antidote for so much dry preaching I'd been hearing lately. Turns out, they were only part of the big picture of my rethinking of narrative preaching.

CHAPTER TWO

Shedding the Veil

The first day of the spring semester I announced, "Finally, a preaching course with the perfect number of students." They assumed I meant seven as in the number for God, and that's partly what I meant. But in the past I'd had so many elective courses in which there were too many students for us to be intimate—seventeen or eighteen, sometimes twenty or more. Deans and registrars like big classes; and I like students, too, don't get me wrong. But in my experience preaching electives are best when smaller. This time around six would have been fine, even eight, maybe nine. The course just needed to be intimate.

PRE 430, "The Story of Narrative Preaching," is a class I teach every couple of years or so, but never before like this. Every time I taught the course previously there was a slightly different focus, enough so that I'd had one or two students take it more than once. This time the lens would be short stories. I did a lot of reading after the trip to Israel, and I was convinced that short stories and narrative preaching really were cousins. Authors such as John Updike and Flannery O'Connor who weren't narrative preachers in the strictest sense but whose stories have deep resonances with the gospel, would join the likes of Barbara Brown Taylor, Gene Lowry, and Tom Long in teaching us how to preach narratively.

Reading great literature—short stories or otherwise—struck me as an endeavor requiring intimacy, so seven really was the perfect number. I thought the course should be intimate as well, including the space. The registrar had assigned us a room that would work, but it wasn't ideal. For starters, it had fluorescent lights, the standard of academia everywhere. If possible, no one should read Scripture and literature under those glowing

7

tubes; chemistry textbooks maybe. The room was also more traditional in layout, rows of chairs facing a desk up front. If I had my way, we would be meeting at the Starbucks down the street, that little nook in the corner by the fireplace, the one with plump leather chairs, and the kind of place where you keep bumping into humanity in all its glory. There were a few windows in the classroom, not enough for sure, and many of them hazy between the panes of glass. In the winter they looked warm and cozy, but other times of the year they looked in need of repair.

Short of meeting in a coffee shop, I thought the perfect room on campus was one of those private conference rooms in the library. With some persuading, we were allowed to switch. The McElvaney Conference Room is appointed with a gorgeous oak table with space for a dozen or so folks, and comfortable armchairs on wheels. Even the carpet gives the room a degree of warmth. I think it's one of the breakout spaces the board of trustees uses when meeting on campus. At the head of the room a thin wooden cabinet is mounted, opening up to reveal a whiteboard and markers. If it were in someone's finished basement, it would contain a dartboard. On the opposite wall a nicely framed commemorative poster celebrates the illuminated St. John's Bible. Floor-to-ceiling windows make up the wall on the left, with a view of the seminary's prayer garden, and beyond that some woods. The wall on the right features two Vincent Van Gogh prints, both of them variations on sunflowers. Between the two prints a plaque gives the name of each piece, as well as a quote by Van Gogh, who started out as a minister himself: "This much I want to tell you—while painting, I feel a power of color in me that I did not possess before, things of broadness and strength." That seemed like a good thought for budding preachers—broadness, strength, and beauty. I told my students how lucky we were, that environment isn't everything but it counts for a lot when thinking about literature and Scripture, or preaching for that matter. I said, "If we weren't in a library, I'd have candles on the table."

"Fat chance, but how about wine and cheese?" joked Cassandra.

"Now that would be perfect," I said. The students knew alcohol isn't allowed on campus at the Saint Paul School of Theology, but I teased them that we might just have to meet at a restaurant from time to time, where drinks and good food could help with ambiance. Everyone looked pleasantly surprised, like this could be a very different seminary experience. And that was precisely my hope. I think narrative sermons should be a very different experience as well.

As we got underway I said, "Before we get to the syllabus and assignments, it would be helpful to hear each other's stories, especially in relation to narrative preaching and literature since that will be the lens by which we look at narrative preaching this semester. I realize most of you know each other but not necessarily all that well. One of my preaching professors used to say that critiquing each other's sermons is like looking through a person's underwear drawer." A few of them giggled nervously.

I said, "If that's true of sermons, it's equally true of talking about literature and how you feel about it. We have to trust each other. As you introduce yourselves, say something about your relationship with narrative preaching and your relationship with literature. Or maybe another way to say it, using Facebook lingo, what's your status with preaching and literature?" Cassandra was the first person to my left, a beautiful young woman of Egyptian descent, and always dressed to the nines. I said, "Why don't you start us off?"

She sat even more upright and said, "I'm Cassandra Samir. As some of you know, my parents moved from Cairo to Peoria, Illinois, shortly before I was born. We are a Christian family from many generations back, and we find the United States an accepting place for the most part. I attended the University of Illinois, where I majored in English." A few of her peers mumbled how that's not fair. She laughed it off. "I love literature, especially poetry and short stories." Before I could say anything or put a star by her name in the grade book, she added, "Preaching and sermons, however, scare the bejesus out of me." Everyone laughed a knowing laugh.

I said, "Preaching and fear do seem to go hand in hand, which probably explains why the first words of Easter—even before the good news of Christ's resurrection—are 'be not afraid.'" They had heard me say this in a previous class, I was sure, but some messages should be repeated regularly.

Joey Lawson, who was seated next to Cassandra, cleared his throat. His OU Sooners cap sat backwards on his head. Joey is not only a sports fan but also an athlete himself, even if slight in stature. He said, "I'm not gonna lie. This class fit my schedule. I've already had my New Testament elective, which meets at the same time, so it was this or watch ESPN on Thursday evenings."

"You mean my class beat out your Sooners?"

He said, "Something like that, I guess." He told us that he was serving a small rural church near the little town of Kearney, on the Missouri side of the state line, so preaching had become an every-week kind of thing. Newly minted ministers often find that a sobering experience. Joey admitted he liked preaching but also that he was highly skeptical of using short stories in sermons. He was not alone.

Next was Lisa, who grew up in Kansas and majored in art history at the University of Kansas. A small-framed young woman, she struck me as someone who had yet to tap into her artistic flair for homiletical purposes, like she was still trying to mimic the male pastors she'd grown up hearing. A

year earlier, in the introductory course, I had them do an informal assignment of sorts, the completion of a sentence, "To me, preaching a sermon is
like . . ." I noted how it's both personal ("to me") and metaphorical ("is like").
I also told them it could be the kind of assignment that takes a lifetime to
complete. Lisa had shared, "To me, preaching a sermon is like leading a
Bible study." It was a fine enough answer, I guess, but I couldn't help thinking she had more to offer.

She said, "My name is Lisa Stewart, and I'm in my final semester." A
mixture of cheers and boos went up. "Yeah, I had to throw that in. I don't
know if I'm a narrative preacher or not. I'm not sure I'm really a preacher for
that matter. I like stories in general, although I don't know if I've really read
any short stories per se. But I'm intrigued by the course." She looked down
nervously, or it felt that way to me.

At the opposite end of the table sat Carlos Alvarez, and to his left, his
wife Rosa. They are originally from Guatemala, but were serving an inner-
city mission in a largely Hispanic part of Kansas City. Carlos said he knew
a great place on Southwest Boulevard where we could eat enchiladas and
drink margaritas for one of our "field trips." Rosa added, "Our real passion,
besides food, is justice ministries." As I recall, Rosa didn't say much of anything about preaching or literature, although Carlos stressed the centrality
of the Bible and wanting to be better at proclaiming the word of God.

Seated next to Rosa was Brock Parker. He is a second-career seminar-
ian, originally from Texas, which annoyed the Sooner Joey right off. Brock
smiled but said he didn't really care about sports. He is a heavy-set fellow,
who was a truck driver for the first half of his life. He said the only thing
harder than the asphalt was life itself, which sounded to me like the chorus
to a country and western song. Brock said he'd been divorced twice, and
was now living in a double-wide trailer in the country where his grandkids
from the first marriage sometimes came to visit. "I love preaching God's
word. Anybody that knows me knows that. And I like stories, just about any
stories. My daddy used to say we are story animals. I don't know anything
about literature, but I'm willing to give it a try. Can't hurt."

The last person was Alesha Phipps, an African American woman
originally from Georgia who moved to Kansas City during high school.
Alesha sometimes wears those brightly colored clothes that remind you of
Africa, and her eyeglasses remind you of Spike Lee. Everyone on campus
knew Alesha, partly because of her work on behalf of LGBT persons but
also because of her warm personality. "Hey, everybody. My name is Alesha,
and Dr. Freeman doesn't know this, but I always wanted to be a writer." She
smiled. I smiled. She said, "Alice Walker is my hero, and I'm so excited about
this semester."

I was thrilled because the last testimony was positive. If a skeptic went last, I would have been tempted to start with apologetics, trying to convince them that sermons and short stories really are cousins. But I wanted to woo them at first, the way literature woos readers and narrative sermons can woo listeners.

I said, "So, I guess it's my turn. What do I bring to a class on narrative preaching, especially one using short stories to help us out? Probably not what you think. I'll share more of my journey into narrative preaching later, but for now my journey with literature, and this is a new thing for me in some ways. I was not exactly an English major back in college. That's an understatement. If confession is good for the soul, then here is mine when it comes to reading literature. I did not read what was assigned in high school." No one seemed alarmed or shocked. "I know, big deal, right? Actually, it turned out to be a big deal. As a child, I read Dr. Seuss feverishly, but by the time high school rolled around, I was no longer interested in literature. Girls and cars, yes; literature, no. Simply put, in high school I did not read."

Joey interrupted, "I can relate to that, dude." He is still the only seminary student I've ever known who called professors "dude," the male ones anyway. I couldn't imagine what he called his female professors.

I smiled and continued. "The one assignment I vividly recall is F. Scott Fitzgerald's *The Great Gatsby*, which I never even cracked open." I was not smiling as I shared this with the class, although several of them seemed to appreciate picturing their professor as a delinquent student back in the day. I said, "These being pre-Internet days, I did what all lazy students did back then, I looked at *Cliff's Notes* and faked it. Hopefully, I did a better job of faking it than the student I heard about who turned in a report on the book *Seagull*, by Jonathan Livingston." I realized even this literary reference may have been lost on them.

"True, these days I read lots of novels and poetry, and of course, short stories. But that wasn't always the case. I still remember the professor in seminary who told us that reading is good for the soul, even when what you're reading doesn't make its way into the sermon. Twenty years ago I thought that was crazy, and now I regard it as some of the best advice for staying alive in ministry: read, read, read!" I continued, "One other confession. Years ago I was reading an essay by Frederick Buechner. Do you know that name?"

Lisa and Cassandra both acted as if it sounded familiar. I said, "He's a Presbyterian minister who was nominated for a Pulitzer Prize in literature for one of his novels. Anyway, he's also an essayist, and in this particular piece he refers to a scene from one of his favorite novels, Graham Greene's *The Power and the Glory.*"

Cassandra said, "I definitely know that novel, about the whiskey priest. Amazing."

I agreed, and then added, "At the time I had never read Greene's novel, but the scene Buechner described seemed like a good fit for the sermon I was working on at the time. I didn't have time to read the novel. Sunday was coming! Ah, the demon of 'no time.' I retold the scene in my sermon, careful not to say I had read the novel, although I'm sure I implied I had. If anyone had asked, I would have told the truth, that I found the reference elsewhere and that I hadn't yet read the book myself.

"Looking back on that event, I am haunted. I wouldn't call my actions unethical; more like pitiful. All these years after that high school book report and that later sermon, I realize a lot of things I didn't know at the time, and not just about cheating or borrowing but more than anything that literature is good for the soul, too. And this is one of the biggest things threatening preachers, dried-up souls. As the American novelist William Burroughs put it, 'Cheat your landlord if you can and must, but do not try to shortchange the Muse. It cannot be done. You can't fake quality any more than you can fake a good meal.'"

Cassandra said, "Wow, that's a great quote. Can you repeat that?"

I did, and added, "Nowadays, I read literature as an attempt to make up for lost time, but more than that, to stay alive. And that is what I hope happens to you during this semester. By the way, I agree with Buechner, Graham Greene's novel is one of my favorites, too. More of that stuff later. The truth is, however, I didn't really recognize the power of short stories for preaching until just this last year on a trip to the Holy Land. Perhaps I'll tell you later what happened there.

"Before we look at the syllabus, one more thing. I'd like for our devotions each week to include not only a passage of Scripture but an excerpt from a literary memoir published a few years back." So I began with some verses from Exodus 35, in which the very same artisans who contribute to the building of the Tabernacle are also inspired to teach, the idea being that teaching and preaching constitute art forms just as much as designing jewelry and other crafts. That still fascinates me.

Then I told them about one of the most amazing books on reading that I've ever encountered. Azar Nafisi's *Reading Lolita in Tehran* is lyrical at times. Vladimir Nabokov's classic novel *Lolita* is about an older man who has illicit relations with a younger girl. The antagonist owns *Lolita.* But Nafisi's work is a kind of commentary on the novel, about what it means to read *Lolita* in another context. She shows how sex isn't the real issue, but power.

I explained, "*Reading Lolita in Tehran* is Nafisi's memoir of teaching Western literature at two different universities in Iran, all of this during the fundamentalist Islamic regime change when the authorities tried to own the people. The powers did not look favorably on Nafisi teaching Western literature, and especially to women. The book celebrates how the best literature sets us free. It's hard to read a memoir out of context, but I'm going to try to find excerpts for each week of the semester.

"This particular passage refers to a clandestine meeting the professor had every Thursday with seven women enrolled in the class." I took a sip of my hot tea and cleared my throat. I looked around to see how many caught the parallels, seven of us meeting on a Thursday. I could tell some got it, but with others I was not so sure. "So listen to her description of two very different photographs and what they symbolize:

> I have the two photographs in front of me now. In the first there are seven women, standing against a white wall. They are, according to the law of the land, dressed in black robes and head scarves, covered except for the oval of their faces and their hands. In the second photograph the same group, in the same position, stands against the same wall. Only they have taken off their coverings. Splashes of color separate one from the next. Each has become distinct through the color and style of her clothes, the color and length of her hair; not even the two who are still wearing their head scarves look the same.

> For nearly two years, almost every Thursday morning, rain or shine, they came to my house, and almost every time, I could not get over the shock of seeing them shed their mandatory veils and robes and burst into color. When my students came into that room, they took off more than their scarves and robes. Gradually, each one gained an outline and a shape, becoming her own inimitable self. Our world in that living room with its window framing my beloved Elburz Mountains became our sanctuary, our self-contained universe, mocking the reality of black-scarved, timid faces in the city that sprawled below.

> The theme of the class was the relation between fiction and reality.

I said, "Isn't that a beautiful image, shedding their robes and bursting into color? That's my hope for us this semester, that the stories we read will set us free and help us to preach a gospel that sets others free." I could sense that a few of them were already inspired, or so I hoped. We prayed, and then got down to the business at hand.

Of course, there's nothing like working through a syllabus to bring folks back to reality. I had the usual list of course objectives, and then some. The usual list read:

a.) Students will learn to appreciate:

- a theology of story

- the narrative quality of Sacred texts

- the sacred nature of short stories

- the theological content of preaching

b.) Students will learn how to:

- read Sacred texts and sacred stories more closely

- pair sacred stories with Sacred texts

- retell these stories and texts more powerfully

- craft sermons that are expositional as well as experiential

The last item under each point was important, even if seemingly separate from the use of short stories. One of the things narrative preaching has been good at is helping listeners *experience* biblical texts and the gospel message, but it's been less than stellar at *exposition* of those texts, exegetically and theologically. This would be an important part of the course as well.

But the lines before these objectives were what I really wanted to high-light on this first night:

1.) That our lives are changed by an encounter with the truth of Sacred texts and sacred stories

2.) That our preaching is changed by telling the truth of these stories more powerfully and deeply

I had never dared to print such things before in a syllabus, even if it ex-pressed my hopes. Who could imagine a preaching course actually chang-ing someone's life? Naturally, I could since it happened to me years before and still did on some occasions.

I said, "Of course, nothing is better than reading actual stories. Before we take a break, I'd like you to read this story by Alice Walker, 'The Welcome Table.'" Alesha was beaming with excitement. "After the break we'll discuss it."

"The Welcome Table"
By Alice Walker

For Sister Clara Ward

I'm going to sit at the Welcome table
Shout my troubles over
Walk and talk with Jesus
Tell God how you treat me
One of these days!
—Spiritual

The old woman stood with eyes uplifted in her Sunday-go-to-meeting clothes: high shoes polished about the tops and toes, a long rusty dress adorned with an old corsage, long withered, and the remnants of an elegant silk scarf as headrag stained with grease from the many oily pigtails underneath. Perhaps she had known suffering. There was a dazed and sleepy look in her aged blue-brown eyes. But for those who searched hastily for "reasons" in that old tight face, shut now like an ancient door, there was nothing to be read. And so they gazed nakedly upon their own fear transferred; a fear of the black and the old, a terror of the unknown as well as of the deeply known. Some of those who saw her there on the church steps spoke words about her that were hardly fit to be heard, others held their pious peace; and some felt vague stirrings of pity, small and persistent and hazy, as if she were an old collie turned out to die.

She was angular and lean and the color of poor gray Georgia earth, beaten by king cotton and the extreme weather. Her elbows were wrinkled and thick, the skin ashen but durable, like the bark of old pines. On her face centuries were folded into the circles around one eye, while around the other, etched and mapped as if for print, ages more threatened again to live. Some of them there at the church saw the age, the dotage, the missing buttons down the front of her mildewed black dress. Others saw cooks, chauffeurs, maids, mistresses, children denied or smothered in the deferential way she held her cheek to the side, toward the ground. Many of them saw jungle orgies in an evil place, while others were reminded of riotous anarchists looting and raping in the streets. Those who knew the hesitant creeping up on them of the law, saw the beginning of the end of the sanctuary of Christian worship, saw the desecration of Holy Church, and saw an invasion of privacy, which they struggled to believe they still kept.

Still she had come down the road toward the big white church alone. Just herself, an old forgetful woman, nearly blind with age. Just her and her eyes raised dully to the glittering cross that crowned the sheer silver steeple. She had walked along the road in a stagger from her house a half mile away. Perspiration, cold and clammy, stood on her brow and along the creases by her thin wasted nose. She stopped to calm herself on the wide front steps, not looking about her as they might have expected her to do, but simply standing quite still, except for a slight quivering of her throat and tremors that shook her cotton-stockinged legs.

The reverend of the church stopped her pleasantly as she stepped into the vestibule. Did he say, as they thought he did, kindly, "Auntie, you know this is not your church?" As if one could choose the wrong one. But no one remembers, for they never spoke of it afterward, and she brushed past him anyway, as if she had been brushing past him all her life, except this time she was in a hurry. Inside the church she sat on the very first bench from the back, gazing with concentration at the stained-glass window over her head. It was cold, even inside the church, and she was shivering. Everybody could see. They stared at her as they came in and sat down near the front. It was cold, very cold to them too; outside the church it was below freezing and not much above inside. But the sight of her, sitting there somehow passionately ignoring them, brought them up short, burning.

The young usher, never having turned anyone out of his church before, but not even considering this job as *that* (after all, she had no right to be there, certainly), went up to her and whispered that she should leave. Did he call her "Grandma," as later he seemed to recall he had? But for those who actually hear such traditional pleasantries and to whom they actually mean something, "Grandma" was not one, for she did not pay him any attention, just muttered, "Go 'way," in a weak sharp *bothered* voice, waving his frozen blond hair and eyes from near her face.

It was the ladies who finally did what to them had to be done. Daring their burly indecisive husbands to throw the old colored women out they made their point. God, mother, country, earth, church. It involved all that, and well they knew it. Leather bagged and shoed, with good calfskin gloves to keep out the cold, they looked with contempt at the bloodless gray arthritic hands of the old woman, clenched loosely, restlessly in her lap. Could their husbands expect them to sit up in church with that? No, no the husbands were quick to answer and even quicker to do their duty.

Under the old woman's arms they placed their hard fists (which afterward smelled of decay and musk—the fermenting scent of onion skins and rotting greens). Under the old woman's arms they raised their fists, flexed their muscular shoulders, and out she flew through the door, back under the cold blue sky. This done, the wives folded their healthy arms across their trim middles and felt at once justified and scornful. But none of them said so, for none of them ever spoke of the incident again. Inside the church it was warmer. They sang, they prayed. The protection and promise of God's impartial love grew more not less desirable as the sermon gathered fury and lashed itself out above their penitent heads.

The old woman stood at the top of the steps looking about in bewilderment. She had been singing in her head. They had interrupted her. Promptly she began to sing again, though this time a sad song. Suddenly, however, she looked down the long gray highway and saw something interesting and delightful coming. She started to grin, toothlessly, with short giggles of joy, jumping about and slapping her hands on her knees. And soon it became apparent why she was so happy. For coming down the highway at a firm though leisurely pace was Jesus. He was wearing an immaculate white, long dress trimmed in gold around the neck and hem, and a red, a bright red, cape. Over his left arm he carried a brilliant blue blanket. He was wearing sandals and a beard and he had long brown hair parted on the right side. His eyes, brown, had wrinkles around them as if he smiled or looked at the sun a lot. She would have known him, recognized him, anywhere. There was a sad but joyful look to his face, like a candle was glowing behind it, and he walked with sure even steps in her direction, as if he were walking on the sea. Except that he was not carrying in his arms a baby sheep, he looked exactly like the picture of him that she had hanging over her bed at home. She had taken it out of a white lady's Bible while she was working for her. She had looked at that picture for more years than she could remember, but never once had she really expected to see him. She squinted her eyes to be sure he wasn't carrying a little sheep in one arm, but he was not. Ecstatically she began to wave her arms for fear he would miss seeing her, for he walked looking straight ahead on the shoulder of the highway, and from time to time looking upward at the sky.

All he said when he got up close to her was "Follow me," and she bounded down to his side with all the bob and speed of one so old. For every one of his long determined steps she made two quick ones. They walked along in deep silence for a long time. Finally she started telling him about how many years she had cooked for them, cleaned for them, nursed them. He looked at her kindly but in silence. She told him indignantly about how they had grabbed her when she was singing in her head and not looking, and how they had tossed her out of his church. A old heifer like me, she said, straightening up next to Jesus, breathing hard. But he smiled down at her and she felt better instantly and time just seemed to fly by. When they passed her house, forlorn and sagging, weatherbeaten and patched, by the side of the road, she did not even notice it, she was so happy to be out walking along the highway with Jesus.

She broke the silence once more to tell Jesus how glad she was that he had come, how she had often looked at his picture hanging on her wall (she hoped he didn't know she had stolen it) over her bed, and how she had never expected to see him down here in person. Jesus gave her one of his beautiful smiles and they walked on. She did not know where they were going; someplace wonderful, she suspected. The ground was like clouds under their feet, and she felt she could walk forever without becoming the least bit tired. She even began to sing out loud some of the old spirituals she loved, but she didn't want to annoy Jesus, who looked so thoughtful, so she quieted down. They walked on, looking straight over the treetops into the sky, and the smiles played over her dry wind-cracked face were first like clean ripples across a stagnant pond. On they walked without stopping.

* * * * * * *

The people in the church never knew what happened to the old woman; they never mentioned her to one another or to anybody else. Most of them heard sometime later that an old colored woman fell dead along the highway. Silly as it seemed, it appeared she had walked herself to death. Many of the black families along the road said they had seen the old lady high-stepping down the highway; sometimes jabbering in a low insistent voice, sometimes singing, sometimes merely gesturing excitedly with her hands. Other times silent and smiling, looking at the sky. She had been alone, they said. Some of them wondered aloud where the old woman had been going so stoutly that it had worn her heart out. They guessed maybe she had relatives across the river, some miles away, but none of them really knew.

CHAPTER THREE

The Sound of Mosquitoes Coughing

Breaks during three-hour block classes at Saint Paul usually last fifteen minutes, with raids on the vending machines and lots of small talk. But it seemed Alice Walker had worked her magic. A few returned with Dr. Peppers and Skittles, but the conversation was anything but small. Cassandra and Alesha were bubbling over. "I know," I heard one of them say to the other, "it's beautiful, poetic in some ways." At least some of them were excited to discuss the piece.

I began, "So what did you think of the story?" I wanted honest, open-ended reflection at that point, no questions about the setting or point of view, just reflection.

Alesha was radiant. "You know I love Alice Walker, but other than her novel *The Color Purple*, I had never read her fiction. Well, I have read some of her essays. This story is beyond description. I don't even know what to say, except I can't imagine a sermon with that kind of impact. What would that . . . how would that work?"

I promised her and the others that we would get to that shortly, but for the moment I just wanted to hear their gut reactions.

Alesha added, "Well, it hit me in the gut for sure." I was tempted to ask when that last happened during a sermon. Writer Janet Burroway claims that the phrase "gut reaction" is not a metaphor.

Joey said the story was cool but didn't care to elaborate much beyond that. He did think the ending was kind of weird, walking on clouds. "Is that supposed to be heaven or something?"

I resisted a direct answer, noting that one of the great things about literature is that anything's possible. Brock, Carlos, and Rosa resisted commenting as well. Entirely. Instead, they looked down at their books and fidgeted with their laptops. Cassandra hesitated too, probably because as a former English major she wanted to give the others a chance. Finally, she broke in. "I love how Walker doesn't give the woman a name and yet she is the one Jesus comes to, not the church that has shunned her. It's also amazing how the story both condemns and lifts up simultaneously, you know, there near the end. It's a gorgeous story."

I said, "Yes, good. Anyone else?" Silence. What I wanted to say is how a moment of silence might be in order, only not this kind; more like the way worshipers pause before eucharistic prayers in the presence of divine mysteries, or the way even tourists with cameras around their necks instinctively become silent when stepping into a grand cathedral, Notre Dame in Paris, for instance. I wanted to say that reading this story makes me ready for the benediction and postlude, how Walker's little story is the literary version of worship for me. But I didn't want to scare them away, claiming to see more than they did, at least not so fast.

So I managed what I hoped were a few less zealous comments. I said, "I was stunned the first time I read 'The Welcome Table.' I was actually in Israel, but I sat immobilized before her wizardry and the story's power the way I used to sit spellbound in the Roman Catholic church of my childhood. I can imagine finding my way into a church's sanctuary midweek and reading this story in a pew. Oh, my God, what a story! I mean this as a prayer. That's how I feel about it.

"But let's go back to Alesha's question. How does one preach using a short story, and especially one the congregation would not have read? What exactly are we talking about, using short stories in narrative sermons? That seems like a legitimate question for this class. Well, to be clear, narrative preaching is not limited to using short stories, that's for sure. But I do think they can be a wonderful window into biblical texts and narrative preaching in general. We can talk about these ideas throughout the semester. For now, let me ask you a question. Did any Scripture passages come to mind while you were reading Walker's story? Did it trigger any biblical connections?"

Lisa said, "What about that parable—I don't remember which Gospel it's in—the one where the Pharisee and tax collector are praying in the temple? Remember, the so-called righteous Pharisee is not the one commended by God but rather the tax collector."

"Great," I said. "Any others?"

Silent Rosa surprised me, "Or what about the Samaritan woman at the well? She is an outsider who is approached by Jesus."

"Yes," I said. I didn't mention how this was my first pairing idea as well. Instead, I said, "And of course there would be many other possibilities. So what if a sermon paired Walker's short story with a biblical story like one of those? And what if the sermon retold both stories in a meaningful way so that listeners entered into both narratives, maybe even making some connections themselves? Far too often, sermons get stuck in the ancient text, and even when illustrations from our day are used, they seem anemic, making only cameo appearances, not really wrestling with the gravity of the text.

"I'm envisioning a kind of narrative sermon that invites listeners into a more extended experience, hearing the biblical text anew and most likely the short story for the first time ever. There are lots of structural possibilities, but that's the basics. And what I hope we will do with the stories we read is brainstorm possible connections with biblical texts."

Cassandra asked, "Isn't that a little backwards since in ministry settings after seminary we'll more than likely start with biblical texts?" I admitted it was a valid point, but that it would have to work for our purposes this semester.

Brock asked, "So, we're really using these stories as illustrations?"

I winced slightly. "Yes and no; I'd like to think it's more than that. Illustrations are often more about understanding ideas, at least in a lot of the preaching I hear. In this course I'm thinking more about the power of juxtaposition." I wrote the word on the board. I said, "Some homileticians have tackled the subject, most notably Paul Scott Wilson, but if you've read any of Gordon Lathrop's work in your worship courses, you may recall his emphasis on juxtaposition, setting one thing next to another." I drew two circles and traced a bolt of lightning between them. I said, "For instance, Lathrop notes how we set the seventh day, the day of resurrection, next to the other six. Or we set Word next to Table. Or if you prefer another edible example, think about the juxtapositions the best chefs employ. Anyone here a big fan of Glacé, the little ice cream shop owned by Christopher Elbow?" Several raised their hands, nodded heads. "Who thinks to put strawberries with Moscato in a sorbet? Or who puts goat cheese with wild flower honey and calls it ice cream? Artists, that's who."

Brock said, "I was going to say a lunatic." But several others chimed in about how good the flavor combinations are there. Someone suggested that would be a good field trip, too.

Resisting the temptation to talk more about ice cream than preaching, I pushed on. "So imagine the creative power of juxtaposing Walker's story with a biblical story. The connections could be obvious, like the ones suggested. Or maybe less so. That's something we'll want to think about throughout the semester, how explicit do sermons have to be? Kierkegaard said literature shouldn't be a 'nursing home for cripples,' but a 'playground

for healthy children.' How might that apply to sermons? Sometimes narratives raise more questions than they answer."

I said, "But just to be clear here about one thing: the people in the congregation wouldn't need to have read the short stories we use any more than
when a preacher tells about her cousin's wedding as a sermon illustration.
The listeners weren't at the wedding, but a good retelling of what happened
can take them there. Same for telling someone about a movie you've seen.
Same with the short story, and this will be a big part of our work together,
learning not only how to make sense of these stories but how to retell them
in a meaningful way. And, I might add, the same should be said not just
for the stories by Alice Walker or John Updike, but John the Evangelist or
whatever biblical writer whose story we are preaching from. And we will
even find time to practice such storytelling in class, with one of the goals
being to invite people into the experience of it all."

I continued, "Only experience isn't the only dimension of narrative
preaching, and I consider this an important part of the course. There's also
the expositional voice, the teaching aspects of preaching, which we'll discuss
throughout the semester. In the end, this is not a class about short stories
per se but how they can help us preach the gospel. So let me say a word
about my own description of narrative preaching. Notice I said 'description.'
I'm avoiding the term *definition* because I find narrative preaching to be
somewhat elusive, certainly flexible. Still, there are some constants for me,
three to be exact." Several of them fired up their laptops and iPads for the
first time, others retrieved a pen and paper. It was time to take some notes.

I said, "In terms of *texture*, narrative preaching is storied." I erased
my diagram of juxtaposition and wrote the terms on the board. "By that
I mean they invite us into an experience of both the ancient biblical text
and the ways in which God is still active in our world. Stories are good at
that, the biblical ones as well as the literary ones we'll be reading. And this
is something illustrations don't always do." I briefly mentioned Patrick Hogan's research on emotions and literature, how he says that stories in every
culture both depict and inspire emotion. I said, "That's a fascinating insight.
Sure, stories *depict* emotions and experience, but they also *inspire* them.
When it comes to narrative preaching, storied texture implies that listeners
feel and experience things in the sermon; they experience the good news
of the gospel. This has been one of the hallmarks of the New Homiletic." I
assumed they remembered some of this from the introductory course.

I said, "Second, in terms of *content*, narrative preaching is theologically and existentially thoughtful," writing this on the board, too. "Narrative
preachers engage biblical texts in meaningful ways and wrestle with the

complexities of the world in which we live. God knows that a lot of preaching these days could use more depth."

And lastly I wrote on the board and noted how narrative preaching is inductive in terms of *flow*. I said, "These sermons *build toward* the point we are trying to make as opposed to announcing it ahead of time. No one writes a murder mystery and calls it *The Butler Did It*." Several of them laughed at the absurdity of such an idea. I said, "I'll have more to say later about structural possibilities in the coming weeks, which to me are secondary to these three constants, but that will do for now."

I paused a moment, and then asked, "So why, then, are we reading short stories? Good question, huh? That's the one remaining task before us tonight, the apologetics question. Why short stories, especially at a time when folks don't read nearly as much as they used to, preachers included?"

"That really is a good question," said Joey. "None of my friends are really into poetry and stuff like that."

"I get that. I'm actually thinking of four reasons we should give this a chance, besides the fact your grade depends on it."

"That's cruel, dude," said Joey.

Several of them laughed. I continued, "I don't know how many of you know the name Krister Stendahl. He was a biblical scholar who loved to quote a proverb from his native Sweden, 'It is pathetic to hear mosquitoes cough.'" Brock let out a belly laugh. He said it sounded like a proverb his dad would have loved. I said, "Stendahl claimed that's what apologetics is like, an insignificant sound. And I tend to agree with him; rarely is anyone persuaded by apologetics. But as I said, there are four good reasons why I think the use of short stories in our preaching is worth the effort."

I said, "For starters, short stories are a great resource of illustrative material, and let's face it, we ministers are always desperate to discover more stories for our sermons."

"Amen to that," chimed in Brock. "I always struggle to find good stories for sermons." Several others agreed.

"All preachers do. And here's a great thing about these stories. They are a relatively untapped resource, which means the stories won't be hackneyed or overused. Walker's 'The Welcome Table' is a million miles removed from that story about 'Footprints in the Sand' or all those email stories folks forward to their ministers."

Joey said, "Oh, my God, can you believe how many of those emails go around? And the stories are pitiful, a lot of them anyway."

I said, "You got that right. These short stories are different. The number of published short stories, new and old, staggers the mind. Granted, not all of the stories published in *The New Yorker* or wherever are 'preachable'; but many of them are." I asked, "Have any of you ever been in a bookstore and come across one of those *Best American Short Stories* collections?" A few of them nodded. "All the stories are interesting in one way or another, or else they wouldn't have been published; but some of them are 'preachable.' And in the last decade alone the number of anthologies slanted toward religion is impressive. I'm thinking here of not just of some of our textbooks, the two anthologies—*God: Stories* and *Faith: Stories*—there are all sorts of similar collections.

"Look back in the syllabus for a moment." I had listed several others, including the collection called *A Celestial Omnibus* and the four volumes in the series *Listening for God.* I said, "Now, more than ever, these 'preachable' short stories have become accessible to preachers. By the way, I have a list of 'preachable' short stories that I'll share with you at some point this semester. I think I'm up to nearly a hundred now. And these stories will preach. Who could doubt the preachability of Walker's 'The Welcome Table'?"

Lisa raised her hand. "Sorry to interrupt. What exactly is your definition of 'preachable'?"

"Good question. Actually, I'm fond of the definition a woman pastor shared with me at a workshop I did a few years back. She said, 'After reading some short stories, it feels like you've been praying.' That description works for me. Or maybe, 'they make you want to start praying.'"

Cassandra smiled. "I love that. It's sort of mystical, and yet you know just what she means. It's that way with some poetry, too, the notions of transcendence or epiphany."

I said, "Yes, exactly. So these stories can serve as illustrations. But as we shall see, these stories have much in common with sermons in the narrative family. None other than Fred Craddock claimed that the sermon and the short story are cousins." I couldn't resist quoting the master any longer. "Craddock even required his students in preaching classes to read a short story every week. That, by the way, would be a great idea even after graduation."

Several of them griped about how much reading is required in seminary. Carlos confessed he wasn't sure he ever wanted to read another book after graduation. Rosa disagreed. "I have lots of things I want to read; it's the books I'm assigned to read that are getting to me." Carlos said that's what he meant.

We talked briefly about reading habits of preachers, some recent studies that were quite alarming. Then I continued. "In other words, these stories are also examples for narrative preachers to emulate. Eugene Lowry, one of the founding fathers of the narrative preaching movement and a longtime professor here at Saint Paul, believes that the two essential characteristics of narrative preaching are conflict and resolution. Sermons must move from itch to scratch, he says, not the other way around. I *know* we talked about this in the intro course. According to Lowry, preachers should muddy the waters a bit before exploring gospel solutions. You've heard the expression, 'the plot thickens.' Plot complication is precisely how short stories work. All right, so what examples in Walker's story complicate the plot?" Silence. "Anybody?"

Brock cleared his throat, "I don't know if this is what you mean, but I got real upset when the men of the church hurled that poor woman out the door."

"That's perfect, Brock. Getting upset often signals a complication in the plot. And the same is true for biblical stories, like when Jesus calls the Canaanite woman a dog, clearly a complication in the plot. And that, by the way, is another text that might work with this story. What about resolution? Where do we see that?"

Lisa suggested that when Jesus shows up and tells her to follow him. "Yes, exactly," I said. "Only this story is slightly more complicated than most in terms of plot because after the resolution we are given yet another twist in the plot with Walker's closing paragraph and that haunting line, 'The people in the church never knew what happened to the old woman.' Is that a great line, or what? There is a kind of 'not knowing,' and then there's another kind of 'not knowing.' So reading short stories can not only give us material for our sermons but teach us how narrative plots might unfold in a given sermon."

I briefly mentioned Alyce McKenzie's book *Novel Preaching*, and the lessons preachers could take to heart from fiction. I said, "With any luck, if we read good writers, some of their artistry will rub off on our preaching. That's the first thing, learning from the writers.

"Second, for those who might claim to have too little time for such indulgent pleasures, these stories can be read in one sitting. That's more important than we might imagine. Edgar Allan Poe, yes, that Edgar Allan Poe, regarded this as one of the essential hallmarks of the short story genre."

Joey said, "That dude was weird."

I said, "Aren't we all? But he was one of the pioneers of the American short story, and he suggested that if a story cannot be read in one sitting, readers would be deprived of what he called 'the immense force derivable from *totality*.' Poe thought it absolutely necessary that readers remained in the grasp of the author for one uninterrupted hour. That's why Alfred Hitchcock believed that short stories, not novels, had more in common with movies, since both could be experienced in one sitting."

Cassandra said, "That's fascinating, how short stories hold us in their grasp at one sitting. I had never thought of that difference between short stories and novels."

I said, "It is fascinating in a way. The writer Hortense Calisher described short stories as 'an apocalypse in a teacup.' Or how about this feature in *The New York Times* by A. O. Scott that I ran across the other day? He wrote, 'the short story may provide a timely antidote to the cultural bloat of the past decade, when it often seemed that every novel needed to be 500 pages long and every movie had to last three hours—or four years, if it took the form of a cable series.'"

"Ain't it the truth," said Brock. "I'm so tired of miniseries that don't tend to be very 'mini.'"

"Precisely. Short stories are the kind of literature we ministers actually do have time to read, while waiting for a colleague who has been delayed or before collapsing into bed at the end of a long day. In that article the essayist Scott even imagines a day when folks will download their own favorite collections of short stories into their Kindle the way music lovers carry their favorite tunes around on iPods. Okay, that's probably a little far-fetched, I admit, but this relative brevity alone makes short stories preacher friendly. Walker's story, for instance, takes only minutes to read but its effects are long lasting. That's quite the contrast with someone telling you on Thursday about a novel that might help with Sunday's sermon. There's not enough time."

I took another sip of tea before continuing. "Even if we decided never to use a single short story from the pulpit, a third reason for us to read these stories is the feeding of our souls. Sad to say, but preacher's souls are often as parched as the Kansas wheat fields near here. Preachers still read of course—emails, minutes from committee meetings, commentaries, textbooks in seminary, even the occasional spy novel or trashy romance on the beach once a year. And we read trade books, titles about preaching, pastoral care, the emerging church movement, postmodernism, and the like. At least I hope ministers are reading such things. But what about literature? How often do we read something that stirs us? When was the last time you read something just for the sheer beauty of reading and not out of obligation or desperation as Sunday approached?"

I wondered with Carlos and Rosa if the reason preachers don't read is that seminary reading burns them out. The Pulitzer Prize-winning Annie Dillard asks, "Why are we reading, if not in hope of beauty laid bare, life heightened and its deepest mystery probed?" Good luck finding that kind of experience in an email, or a commentary, or one of those online resources for preachers desperate on a Saturday night to put together some kind of sermon. I said, "Walker's story speaks to the deepest parts of our being, and from a well-watered soul comes the best sermons. And there are many other stories like hers out there, waiting to offer us refreshment for the journey called life.

"One more thing, and then we're out of here for the evening. A final way that short stories can affect us and our preaching—and in my mind this is the most important reason—is noticing how richly textured and honest these stories are. No, even that description doesn't do it justice; these stories are messy. Even the word *messy* may be too clean. A few select four-letter words come to mind; use your imaginations."

Alesha said, "Be my guest."

I just smiled. In Tim O'Brien's story about the Vietnam War, *The Things They Carried*, he writes, "If you don't care for obscenity, you don't care for the truth." Some Christians find that a hard pill to swallow. I said, "The critic Mavis Gallant refers to this messiness as 'the fatal untidiness of life.' How that's for a description? Far too often when preachers want to tackle the kinds of injustices we see in Walker's story, we resort to stock phrases and clichés instead of stories. We use expressions such as 'playing church,' 'the judgmental nature of so many Christians,' 'the need for peace and justice,' and on the list goes. All of these *ideas* are in the story, but not in the form of *ideas*. No one has ever been moved by abstract phrases, and good preaching should move folks. Writers could never get away with such vague phrases; instead they address the hidden places of our souls even as the stories are set in the everydayness of our lives. As the Russian writer Anton Chekhov wrote, 'God save us from vague generalizations!' We should print that on placards and post them above our desks." A few of them smiled at the suggestion, even if I meant it literally.

"Consider just two examples of realism from Walker's story: 'The reverend of the church stopped her pleasantly as she stepped into the vestibule. Did he say, as they thought he did, kindly, "Auntie, you know this is not your church?"' Or later, 'It was the ladies who finally did what to them had to be done. Daring their burly indecisive husbands to throw the old colored woman out they made their point. God, mother, country, earth, church. It involved all that, and well they knew it.'

"I don't want to get into technical literary jargon at this point, but 'texture' is one of the things we'll want to pay close attention to in these stories. Texture, or what some call tone, is not just how a story feels to the reader but how it makes you feel when reading it. Much of the so-called Christian fiction published these days is a black-and-white caricature of our world, lacking in the texture of real life. Their stories are like stick figure drawings, or maybe Normal Rockwell, but definitely not the whole story of our lives." I paused, and then added, "You may not believe this, but at the public library near my house, they have conveniently put fish-shaped stickers on the bindings of Christian books so that readers won't have to be subjected to the messiness of life found in much non-Christian fiction. After all, so the argument goes, Christians don't want to read about extramarital affairs or domestic violence; never mind the fact that both of these taboos are portrayed in Scripture."

Cassandra interrupted, "I guess you could say there's no fish symbol on the binding of the Bible." Several of us pondered the wisdom of that observation.

"Great point," I said. "But while some readers avoid such messes, the best writers don't. To borrow a phrase from C. S. Lewis, the short stories we will read are like the lion Aslan in the Narnia stories, 'not safe, but good.' And the lion of course symbolizes God."

Carlos said, "I don't disagree completely, but going back to what you said about certain trashy novels as opposed to the ones with fish on the outside, it seems to me that novels today are more graphic than they need to be. And the same for movies as well."

I said, "You make a good point, although I would note two things. One, the Bible is messier than you might think. Translators have cleaned up a lot of the biblical stories. There is much more earthy language in Scripture than we imagine, and in both testaments. That doesn't mean I'm advocating for a measure of obscenity in our preaching, not at all. But, and this would be the second thing, I am advocating for a kind of preaching that is real. Think about the need for an honest portrayal of our lives like this: In a world where people watch local and global tragedies on their nightly news, perhaps our preaching should be so honest. As I mentioned before, this attention to honest portrayals of life's messiness may well be the most important reason for preachers to consider short stories. Churchgoers who experience the realistic power of movies on Saturday nights rarely experience anything close to that on Sunday mornings in church. How tragic! Short stories are the literary version of those powerful movies."

I looked at them and smiled. "See you next Thursday. Go in peace."

Chapter Four

The Organic Movement

The following Wednesday I got an email from Lisa, asking for clarification on one of the assignments. She remembered how in her first year of seminary, when her New Testament professor said something about "exegesis," she thought he was saying "exe-Jesus." And now in this class, she noted, they were going to have to learn how to do "literary exegesis." While she claimed to be more concerned with learning than grades, both things seemed to be on her mind.

I emailed her back, saying it was a valid question, even if the syllabus stated we would go over it in class. In fact, I told her we would cover it this coming Thursday after some more introductory material. I also said it was the same question everyone had, so wait until class and if she still had questions, ask away. And I reminded her we would get to do a practice exegesis without a grade.

I met David, my co-leader from Israel, for lunch at Chipotle's before class on Thursday. A burrito, chips and guacamole, and good conversation are all sacraments in my book. Besides, the Kansas City winter had settled in for the long haul at the beginning of the so-called spring semester, and some hot sauce couldn't hurt in taking off the sting. I mentioned Lisa's email and griped to David for the umpteenth time about what grades do to theological education, stifling students out of fear and the need to conform.

He said, "Yeah, but remember when you made that one course pass/fail as an experiment with the dean's permission? You said some of them didn't seem to try as hard."

I took a sip of my Arnold Palmer concoction and said, "I know, I know. But I also remember some students who 'found themselves' along the way, no longer afraid. And it's not just grades, but papers too. The longer I teach preaching, the more I realize it is not only built on the foundations of biblical and theological studies but must overcome the straitjacket of term papers and book reports that stifle creativity. Teaching students to become scholars often means forfeiting their imaginations, whereas fostering creativity often results in neglecting scholarship."

David knew that I would never question the validity of exegesis papers or any other foundational course work, so he appreciated my emphasis on creativity and scholarship. He said, "Irresponsible exegesis and inept homiletics are the bane of the church's existence."

I said, "Dr. Hayes, you should write that down."

I began class that week with some "housekeeping" matters, reminders to sign up for preaching slots later in the semester, and to be sure to turn in their reading reports. I mentioned an email from someone in the class about the two required "literary exegesis" papers, and how we would get to that during the second half of class.

For our devotional time, I read from Genesis, about the plight of Hagar when Sarah sends her away. I also shared another lengthy passage from *Reading Lolita in Tehran*, this one about Nafisi's first clandestine meeting with her seven female students:

> The first work we discussed was *A Thousand and One Nights*, the familiar tale of the cuckolded king who slew successive virgin wives as revenge for his queen's betrayal, and whose murderous hand was finally stayed by the entrancing storyteller Scheherazade. I formulated certain general questions for them to consider, the most central of which was how these great works of imagination could help us in our present trapped situation as women. We were not looking for blueprints, for an easy solution, but we did hope to find a link between the open spaces the novels provided and the closed ones we were confined to. I remember reading to my girls Nabokov's claim that "readers were born free and ought to remain free."
>
> What had most intrigued me about the frame story of *A Thousand and One Nights* were the three kinds of women it portrayed—all victims of a king's unreasonable rule. Before Scheherazade enters the scene, the women in the story are divided into those who betray and then are killed (the queen) and those who are killed before they have a chance to betray (the virgins). The virgins, unlike Scheherazade, have no voice in the story, are mostly ignored by the critics. Their silence, however, is significant. They surrender their virginity, and their lives, without resistance or protest. They do not quite exist, because they leave

no trace in their anonymous death. The queen's infidelity does not rob the king of his absolute authority; it throws him off balance. Both types of women—the queen and the virgins—tacitly accept the king's public authority by acting within the confines of his domain and by accepting its arbitrary laws.

Scheherazade breaks the cycle of violence by choosing to embrace different terms of engagement. She fashions her universe not through physical force, as does the king, but through imagination and reflection. This gives her the courage to risk her life and sets her apart from the other characters in the tale.

We sat in silence for a moment. I said, "Let's pray. O Holy One, God of Sarah and Hagar, God of the exodus, the wilderness, and a promised land, we confess that we live in a world of bondage. We think of your children in the Arab Spring, and we think of our friends trapped in addictions. We think of sex slaves in Asia and here at home, and we think of acquaintances trapped in dead-end marriages. We think of prisoners jailed unfairly, and we think of the poor trapped in their lives of little. Free us, we pray, from that which keeps us from living in the freedom of your Spirit. May this Arab Spring become an Arab Summer, an Arab Fall and more—a future of peace and hope and freedom. Guide us, we pray, in our journey this semester. And help us never to forget those who remain ensnared. Inspire us to work on their behalf, even as you continue to set us free. For this is our prayer in the name of the Christ. Amen."

Then I had a surprise. I said, "You know how I'd just as soon be meeting in a coffee shop, or maybe a living room like Nafisi did with her students. Well, part of the genius of Nafisi's arrangement was the food she served. So I brought some treats for us. I should have done this last week." I placed tube-shaped packages on the table, and explained what digestives are. "Leave it to the British to call cookies digestives. It makes you feel healthy eating them. I brought two kinds with me, the plain shortbread version and the ones dipped in chocolate. You'll have to bring your own drinks, but at least we can have some food. In fact, I'm passing around a sheet if you want to sign up to bring a treat one or more weeks. Your option. Enjoy the cookies, I mean, digestives."

After all the excitement over food, I reminded them how during our introductions last week it became apparent that all of them were at different places on the homiletical journey. All of them had taken the introductory preaching course, true, but it had been awhile for some and not everyone was preaching weekly. I said, "Let's do a brief review of homiletical history."

I hoped none of them were allergic to history. Then I told them a story from when I served as pastor at a church in Fayetteville, Arkansas, about a woman in that church who had retired from teaching in the university. Not surprisingly, she was an avid reader, and we often compared notes on books we were reading. One Sunday she told me the story of going to the Barnes and Noble near her house that past week. She didn't have a particular title in mind, just a particular subject. She asked the coed at the help desk where she might find a book on the Great Depression. The girl said, "Sure, right this way." My friend was confused at first, then amused. They were standing in the self-help section. She said, "No, I think you misunderstood me. I don't need a book on depression. I'm looking for something on the Great Depression. You know, the Great Depression." With hands on her hips, the girl said, "Look, there are all kinds of depression. You'll have to figure out which one you have." My students roared with laughter. Ever since my friend told me that story, I decided historical reviews are never a waste of time.

I said, "So here's my *Reader's Digest* version of recent homiletical history. You'll want to write down this date: April 15, 1986. Most people don't know it, but that is when narrative preaching was born." I paused; they jotted it down. "OK, let me come clean. That's not the beginning of narrative preaching; that's when our first child was born." Several of them made faces, hitting the delete key. I said, "Hang on. The date coincides nicely with my own introduction to narrative preaching. It's the date when narrative preaching was born in me. Here's what happened: I was nearing my last year of doctoral work in preaching, an approach heavier on the older forms of exposition than the newer forms of narrative. I ventured into the bookstore on campus shortly after our son was born, and by the grace of God found a copy of Fred Craddock's *As One without Authority*. It might be more accurate to say it found me. Shortly thereafter, I discovered Eugene Lowry's *The Homiletical Plot*. Never has someone's world been more upturned than in my encounter with those two books.

"To his credit, my major professor suggested I should do research papers and presentations in my last doctoral seminar on what I learned was called the New Homiletic. So that's what I did, and here's the funny thing. As I recall, my colleagues in the doctoral program were not persuaded, not in the least. Remember, this New Homiletic really was new stuff. Normally, such resistance would have derailed me. Not this time. I knew I had stumbled onto another way of being in the world, another way of preaching. It felt like stumbling upon the Holy Grail, certainly not an inferior way of preaching. Not hardly. Bottom line, it was a way that felt right to me. Over the next few years as I began to read bedtime stories and tell Bible stories to our son and later to our two daughters, my own approach to preaching began to change. For me, narrative preaching was born on April 15, 1986. That, however, is not when most scholars date its birth."

Cassandra said, "Really? I would have thought all homiletical theories were based on the events of your own life."

We all got a laugh out of that. Getting us back on track, I said, "Actually, it's hard to know where to jump in, but 1958 is as good a place as any in terms of contemporary homiletical theory. And no, that's not the year I was born. That's the year when H. Grady Davis published a book with the shocking title *Design for Preaching*." I paused. "So, how come none of you gasped?"

Alesha pretended to be shocked. Joey said, "Didn't sound shocking, that's why." Several others shrugged.

I said, "I know, not to our ears, not now. But you have to realize that the word *design* was scandalous in preaching lingo back then. Prior to Davis, preaching books used more masculine metaphors, terms from the courtroom (arguing for a verdict, that sort of thing) or from construction (like books by the British preacher W. E. Sangster, such as *The Craft of Sermon Construction*). It's a little crass, but picture a worker with his tool belt and pants too low. He's building a sermon, and showing us how to build one in the process. The message will need a good foundation, lots of lumber, and there will be dust in the air. You can count on that.

"Then along comes Davis going on about *design*. In fact, he starts his book with a poem about how sermons should come from the soil of the text, much the way trees spring up from the soil. This was the beginning of the organic movement in preaching. In a world of two-by-fours, Davis was talking about trees. And in many ways, that was the beginning of what we now call the New Homiletic.

"Of course, the name synonymous with the New Homiletic and attention to sermon design is Fred Craddock. You know the phrase, 'turned the world upside down'? Well, Craddock turned the homiletical world upside down, figuratively but also literally. What I mean by literally is his notion of inductive preaching, which I mentioned briefly last week. Remember, I said in terms of flow, narrative sermons should be inductive. Prior to Craddock, sermons were largely deductive, starting with some announcement of where the sermon was headed. You've heard those sermons, right? The preacher begins: 'This morning, I want to talk to you about discipleship and what Jesus says in Matthew's gospel about renouncing our selfish agendas to follow God. Many of us really are selfish . . .'

"Craddock said this was like starting a joke with the punch line. He said ministers use inductive inquiry in the study, wrestling all week with a text, hoping like Jacob wrestling in the dark mud that a blessing will be forthcoming. After all the wrestling, then comes the insight. So far, so good, only then the preacher robs the listeners of the same journey. Craddock suggested preachers should do in the pulpit what they do in their studies, invite listeners to wrestle with the text as well, arriving at conclusions where conclusions belong, nearer the end of the sermon. This really is crucial. Again, in terms of *flow*, narrative sermons should move inductively."

I saw heads nodding yes, as if this were the most obvious truth in the world, like I'd been describing gravity's pull on earth. Others looked at me the way a calf looks at a new gate on a ranch, head turned sideways and definitely puzzled. I asked, "OK, so what makes sense to you about Craddock's approach, and what's not so clear?"

Carlos volunteered, "I remember when we covered some of this in the first class. It makes perfect sense to me in theory. I get it, the idea. I just don't know how to do it. For some reason, I want to give away the sermon's main idea earlier rather than later. Then again, to be honest, I'm not sure what's wrong with that anyway."

I said, "Carlos, good questions. Really. Sermons don't have to be inductive, that's for sure. Preachers can preach quite compelling messages with the thesis stated up front. Lately, I've noticed at least two exceptions to the inductive rule, the kind of preaching that even though deductive in nature is still quite compelling. The first exception is when the topic is so compelling it doesn't matter if the preacher gives it away. The preacher begins, 'It's been in the news every day this week, and so this morning I want us as the church gathered to talk about gay marriage. I believe God wants all of us to be blessed and happy, gay or straight.' At that point, one could expect to have everyone's attention even if the preacher has given away the thesis."

Several of them commented on the example. A few said something about being called before committees or boards for controversial views, that sort of thing.

I said, "The second exception I see more frequently these days is the charismatic personalities in megachurches who announce their thesis right up front. And folks gather by the thousands for forty-five minutes of deductive exposition, more of a study than sermon in some ways. While I could say a lot about that sort of thing, for now I would simply note that not very many of us have the charisma to pull off something like that."

Lisa said, "Oh, I don't know, maybe Joey could." He blushed and smiled.

Alesha said, "I see what you're saying, but I'm thinking about some of the black preachers I know. How would you characterize them in terms of deductive/inductive?"

"That is such a good point, Alesha, and thanks for bringing that up. As you well know, there is no such thing as one kind of preaching tradition in African American churches. Not even close. But it's true that some of the best black preachers, even the deductive ones, preach a compelling kind of narrative sermon. Somehow they announce the sermon's focus up front and yet still command attention as they invite listeners on a kind of narrative journey. I don't know for sure, but in a way I think it's because they invite listeners to enter into an exploration that they've experienced many times, but to do so anew. I don't know, honestly. We should explore that this semester along the way. I do know this: building toward suspense is a powerful thing. It's how stories work."

Lisa said, "My question is about the sermon's focus and clarity. How are we supposed to be clear as to the sermon's focus if things don't become clear until late in the sermon? Won't listeners be lost along the way?" Several nodded in agreement.

I said, "Another good question. It is possible for inductive sermons to lose folks. Of course, I've heard deductive sermons do that as well. It helps to think about the difference between a sermon's *topic* and its *focus*. Early in the message listeners have to be clear what the sermon is about, the topic. Messages don't make sense if listeners are clueless as to what we're saying. People naturally try to make sense of the sermons they hear, the world they live in. Hans Gadamer said interpretation is not something people *do*; it's who we *are*.

"Think of it like this. When someone strolls through a museum, for every piece she encounters, she tries to make sense of it. Here's a painting of a landscape with our eyes directed toward one tree, or here's a piece of modern sculpture in which a person's stomach is actually a hole. So we ask ourselves what these things mean. It's the same for sermons. People want to know why the preacher has positioned us in front of this text, what the preacher wants to say about it.

"So the topic has to be clear from the start. But the focus, the punch line, comes later. If we wanted to share an artistic insight into why the artist has a hole where the person's stomach should be, we would wait a while. We would ask questions, let people ponder that. Or to use a preaching example, if our sermon was going to explore gay marriage, announcing the topic up front would create tremendous amounts of tension, even if the preacher didn't give away her/his take on it until near the end. Or not at all, letting listeners wrestle with the topic."

Then I thought of another example. I said, "Or what if the text for a sermon were the widow's mite. We would be clear from the beginning we are wrestling with matters of financial stewardship. That's our topic. But if our take on that passage, our focus, is about how maybe Jesus isn't commending her for giving her last two cents but condemning the religious establishment for 'devouring widows' houses,' that would come out later, as the sermon progressed, not up front." Several of them were stunned at that idea, the text as indictment. I noted that being stunned by such an insight is what inductive preaching does so well, that if a sermon started with it, the cat would be let out of the bag too soon.

I also wanted them to see how the short stories we'd be reading model a form of narrative preaching for us. I said, "Think about Walker's story. At what point do you get a sense of what the story is about, the topic? Early on, right? We know this is a marginalized woman, nameless and black, heading to the white church down the road. But when do we see what happens to her? And when do we discover God's perspective on her suffering?"

Brock said, "At the end, of course. I don't know if this analogy works, but when I drove trucks for a living, I knew if I was headed west on I-40 or whatever, that by evening I would pull into Albuquerque, but I didn't know what I would encounter along the way until I got there. Is that what you're saying?"

"Very much so," I said. "And Joey, when you watch your Sooners play basketball on TV, you know they have the ball with three seconds left, that the point guard is about to jack up a long three-pointer. What you don't know is whether they will win. It's why we watch sports."

Joey was excited. "Cool, dude. I'm tempted to say that of course the Sooners will win. But I get what you're saying."

I added, "But here's the difference. Unlike the sportscaster, the preacher knows the final score, how the sermon will end. And the listeners in church do as well. I mean, they know the preacher will come down on the side of peace and justice, or what have you. But who recaps a game they've seen by giving away the final score up front, then summarizing the final moments? No one. Instead, when we want to tell someone about how the game ended, we describe the scene and build up to it."

Now everyone seemed to nod, even Carlos, who had been skeptical. I said, "This was one of Craddock's main contributions, inductive sermons. But it wasn't his only contribution. Not hardly. In his textbook, *Preaching*, which was recently re-released in a twenty-fifth anniversary edition, Craddock said, 'Unless the minister has two eurekas, it is unlikely the listeners will have one.'"

Cassandra said, "Ouch. That hurts."

I smiled. "Maybe so, although I don't think it's intended to hurt." I continued, "In other words, ministers must have two epiphanies, the first, when they know what their sermon is about, and the second, when they determine how they will say it. In a way, all that preaching professors really want is sermons that have something to say and say it well. That's not asking too much, is it?" Several of them laughed at the simplicity of it all, knowing of course that pulling off those two things is anything but easy.

I also reminded them how Craddock asked why all our sermons sound the same, given how many different genres of texts there are in Scripture. It's almost as if for generations preachers knew weeks in advance that their sermons would have three points even if they didn't yet know which texts they would be preaching from. And this question of Craddock's was very instrumental in launching the next big movement in preaching, the narrative sermon.

I knew we would have to say more about these developments throughout the semester, especially given how few of my students actually used points any more. Times had changed, and I wanted to know how they viewed sermon styles. Outside, a light snow was falling. Several of us were ready for a cup of coffee or hot tea on break. But we still had some work to do. I briefly rehashed the advent of the modern narrative movement, Lowry's *The Homiletical Plot*; *Preaching the Story* by Steimle, Niedenthal, and Rice; and Jensen's *Telling the Story*, all of which were published in 1980. I mentioned the collection of essays Wayne Bradley Robinson had edited, *Journeys toward Narrative Preaching*, which explored six distinct approaches. But more discussion would be the key to keeping them involved. I asked, "So what do you remember about narrative preaching?" This was a crucial question, maybe the crucial question. After all, this was a class on narrative preaching, even if we were using short stories to explore the topic.

I decided everyone needed to be involved, so I did what I do in workshop settings when there are a few pastors who dominate the conversation and some who never say a word. I paired them off, and said, "Okay, take five minutes or so to discuss what you remember about narrative preaching." I suggested Carlos and Rosa split up and meet with others.

Lisa said she and Rosa could be discussion partners, as did Brock with Joey. Carlos paired off with Alesha. Cassandra appeared to be stuck with me, but I urged her to join with Carlos and Alesha. I wanted to roam the room, listening in to their conversations. But I knew that could be intimidating. Instead, I sat in my chair and overheard several conversations, only some of which made it to our class discussion.

One person, I think it was Alesha, told her group, "I know this much for sure, it's not about how many stories are in the sermon. That's what Eugene Lowry says."

Carlos asked, "How could it be a narrative sermon without stories? That doesn't sound very narrative. Professor Freeman said last week that narrative sermons are stories."

Alesha said, "Actually, he said *storied*, not stories."

Carlos said, "Anyway, I'm not sure how biblical this narrative preaching is in the first place. The Apostle Paul wasn't a narrative preacher." I would love to have jumped in and asked, "But what about Jesus?" I didn't.

Pushing a strand of hair behind her ears, Cassandra said, "I think for Lowry the essence of narrative is the plot of the sermon overall. It needs to have tension. That's what stories do, and I get it when it comes to stories like Walker's. But I don't have a clue how that works with sermons. Or maybe I have a clue, but the actual doing of it is difficult for me."

In another group I heard Joey's Oklahoma drawl, "I know this much, on Sundays when I preach, people comment afterwards on the stories. They hardly ever say anything about other parts, but definitely the stories. I just don't know if that's what I want them remembering, you know what I mean." I didn't hear Brock's response to that. Rosa and Lisa were engaged with each other, although I couldn't hear them either.

It had taken a few minutes to get them going, and then it was hard to get them to quit talking; or at least to quit talking in groups and share with the whole class. I said, "So what were you saying amongst yourselves? What do you remember about narrative preaching? Alesha, what about your group?"

She said how they debated Lowry's idea that narrative preaching isn't about how many stories get told or not, but the sermon's overall plot. I said, "Yes, that's key for him. What does that mean, a sermon's overall plot? Anybody?"

A few looked at their notes, hoping not to be called on. Cassandra reiterated what she'd said in the small group, how it's about tension. She said she understood it when it came to stories, but not sermons. I asked, "Anyone remember Lowry's pithy quote about 'scratch' and 'itch'? Remember, he said sermons should move from itch to scratch. In a way, that's another description of inductive movement because Lowry was greatly influenced by Craddock. Who wasn't? But 'itch to scratch' is Lowry's way of saying sermons should work the way all good plots do. They complicate things. Even Disney movies do this. In *The Lion King*, Mufasa dies, and we're not sure Simba will survive. Later, we think Simba is in the clear, but along comes more trouble in the form of Scar. The same with genies and princes, and the like. The same with *The Grapes of Wrath* or *War and Peace*. And the same for 'The Welcome Table.' All good stories have plots with twists.

"Scriptural stories do, too, only we have domesticated those. We're no longer surprised by the twists and turns. We know the traveler in the parable will fall among thieves, that the first two passersby will do just that, pass on by. We also know the Samaritan will stop. We even dare to name the story ahead of time, 'the Good Samaritan.' No tension, no plot. No sermon, according to Lowry. So he invites us to listen for the complications in the text or to bring them to the text from the messiness of our lives. The preacher might ask, 'I know Jesus wants us to go and do likewise, but does he have any idea how dangerous that can be in modern America?' That's a complication from outside the text. Or how about this complication from within the text, 'If this is a parable on being neighborly to the despised, wouldn't it make more sense for the man in the ditch to be Samaritan, not the one who helps?' Now the listeners are itching." It was obvious that for several of them I had muddied the waters for sure.

"Obviously, there is much more to narrative preaching and we'll have a semester to explore it, celebrating its strengths but also critiquing aspects of it. And I can see that several of you are ready for a break, but one more thing before we pause. It's part of our review of preaching overall."

I went to the board and wrote two words, *text* and *today*. I said, "Now, at the risk of making my job and your calling sound way too easy, think about these two words as the essence of preaching. There is the text and there is today. That's all there is, really. The first words out of our mouths on Sunday come from one of these two worlds. And the next words as well. Preachers weave their way between these two worlds, seeking to show how the ancient text still speaks a relevant word to folks like us. (The word, *text*, by the way, comes from the Latin term 'to weave.') The texts direct us to prophets and apostles who lived in a different world than we do. I don't know anyone who struggles with eating meat sacrificed to idols as was the case in Corinth. The grocery store I shop in doesn't even carry idol meat. But the sermon isn't only about our times either, a homiletical version of reading the editorial page in *Time* or *Newsweek*. So the preacher explores the church's Scriptures in hopes of finding a word from God that can address our lives. One of the ways to do that is called narrative preaching, and we're going to look at how short story writers can help us in our task. All right, let's be back in fifteen minutes."

Chapter Five

Breathing in the Experience

When everyone had returned from the restrooms and the break room, I asked, "Okay, so be truthful, when you started seminary how many thought the Bible professors' references to 'exegesis' had something to do with 'Jesus'?" Several nodded in agreement. "I get that. I was in the same boat when I started seminary. But our vocabulary eventually caught up with us on the journey. We learned the basics of biblical exegesis. Well, in this course we're going to be doing the traditional kind of exegesis with biblical texts in hopes of arriving at a focus for our sermons, and that's very important for all styles of preaching, narrative maybe even more so than others. I'll explain that in more detail later. But we're also going to be doing a different kind of exegesis, 'literary exegesis.' Or to paraphrase one of our textbooks," and here I pointed to Thomas Foster's book, *How to Read Literature Like a Professor*, "we're going to be learning to 'read literature like a preacher.' In fact, it could be to our advantage not to be trained literary critics."

Joey said, "Yeah, Cassandra. We just might have the advantage over you this time." She simply smiled.

I said, "Check out this line by the essayist Cynthia Ozick. It's in an article with the title, "God Saw Literature, That It Was Good." I love the title alone, but here's the line, 'The earth is flooded with stories, hymns, and parables regarded as holy in their origins. The literary approach can deflate them all.'" Several of them chuckled. I said, "Is that great, or what? All these beautiful stories, and if we're not careful, the literary approach can let the air out of them all. And that air is the very breath of God who breathed life into them in the first place. And I'm not just talking about the short stories but

Scripture too. In fact, reading these stories more closely may teach us how to read the Scriptures more closely."

I continued, "What we're really talking about is a combination of being critical and possessing a degree of naiveté, what Paul Ricoeur called the second naiveté. There are techniques that English professors and biblical critics use that we'll want to utilize. But we'll also want to reclaim the childlike power of entering into these stories, and letting them enter into us. So I have a handout for how we're going to do literary exegesis, and we'll try our hand at the Alice Walker story we read last week. But first, a few passages from Nafisi to whet our literary appetites." With that, a couple of them popped a digestive cookie in their mouths or took a sip of coffee.

I read several quotes from *Reading Lolita in Tehran*:

> *Do not*, under *any* circumstances, belittle a work of fiction by trying to turn it into a carbon copy of real life; what we search for in fiction is not so much reality but the epiphany of truth.

> In all great works of fiction, regardless of the grim reality they present, there is an affirmation of life against the transience of that life, an essential defiance.

> Don't go chasing after the grand theme, the idea, I told my students, as if it is separate from the story itself. The idea or ideas behind the story must come to you through the experience of the novel and not as something tacked on to it.

> A novel is not an allegory, I said, as the period was about to come to an end. It is the sensual experience of another world. If you don't enter that world, hold your breath with the characters and become involved in their destiny, you won't be able to empathize, and empathy is at the heart of the novel. This is how you read a novel: you inhale the experience. So start breathing.

Alesha said, "I know you're not requiring us to read that, but I have to get that book." Cassandra agreed. I just smiled. I had thought of requiring it, but it seemed like the kind of book that would work its magic best if they wanted to read it. Now at least a couple of them would do just that.

I passed around copies of a handout. I said, "Take a few minutes to look over these questions. We'll go over them in a minute. These are the questions that will guide the way we do literary exegesis."

QUESTIONS FOR LITERARY EXEGESIS

Reflection Questions

Personal

When you read this story and simply breathe in the experience, how does it speak to you? Not as pastor but personally, how does it touch you?

Homiletical

Brainstorming multiple possibilities, what passages of Scripture are brought to mind that might be paired with the story?

Literary

Keeping in mind how the story complicates an issue and moves toward resolution, what is the basic plot? Who are the main characters and what happens to them?

Critical Questions

Homiletical

Of the biblical passages you brainstormed, what text do you intend to use in a sermon? What would be the focus of the sermon?

Literary

Given the proposed sermon focus, what scenes are revelatory? What is the story's point of view, and what difference does that make? Using sensory language, what is the story's tone or texture? How does the story end, and what difference does that make?

Theological

Given the proposed sermon focus, what glimpses of deity do we see explicitly or sense implicitly? What would your use of the text and story say about the human condition? Given your focus, where in the text and story do you see grace breaking in? How does your theological perspective address the issues this text and story raises?

Homiletical

How might the text and story interact in your sermon? What kind of sermon flow or structure might work best? Given your reflections on this story, share a retelling of it.

Reflection Questions

Personal/Pastoral

What do you believe about what this text and story says to you? What do you hope happens for those who listen to this text and story sermon?

When everyone seemed ready, I asked, "So what do you make of the questions listed for us? What stands out for you?"

Lisa said something about the open-ended, almost impressionistic, nature of the questions. She thought it was great to play with ideas before sweating out what a sermon might actually look like.

"Yes," I said, "that's exactly the idea. Some of you may even recall that essay by Anna Carter Florence we read in the introductory class. She says that her students in preaching classes are good at playing with texts and possible ideas, until they suddenly remember they have sermons to write. Then they get nervous and occasionally resemble executioners bearing swords. And it can happen with the texts of short stories, too. Give yourself room to play with the stories and possible texts. That's something of what we did with Walker's story right off. I didn't ask about the point of view, the protagonist, flashbacks, and foreshadowing. I asked what spoke to you in the story.

"Good. So after the initial reflection questions, we move to the more critical questions. What stands out to you about that set of questions?"

Cassandra said, "The same thing that always stands out for me in preaching. I don't know how to decide on the sermon's focus, and that's without the complication of having a short story to deal with at the same time." Several others nodded agreement. Suddenly, it seemed we were dealing with brain surgery or rocket science, or what a friend of mine calls *rocket surgery*. He would say of something, "It's not like we're doing rocket surgery."

But I agreed that this homiletical move is complex, certainly crucial. I said, "So let's get a handle on the big picture here. Starting with a short story isn't the norm, as we noted the first week of class. Most of us start with biblical texts, lectionary or not, then among other things we go looking for stories. But here's the thing: starting with a sermon idea that originates in a story, or starting with a biblical text, either approach is equally valid. Not all teachers of preaching would agree, but the reason I say that is because faulty exegesis, or what we usually call eisegesis (reading into the text) is possible either way. And so is responsible interpretation. The key is treating the text with respect and interpreting theologically.

"But here's the real point," I added. "We play with texts and we study texts rigorously, but eventually we have to decide what the sermon will be about. There are lots of possibilities in every biblical text, and in every short story for that matter. But the other exegesis we always do is congregational. The sermon occurs at the intersection of textual and congregational exegesis. What complicates this just a bit more is the short story."

Joey scratched his head, "Dude, I'm sorry, but I'm lost. Do we start with what the story means, what the text means, what?"

I said, "No need to apologize. When we read Walker's 'The Welcome Table,' we encountered several possible themes. Okay, so what is one of the themes you saw there? Joey?"

He said, "Uh, I don't know. Well, there's the part about the church being judgmental toward the woman."

"Good," I answered, "very good. And that's an idea for a sermon. Can you think of texts about the judgmental nature of the church? Anyone?"

Carlos, who knows his Bible better than most seminarians, said, "There are plenty such passages. In the Sermon on the Mount, Jesus warns against judging one another until we have removed the log from our own eye. Or there's the story in Luke when Simon the Pharisee looks down on a sinful woman who is washing Jesus' feet. Or Paul writes about . . ."

I interrupted, "Fantastic. Well, you know what I mean. Unfortunately, we have lots of biblical texts about the church's judgmental nature. It seems to be in our DNA. So we would do some preliminary readings on these texts, making sure the one we select fits well with the story's emphasis. We're not interested in forcing square pegs into round holes. Big mistake. But we would also think about the congregations to whom we preach. Are they like that church in Walker's story, or are they more like the woman herself? That's a crucial question in helping to shape the focus for the sermon. Sometimes, asking which character in a story our listeners might most readily identify with is a key question. All in all, this is a dynamic process, a kind of homiletical dance in which we move between text, story, and the people."

I was hesitant to ask, but said, "Does that help?" It seemed to do the trick, or at least no one asked any more questions at that point. The longer I teach, the more convinced I am that focusing the sermon is the hardest thing for preachers to do, and maybe the most important. I continued, "Okay, so we would settle upon a text and a focus. After that, we are back to asking questions of the short story. And to me, one of the primary ones has to do with revelatory scenes. Do you see that question? 'Given the proposed sermon focus, what scenes are revelatory?' What does that mean?"

Brock said, "To me it means what stood out."

"Yes," I said, "what stood out. Theologians refer to the idea of *epiphany*. Turns out, so do writers. The Irish writer James Joyce used the term in relation to short stories, describing an epiphany as 'a sudden spiritual manifestation.' Of course, some contemporary writers use different terms. Wordsworth referred to epiphanies as 'spots of time,' Virginia Woolf, 'moments of being.' I especially like Betty Freidan's term, 'click moment.' And there are usually many such moments in a story. It's like going to see a movie with friends and how there are certain scenes that cause something to click. We rented *The Help* the other night. If you see a movie with friends, then go to dinner, and someone says, 'Wow, imagine having to use an outhouse or separate bathroom because of the color of your skin.' Or 'Can you believe that part where the maid Minny bakes that pie for Miss Hilly?' Most of the time, the scenes we discuss afterwards are the revelatory ones, the moments when something big happened."

Several of them commented on the pie scene. With a dry wit, Brock said, "I hope no one signed up to bring chocolate pie to this class anytime soon."

Like the others, I laughed, and then asked, "So what are some revelatory scenes in Walker's story? If it were a movie, what would have you talking?"

Rosa said, "When Jesus comes walking down the road and tells her to follow him."

Joey said, "Yeah, and before that, when the ladies of the church have their husbands throw her down the steps."

Cassandra added, "Of course, when the two of them walk on clouds. And even the last paragraph about how the church folks never did know what happened to her."

"Great," I said. "And because this story is shorter than most, it almost sounds like everything is revelatory; but not quite. Here's a really important point for determining revelatory scenes: it depends on your focus. If our hypothetical sermon is going to be a word of grace for those abused by the church, the walk on clouds is crucial but maybe not the last piece about the church's ignorance. But if our sermon is an indictment against religious abuse, that last piece is essential. Do you see that? Or maybe another way to say it is that there are revelatory scenes and relevant scenes. A key question is figuring out what is revelatory because it is an epiphany of sorts and what is relevant for your sermon." Suddenly, light bulbs appeared over most of their heads; they were catching on. I said, "In other words, we don't have to treat every aspect of the short story, any more than we have to treat every aspect of a biblical text."

"I sometimes hear preachers who think that everything they read in the commentaries has to show up in the sermon. Definitely not. I think it was Lowry who said that putting a sermon together isn't like building a dog house, nailing on boards willy-nilly; no, it's more like a sculpture from which you remove and take away the extraneous until the sermon takes shape before you.

I continued, "Next, we have theological issues at stake. This is very important as well, especially since one of the correctives needed in much narrative preaching relates to a lack of theological discourse. Remember, in terms of *content*, narrative sermons should be theologically thoughtful. We'll read more about that in the weeks to come and think about some deficiencies in certain types of narrative preaching. But for now, let's look at a couple of key theological questions. The first one is about where we see God in the story."

"That's easy," several of them said in unison. "Jesus walks into the story."

"Ah, you noticed that, huh? Yeah, this one is a little easier in that department than most. All of the stories we read will have 'glimpses of deity' in them, or else I wouldn't have selected them. But sometimes it will be just that, a glimpse, the backside of God, so to speak, or a still, small voice. Other times these glimpses will be explicit, like when a character prays, goes to church, that sort of thing.

"I'll give you a classic example, and I only discovered this recently. We're not reading Raymond Carver's story 'A Small Good Thing,' although it pains me to omit it. It's a fairly well-known story that a lot of preachers have used when preaching on the Eucharist. I won't give it away, except to say there's a great closing scene in which a bereaved couple and baker eat some hot coffee rolls together. It's a communion scene of sorts, no question. But a minister friend of mine recently shared with me an earlier published version called 'The Bath,' and there's not even a hint of that eating scene. In some ways, as religious as the one story is, the earlier version is almost totally bleak. We won't limit ourselves to explicitly religious stories, but we will read ones that at least hint at God's presence in our lives."

I said, "Okay, back to the handout. What about the human condition? That's another question."

Carlos said, "The Apostle Paul says that 'all have sinned and come short of the glory of God.'"

I said, "Okay, but that's only one line about the human condition. What else does Scripture say about us?"

Lisa said, "Genesis describes humanity as made in the image of God."

Cassandra remembered part of Marcus Borg's scheme of the human condition, that humans are sometimes portrayed in bondage as in the exodus story or despair as in the exile story.

"Excellent," I said. "In other words, the human condition is multifaceted."

I recalled Martin Luther's line, "simultaneously justified and sinners." Preachers who use short stories have to look at what aspect of the human condition the author has tapped into, even if they don't use theological language to do so. Writers like John Updike were well versed in theology, the works of Barth, Niebuhr, and Tillich. But not most writers. But the short stories we would be reading in class deal with what Tillich called matters of "ultimate concern." He claimed that was the essence of religion. People care about relationships, forgiveness, alienation, the meaning of life, and so forth. I told them we would read more about these matters in the coming weeks.

I continued, "Looking at Walker's story, what are the classical doctrines of anthropology that we see coming to the surface? What does she say about the human condition?"

Carlos said, "Well, we see how the church is full of sinners. They definitely fall short of God's glory."

"Absolutely," I said. "And of course the church in her story is a kind of character unto itself, so-called saints who sin egregiously. What about the woman's condition though?"

Rosa cleared her throat. "She is a victim." Carlos nodded in agreement.

Alesha added, "Yes. She has been marginalized by the system. Her plight is the plight of many African Americans in our nation's history."

I appreciated Alesha being the one to point this out. It carried a certain clout. I said, "And of course we see grace breaking in with the gift of Jesus' presence."

Cassandra added, "And not just his presence, but his smile and listening ear. Plus, he does not condemn her for taking that picture from a white lady's Bible. I love that part. He comes in peace and with grace."

"Again," I said, "it won't always be so obvious. But the grace does come in these stories. Listen to how Flannery O'Connor put it. She's one of the authors we'll read." I flipped through my notes and found the quote. "Here it is: 'In my stories a reader will find that the devil accomplishes a good deal of groundwork that seems to be necessary before grace is effective.'

"Now, I haven't spelled this out specifically on the handout, but in learning to exegete these stories, there is an underlying skill that is also applicable to interpreting biblical texts. That skill is what some have called a 'close reading' of the text."

Joey said, "Did you say a 'close' or 'closed' reading of the text?"

At first I thought he was joking since it was hard to imagine anything positive about a "closed" reading of anything. But he was serious. I said, "No, a 'close' reading, looking closely at what it really says. And this is a carry-over skill from biblical interpretation. For instance, suppose we were reading the parable of the Prodigal Son, and I said, 'What do you think of that scene when the father throws a party for his son who's come home?' It would not be a satisfactory answer to respond, 'Well, I know when I was a teenager, if I had run away one summer, my parents would have . . .' No, that kind of reading strategy won't work. And why would that be inappropriate? Because while the story might generate that memory in you, those things need to come later in the reading process. We wouldn't want to ignore what the story triggered in you, as reader-response theories rightly remind us, but from a hermeneutical standpoint, we wouldn't be reading the text closely. A close reading would suggest we see how Luke, the writer of the Gospel, wants us to understand first-century customs, and so forth."

Alesha said, "So what role does reader-response play?"

I said, "In my opinion, it's very important for the preacher, only later in the process. I need to wrestle with the first-century customs before I start importing our contemporary ones into the ancient world." It was fairly obvious in looking around the room that some of them found this conversation over their heads.

I continued, "Back to the handout, because after those interpretive questions, we have homiletical questions, patterns of narrative preaching that we'll consider more closely as well in the coming weeks. But don't let this one little piece escape your attention. It says, 'Given your reflections on this story, share your retelling here.' That is huge. One of the skills we need to develop is retelling these stories. How do I tell Walker's story so that a congregation that has not even heard of it enters into the experience?"

Once again Joey said, "Good question, dude. So what's the answer?" While Joey could easily get on a person's nerves, we all realized he was going to keep us honest.

I said, "Before I answer that, let me share a scene from early on in Foster's *How to Read Literature Like a Professor*. You'll read it later, but it fits nicely here. Remember, he's trying to teach literary criticism to college freshmen, which is no small feat. A friend of mine who teaches at a liberal arts college refers to freshmen as 'thirteenth graders.' Anyway, Foster says that early on in every semester there comes a moment when the English professor says, 'What, don't you get it?' And at the same time, the students say, 'We don't get it. And we think you're making it up.' According to Foster, they eventually concede that there really must be certain conventions and techniques by which to read well. And when they ask for the secret, he says, 'Same way you get to Carnegie Hall. Practice.'

"What a profoundly simple but helpful reminder. Practice. If you want to play oboe in Carnegie Hall, you'd better practice. Same for deciphering literature, and it's the same for learning how to tell these stories effectively. It takes time. We will practice doing literary exegesis, and we will practice telling these stories. Don't be too hard on yourselves at first."

I said, "So before we go, let me share my own retelling of Walker's story. I've used Walker's 'The Welcome Table' a couple of times now, so let me share my retelling of it."

Several of them smiled in anticipation. Others were mildly curious. I stood up, since performing a story takes our whole bodies. I briefly noted that my retelling would have been paired with John 4, the story of the Samaritan woman, and that helping listeners enter into that story would also be crucial. I also noted that in this case, the sermon's narrative structure stuck with the biblical text almost exclusively throughout, but ended with the short story. Then I shared what would have been the ending of the sermon.

> When I read stories of Jesus eating or drinking with folks, I think of a short story by Alice Walker. Most of us know her as the author of *The Color Purple*, which was made into a movie. But her short story 'The Welcome Table' is just as powerful. It's the story of a woman, nameless and black, whom Walker describes as 'the color of poor gray Georgia earth, beaten by king cotton and the extreme weather.'
>
> On this particular fine Sunday morning she starts off to worship at the big white church down the road, a church that is white in many ways. The good religious folks are shocked when she appears. The reverend kindly reminds her this is not her church, as if one could choose the wrong church. The young usher tries as well to persuade her to leave, but she has come to worship God. She settles into a pew near the back, noting to herself how cold it feels inside. Finally, the respectable ladies have had enough, and their husbands hurl the poor woman out onto the porch.
>
> She is speechless. Only moments ago she was worshiping God. Then something happens. She gets this big grin on her face, a toothless grin. And she starts giggling and slapping her hands on her knees, because 'coming down the highway at a firm though leisurely pace [is] Jesus.' I mean, the real Jesus. She

recognizes him from a picture in the Bible. As he approaches, he says, 'Follow me,' and without hesitation she joins him there on the road, although she has no idea where they are headed. She hums. She sings. She tells Jesus all about her troubles, including how they threw her out of his church. He listens. He listens and smiles. And the two of them walk on until the ground beneath their feet gives way to clouds. And she is truly home!"

I paused for a few seconds, and then added an "Amen." Even in class, it felt like we should sing a hymn next. Walker's story is powerful, even a retelling of it. I finally asked for comments, questions. Alesha was moved by it, but she wondered about what I had left out, what I had added. She said, "I loved what you did, especially the way you made it your own. It wasn't a duplicate, that's for sure."

That is an important distinction. If a preacher decides to use a short story in a sermon, the idea isn't to duplicate the story. Might as well read the whole thing word for word in that case. No, replicating seems more appropriate. The congregation is invited into an experience of the story as the preacher retells it, or replicates what she/he experienced reading it in the first place. Capturing the power of narratives, the biblical ones as well as the literary ones, is crucial.

I said, "Helping listeners experience something of what you experienced is crucial. Storied texture, or experience, that's the real deal in narrative preaching. It's not the only thing that matters, but experience matters. We'll see you next week. Go in peace."

CHAPTER SIX

Whale Watching

I usually date the end of winter in Kansas City the last day of February, even if we still have a few weeks to go and even if March can still freeze a person's buns off. It's a morale booster if nothing else. Either way, we were smack dab in the middle of the season of Epiphany. I kept hoping the Christ would showing up—in churches on Sundays, in classes on Thursdays, and every other day of the week for that matter. My wife and I had attended a wedding over the weekend. The minister had not turned water into wine or anything like that, but she'd done a nice job. The presence of Christ was fully evident.

Joanna Harris, the presiding minister, had earned her DMin at Saint Paul a few years back, in the Revitalizing Congregations track. In the "Biblical Preaching" seminar we had looked at two sample wedding homilies by Tom Troeger. Both stress how marriage is about "promise and covenant." In fact, in the first homily the words appear several times, and it is an example of what Troeger calls a "rhetorical sermon." Even without the stereotypical three points and a poem, the homily is meant to represent traditional propositional approaches to preaching. In other words, the focus is on ideas. In the second homily, the words don't appear at all, at least not in so many words. Instead, in this "visual style" message Troeger tells the story of a couple who decided that every year on their anniversary they would don their wedding clothes and have their picture taken. The photographs would be collected in one single anniversary album. The story goes something like this. Troeger imagines them on their fifth anniversary. The professional photographer will arrive shortly. Their new home sparkles, as do their hopes for a bright future together. Life is great. "Smile!" As he snaps the picture they repeat their vows. The phrase "for better for worse" stands out, especially the word "better."

Next, he pictures them on their fifteenth anniversary. They no longer have a professional photographer. The husband has lost his job, just a temporary layoff—but still. So a neighbor is coming to take the picture. They squeeze into their wedding garments. As they pose, the wife notices a couch in need of reupholstering. The flash goes off as they repeat their vows, the phrase "for richer for poorer" sticks in their throats.

Years go by and it's their forty-seventh anniversary. Forty-seven years. They wonder if they'll make it to their fiftieth. He's had two heart attacks and one triple bypass surgery. They pose before the fireplace. He takes her hand, wrinkled and bent with arthritis. Their granddaughter snaps the picture as they vow, "in sickness and in health." The granddaughter runs upstairs to get fresh batteries for the camera. "Be back down in a minute." But they're not listening. The two of them look into each other's eyes and see something more beautiful than the prized pictures in their anniversary album, for what they see is the beauty of a promise kept.

Joanna, like other students I've had, thought that was one of the best things she had read in seminary, certainly the most memorable. She used it in her wedding sermon. I commented afterwards about how her telling of it had been quite effective. Clearly, the families of the bride and groom were touched as well. The timing could not have been better. In class the next week we would be discussing what stories can and can't do, a common theme for the remainder of the semester.

Alesha brought pita bread and fresh hummus with hints of cilantro to share. So as everyone grabbed a bite and settled into their seats, I shared another passage from Azar Nafisi's memoir, this one about how the chief film censor in Iran was nearly blind. Literally.

> We lived in a culture that denied any merit to literary works, considering them important only when they were handmaidens to something seemingly more urgent—namely ideology. This was a country where all gestures, even the most private, were interpreted in political terms. The colors of my head scarf or my father's ties were symbols of Western decadence and imperialist tendencies. Not wearing a beard, shaking hands with members of the opposite sex, clapping or whistling in public meetings, were likewise considered Western and therefore decadent, part of the plot by imperialists to bring down our culture.

There, in that living room, we rediscovered that we were also living, breathing human beings; and no matter how repressive the state became, no matter how intimidated and frightened we were, like Lolita we tried to escape and to create our own little pockets of freedom. And like Lolita, we took every opportunity to flaunt our insubordination: by showing a little hair from under our scarves, insinuating a little color into the drab uniformity of our appearances, growing our nails, falling in love and listening to forbidden music.

After praying together, I said, "I have a plan for discussing our readings, but first, I have a story." I would have added something about how this is a true story, but as they've heard me say many times before, "All good stories are true; and some of them really happened."

I said, "Several years ago now, I was invited to lead a week-long summer workshop at Princeton Theological Seminary. The emails from the director of Continuing Education contained the usual information, including travel instructions. After taking the train from the Newark airport, I was to change trains and catch 'the Dinky,' the affectionate nickname for the two-car train that delivers students and professors onto the edge of Princeton University's campus.

"Towing a wheelie suitcase in one hand and my golf clubs in a wheelie bag with the other, I began the walk up the hill from 'the Dinky.' My laptop was in a satchel around my shoulders. The weather was hot, so when a friendly stranger in an early model station wagon asked if I needed a lift, I said sure. I know, you're not supposed to take rides from strangers. Turns out, he was on faculty at the seminary. And this is how he introduced himself to me. He said, 'My name is _____. I teach in the area of _____. And I am not a Barthian.'"

Incredulously, Alesha and several others commented at the same time, "He said what? No way!"

"You heard me," I said. "His introduction to another seminary professor, although a perfect stranger, was to give me his name, his discipline, and to clarify he was not a Barthian."

Joey said, "Oh, at first I thought you said 'not a Martian.'" Now we were all rolling, laughing nearly to the point of tears.

When I regained some control of the situation I held up a copy of Will Willimon's *Conversations with Barth on Preaching*. I said, "Willimon claims that whether we know it or not, we are all of us in conversation with Barth. We might be infatuated with the Swiss theologian, even president of his fan club like Willimon. Or we might be giving him the silent treatment.

We might be somewhere in between. But all preachers are in conversation with Barth."

The students were not assigned readings from Willimon, but rather from Charles Rice's *Interpretation and Imagination* and Charles Campbell's *Preaching Jesus*. In a way, both are conversations with Barth's work, albeit with very different appraisals of the dean of neoorthodoxy.

I began, "So here's what I propose we do the first half of class this evening. Instead of pairs, I'd like to divide us into two groups. One will take the chapters we read in Rice's book, the other the chapters from Campbell. You don't have to agree with the viewpoint you're assigned for discussion. In fact, it might help to take the opposite view. But before you discuss the authors and their respective theses, each group should address the questions I've written on the board. Don't think about the authors. Think about your views. Is that clear? Take about ten minutes."

On the board I had written the following questions:

1. What contemporary story did you tell or hear in Sunday's sermon?

2. Why do preachers tell stories that come from outside of the canon?

3. Why read short stories for preaching?

I nibbled on some pita bread and hummus, drifting to both sides of the room, listening in on their conversations. Ten minutes later, I went to the board and asked them to share. "What did you come up with? We probably don't need to hear the stories themselves from all those Sunday sermons, but let's start with the kinds of stories. What kinds of things were the stories about?"

Joey said, "I don't know if this is right or not, but I started with a joke about a priest, rabbi, and minister." Joey should have known better, since in the introductory course I had gone on a tear against preachers starting sermons with jokes since they're usually not only lame but also unrelated to the sermon's focus.

Rosa shared that Carlos had told the story of the prodigal son. Carlos added, "My sermon was from Ephesians, but I used the prodigal son's story to talk about how God receives us back when we repent."

I said, "Okay, but notice how that's not a story from outside of the canon. Did you tell any stories from your own life or from happenings in the news lately, that sort of thing?"

He pushed his reading glasses back up his nose and thought for a moment. He said he mostly uses biblical stories, but the Sunday before last he did tell about an Alvarez family reunion a few years back. I couldn't tell if he felt slightly guilty or not for telling such a story in the pulpit.

Brock said, "I told a story about shopping for antiques, how you never know what you might find."

Several others shared similar things. I said, "OK, it's a good representative list. So the question then is: Why? Why do preachers . . ."

Brock interrupted, "Sorry, but I just remembered how a pastor I once knew told about the results of his prostate exam."

"No way," several of them shouted. Brock said it was the most bizarre thing he'd ever experienced in church. We briefly discussed how ministers can abuse their powers, sharing inappropriate things from the pulpit.

Of course, it's fairly well known that David Buttrick believes ministers should never tell personal stories, echoing the refrain of clinical pastoral education instructors everywhere: "It's not about you!" Buttrick even formulated a way to convert personal stories into more universal ones, with all hints of the preacher's presence removed. Fred Craddock, however, practically made a cottage industry out of telling personal stories. But even his personal stories were rarely about him so much as something that happened to him. Most listeners can tell when a preacher's stories are used in service of themselves as opposed to pointing to the good news of God. I thought we would need to explore this topic in more detail later.

After Brock's prostate story, I tried to get us back on track. "So why do we tell these kinds of stories? Not the inappropriate ones, but the ones that fit. Why do we tell stories?" Everyone was silent. I said, "You do realize there are schools of thought where only stories from the Bible are allowed? That's not our philosophy, obviously; but what did you come up with?"

Cassandra said, "To evoke feelings. Stories are good at that. I think it's one of the reasons people read novels and go to movies. We are numb and want to feel alive."

"So true," I said. "Do you know that story about the Jewish novelist Chaim Potok? He used to tell his mother that when he grew up he was going to be a writer. His mother would say, 'Become a doctor; you'll make a lot of money and you'll keep people from dying.' All of his growing up years she would say the same thing, 'Become a doctor; you'll make a lot of money and you'll keep people from dying.' He finally protested, 'Mother, I'm going to be a writer. I don't want to keep people from dying; I want to teach them how to live.' That is what the best writers do, teach us how to live, or at the very least how not to live."

I added, "Of course, you realize that homileticians would be divided over this, evoking feelings. Nobody wants listeners to be numb, emotionless; but evoking feelings sounds shallow at the very least, maybe even manipulative at worst. And that may be our real problem with sermons touching people. Not wanting to be manipulative, we have decided to not move people at all. However, some black homileticians—Henry Mitchell and more recently, Frank Thomas—have argued that emotion is part of our faith response. And John Wesley argued that the affections are part of what it means to respond to God. Remember, his heart was strangely warmed. As Andre Dubus writes, "I cannot feel joy with my brain alone." These are things we need to talk about during the semester."

I asked, "Why else do we tell stories?"

A couple of them in one group said, "To make the Bible come alive." Even as I wrote their response on the board, I could hear the class was divided on this one. Lisa said, "I think I know what you mean by that, but the Bible is alive already." We discussed the observation Tom Long makes, how some preachers only become animated during the contemporary illustrations and often make the Scriptures sound dull by comparison. I mentioned how Willimon and others believe it's not the Scriptures that need to be made alive but how we can be made alive in the hearing of them.

Alesha said, "Stories are interesting. They keep people from being bored. The people who fall asleep in churches rarely do so while the choir is singing or we are praying, but they sure do during sermons. Stories keep people engaged."

I said, "Ah, boredom. Do you remember that line from Garrison Keillor, how if you took all the people who fall asleep during sermons and laid them end to end, they'd be a whole lot more comfortable?" A few of them chuckled at that. "Let's face it, we don't want our sermons to be boring. What else?"

Lisa remembered how the very word *illustration* comes from the word *luster*, how sermons illuminate ideas. She said, "They're like windows, letting light into the sanctuaries of our lives." Someone noted how the windows in our room were like that.

I said, "So are you saying this class would be boring without the windows?" We did agree that looking out on the woods, even the bare trees in winter, was a nice break from academia. The squirrels sure seemed to be having fun.

Several other answers were shared, then I said, "There's still one thing missing from our list, and to me, it's the most important reason for including stories in sermons." I waited, but sensed fear on the part of several that they might get it wrong. "I think I'll wait, though, to share it. Let's do some more work in groups first."

Several of them protested, "You can't do that, bait us like that, then move on to something else."

I noted how their comments were homiletical in nature, having to do with rhetoric and how people listen. I claimed I was just using inductive tension, even if somewhat flagrantly. I said, "It's amazing, isn't it, how we put things together in speech and can create a response? I promise we'll come back to it. But let's do some more work in our two groups." They still weren't thrilled with my delay tactics, but we pushed ahead. I said, "Take the set of questions about stories and think about the readings from Rice and Campbell. How might they address these issues? Take fifteen minutes this time."

I left them alone in the room, refreshed my cup of Earl Grey, and made small talk with some folks in the library. I ran into a colleague who teaches theology and shared how among other things we were wrestling with Barth this evening. She said, "I've wrestled with Barth a lot myself, having done my dissertation on him. And I can show you the bruises to prove it."

When I returned, the conversations were animated. I brought us back together and wrote the names Rice and Campbell on the board a few feet apart. Beside Rice's name I also added in parentheses: (Revisionist/Chicago School/Schleiermacher/Tillich). Beside Campbell I wrote: (Postliberal/Yale School/Barth/Frei/Lindbeck). I said, "Many of you will recognize these names and terms from other course work. You don't really need to concern yourselves with all the details, just the broad movements here. None of these thinkers held to or hold to identical ideologies, but they are related in a broad sense. So what did you come up with in Campbell's group? Let's start there. Do you have a reporter from the group?"

Alesha said, "I'm happy to report if no one else wants to." Nobody objected. She said, "As the subtitle of Campbell's book suggests, he's interested in applying the postliberal thought of Hans Frei to preaching theory. I am probably more familiar with Karl Barth than Frei, but they seem to be closely related." I noted that Frei had done his doctoral dissertation on Barth, and thus the unmistakable similarities. Alesha continued, "Campbell doesn't have a problem with the narrative genre. He's all in favor of it, and he even lists several contributions of the New Homiletic with regards to narrative and narrative preaching, things like . . . hang on, just a sec. Oh, here; things like: a return to Scripture which is largely narrative; new, innovative forms for preaching; and the holistic nature of preaching so that it's more than cognitive. I think he had some others. But I found one line very powerful." She flipped a few pages. "Here it is: 'It is questionable whether many forms of narrative preaching are adequate for the current American context, in which a biblically illiterate church finds itself in an increasingly minority situation in an increasingly secular culture.'" Alesha added, "I really like stories, but this makes me stop and think."

Brock said, "I think that's the point, stopping to think." I wondered if Brock's time spent on the road as truck driver was part of what led him to be so reflective.

"Absolutely," I said, "serious reflection is vital in good preaching. And this is one of those critiques of narrative preaching we will have to take seriously during the semester, but also in our ministries. I would note, however, that Campbell does stipulate 'many forms of narrative preaching' may not be up to the task; that doesn't mean all of them." I added, "We didn't read one of Campbell's later chapters, but let me share another quote. Here it is. Early in chapter seven he writes, 'Homiletics has focused far more on narrative form than on the content and function of the biblical narrative.' That is a key concept with Frei and with Campbell. Jesus has been made known to us in story, and at times we have worshiped the genre more than the revelation to which the story points."

Alesha said, "Wow, that's a powerful indictment. One more thing, and several of us in our group commented on this, especially in light of the readings in Rice. Campbell critiques narrative preaching for its unhealthy fascination with experience. He notes how Craddock and other pioneers favored preaching as an event."

I said, "Good work. No question, the New Homiletic has emphasized preaching as experience. And we will need to nail down what that means. You bring up Rice's work by way of contrast. So let's hear from the other side of the room. What do y'all have to say to that?"

Cassandra said, "Y'all? Did you say y'all'?"

I said, "Yes. That's Greek, don't you know? The New Testament uses 'you' plural almost exclusively, and the Greek word is y'all.'"

Joey said, "Amen, brother. That's the way we talk in Oklahoma." Cassandra just smiled.

"Okay" I said, "what did *you guys* come up with? Cassandra, you can be the spokesperson."

Suddenly she was all business. "I don't know if Rice would give you a ride up the hill in Princeton, but he's definitely not a Barthian." I said something about the gracious spirits of Charles Rice and Chuck Campbell, but that she was spot on when it came to Rice's theology. She continued, "He's more in the camp of Paul Tillich." She asked, "Didn't he have an ongoing debate with Barth?"

I said, "Actually, Barth's most famous ongoing debate was with Emil Brunner. Their spat was among other things about whether being made in the image of God is something that survived the fall of Genesis 3. Brunner said yes; Barth said no. Tom Long has a wonderful essay about that. But you're right about Rice not being a Barthian. Go ahead."

She said, "Following Tillich's lead, Rice thinks human experience and culture are excellent starting points for a theological encounter. I love that quote on the first page of the chapter we read, 'It is clear that the Bible reflects vastly more of the culture in which it was born than does much contemporary preaching.' Or a page or so later," and here she looked at notes on her laptop, "Here it is: 'Without equating religion and culture, Tillich learned by unimpeachable human experience that they are inextricable.' That's powerful stuff."

Lisa added, "Yes, and for Rice and Tillich, the symbols of culture, whether that's short stories or whatever, are to be taken seriously because they participate in the very religious thing to which they point."

Joey, always the one to keep us honest, said, "Okay, I think I get what he's saying. But I gotta be honest with you; I don't think I get all of it. My brain is fried, especially when it's close to break time. What's his deal with culture?"

I said, "Good question. In fact, it may well be *the* question. We rushed over that earlier quote from Rice, the one about sermons reflecting more of the biblical culture than ours. As far as I'm concerned, that's a key insight. Lots of sermons I hear and read seem to get stuck in Thessalonica or wherever, forgetting we live here. Sure, the ancient world of the biblical texts is crucial; no doubt about it. But so is the one we live in today. For some reason, preachers always feel the need to pick one of those over the other."

I said, "Joey, in response to your question, we need to turn to page 3 in Rice's book. Near the bottom he writes, 'To be religious, said Tillich, is to be ultimately concerned.' Or a few pages later, Rice actually quotes Tillich, 'Religion is the substance of culture and culture the form of religion.' In other words, cultural expressions like the ones we are reading in these short stories are one of the ways people grapple with religious matters, with things of ultimate concern. People care about relationships, love, forgiveness, alienation, purpose in life; the list goes on and on. Think about Walker's short story. It deals with some of these religious matters."

I moved over to a blank section of the white board and drew two columns:

	Postliberal	Revisionist
Aim	Dogmatic	apologetic
Method	Anselmian	correlating
Content	Christological	anthropological

I said, "I think this will help answer Joey's question and provide some clarity for all of us. The postliberal position takes a dogmatic stance in its aim; the revisionist, an apologetic stance. In other words, the first starts with Scripture and theological thought, whereas the latter begins with experience. Both view revelation as coming from God, but where that revelation may be found is a different matter. As for method, the postliberal is Anselmian, 'faith seeking understanding,' whereas the revisionist approach believes there is a correlation between the things of experience and culture that can help us in our seeking after God. According to Campbell, the resulting content is either Christological or anthropological. Personally, I find this chart somewhat helpful, but do not agree with Campbell's conclusions. Let me explain."

I continued, "Just prior to this chapter in Campbell, he tells about a preacher whose sermon included stories about a whale watching trip off the New England coastline. Later, he commented it would be nice for a change to hear someone preach about Jesus, and not so much on whales. Now I didn't hear the sermon, so I can't pass judgment on it, but here's my point: I think a whale story can be christological or more generally theological, and I'm not just thinking of Jonah's story but Melville's *Moby Dick*. Telling stories of God's ongoing work in the world need not be exclusively anthropological."

Preachers have always had to navigate the valley between the mountain ranges of Barth with his followers on one side and Tillich with his followers on the other. I think the valley is where we belong, the via media, a kind of dialectical tension rather than a dualistic choosing. On the one hand, Barth's primacy on the preaching event *as event* is a reminder that it is God who makes such a thing possible. On the other hand, there are problems homiletically when Barth's theory is pushed too far in practice, which is what happens sometimes. Even Stanley Hauerwas notes that a stress on God's otherness shouldn't eliminate the need for analogies of faith, connections between God and us. This is why Tillich's reminder that human experience also testifies to the God event is helpful as well. For some reason, we are uncomfortable with dialectical tension (this *and* that), wanting instead to choose (this *or* that).

I said, "I remember having a theological discussion with a colleague as we boarded a flight out of Kansas City. I said, 'When I get on a plane, I'm glad for wings on both sides.' He reminded me that there's really only one huge wing running through the fuselage. I said, 'Touche.' And with that, I think we need some more pita bread and hummus."

CHAPTER SEVEN

Now in Flesh Appearing

E ventually, we all traipsed back into the McElvaney Conference Room. Several of the students were hyped up about the Super Bowl, cultural competition for the season of Epiphany, as if that were a fair contest. I said, "Remember how I promised to come back to the role of stories and the number one reason why I value them so much? Drum roll, please." Joey obliged with a set of pencils. "Well, I don't want to downplay the suggestions all of you offered earlier, but those were largely rhetorical in nature, keeping interest and so forth. But what about theological reasons? Preaching is not only rhetorical in nature; it's theological too. Or theo-rhetorical. My answer to the question: stories testify to the ongoing presence of God in our lives. Stories remind us that God is still active, still welcoming prodigal sons and daughters, still breaking bread with disciples. Otherwise, we give the impression that the first-century Mediterranean world was a more holy place and time than here and now. 'Too bad we couldn't live during the time of Jesus. At least we have our history.' No, no, definitely not; that won't do. Christ is still present. God still speaks in unlikely burning bushes, and in books that some folks would like to see burned for that matter. To paraphrase Charles Rice, 'God did not stop speaking when the Good Book went to press.'"

I continued, "Do you remember those books I told you about, the ones in the public library with the fish symbols on the binding? What they are claiming, though I doubt they would have the vocabulary to put it this way, is that the Christian faith is really a Gnostic one. More than that, it's a docetic form of Gnosticism. So, let's do some review of your 'Christian Traditions' course work."

I said, "When the Council of Nicaea convened in the early part of the fourth century, roughly 300 bishops attempted to hash out beliefs about the nature of Christ, in particular the nature of his divinity. The question was whether he was of the 'same substance' as God (*homoousios*) or a 'similar and subordinate substance' as God (*homooisios*). Do you remember trying to learn the different terms for an exam?"

Joey said, "Oh yeah, dude. It was not a pretty picture."

"The difference," I said, "between the two terms was literally one *iota*, the Greek letter 'i'; but the theological significance was monumental. The bishops of course eventually settled upon his being the 'same substance,' but the controversy was far from settled. Everyone it seems had their own opinions. According to at least one bishop, he couldn't even get his hair cut without having to listen to folks in the barbershop debate the divinity of the Christ."

Brock said, "Are you serious? You're joking, right?"

I said, "No joke."

Brock said, "It was barbershop talk?"

I said, "It was the talk of the town. What, the person who cuts your hair doesn't bring that up in conversation?"

Brock said, "Not exactly. Most of the time it's politics or dirty jokes."

I said, "Well, truthfully, most Christians today probably have never heard the term *Gnosticism*, which may say something about our lack of theological thoughtfulness in much preaching. As for Gnosticism, one modern theologian believes it was more dangerous to the early Christian movement than martyrdom, since the latter often inspired believers, whereas the former was 'like a vampire,' sucking the very life out of Christianity."

I said, "This is the kind of thing we learn in seminary but can't imagine being important for ministry. But coming to terms with Gnosticism is still vitally important. There is much to be said about that ancient heresy, but I'm focusing on one aspect in particular. Gnostics claimed that a secret knowledge was required to understand God and God's ways. Remember, the term *Gnostic* comes from the Greek word for knowledge. Part of this knowledge was a dualistic view of deity, that this messed-up world in which we live is the creative product of a God (god?) somewhat less in stature than the real God. This real God couldn't have anything to do with a world like this one. And so while this has consequences for how contemporary preachers deal with human suffering, the environment, and a host of other issues, there is another facet of Gnosticism that I find prevalent in much Christian thinking and preaching, namely the denial of the goodness of this world and our fleshly existence." I said, "Why do they put fish bindings on those books in the public library? What are they trying to avoid?"

Cassandra said, "Sex."

I said, "I suspect you're right. There would be other things, like violence and crude language, but mostly sex. Too much flesh. If, according to Gnostic teaching, this world was not the product of the real God, you can see how they came to value spiritual matter over earthly matter. These early Gnostics believed that the flesh is evil. They viewed the body as a prison in which the human spirit or soul was imprisoned. As for *docetic* Gnosticism, the term comes from the Greek word meaning 'to appear.'"

Lisa interrupted, "Sorry, but could you spell that?"

I said, "No problem." I erased the Campbell/Rice chart and wrote *docetic* on the white board. I continued, "Docetics argued that the Christ *appeared* to be human but was not really human. If he walked on the shores of Galilee, they said, he wouldn't even make footprints in the sand. As Irenaeus put it, 'Not one of the heretics is of the opinion that the Word was made flesh.' Their high view of his divinity came at the expense of his humanity. Although docetic Gnosticism is no longer the topic of conversation in barbershops and beauty shops, or churches for that matter, it is definitely present in much popular Christian thinking. Gnosticism allows Christians to be so focused on the next life that they are of little good in this present one. Who cares about school boards when someday we'll be singing with angels? In Gnostic thought, prayer is more spiritual than working in a soup kitchen, meditating more significant than caring for the earth. Gnosticism rears its ugly head all the time, even in that hymn most of us sung a few weeks ago during the season of Christmas, 'Away in a Manger': 'The cattle are lowing, the baby awakes/But little Lord Jesus, no crying he makes.' Now tell me, what kind of baby doesn't cry?"

Brock said, "I once heard a radio preacher claim, unless your Jesus passed gas, he wasn't really human. Normally, I don't go in for those radio preachers, but I thought he had a good point."

Lisa said, "The problem is that too much humanity makes people uncomfortable."

I said, "Precisely. We're uncomfortable with our own bodily functions, never mind the bodily functions of the Son of God."

I remembered how in Barbara Brown Taylor's wonderful book, *An Altar in the World*, she has a chapter on incarnation called "The Practice of Wearing Skin." She tells a story about going as guest preacher to an Episcopal church in Alabama. She arrived forty-five minutes early, something like that, so she decided to look around the empty sanctuary. Only one older refined lady was there already, and she was polishing silver in the sacristy. Taylor noticed a painting above the altar, a larger-than-life painting of Jesus emerging from the tomb. She could never remember seeing a painting featuring so much of Jesus' skin. The woman said, "It's beautiful, isn't it?" Taylor agreed, then added, "But did you notice he has no body hair? He has the underarms of a six-year old. And his chest is smooth as a peach." The woman nearly went into apoplectic shock. Without ever uttering a word, that woman was protesting, "I can't believe you're saying this to me. I can't believe you're saying this to me." Too much talk of realistic, even hairy, skin.

I continued, "Flannery O'Connor, the great southern writer, said a lot of so-called Christian writers are really Manicheans, a school of Gnosticism. Her advice to writers was that writing is difficult because it is incarnational. She said, 'Fiction is about everything human and we are made out of dust, and if you scorn getting yourself dusty, then you shouldn't try to write fiction.'"

Brock said, "The way I see it, folks can't get saved if they're not lost; can't get clean if they're not dirty."

I agreed, and let these ideas sink in a moment. We had been wrestling all evening with heavy concepts. It seemed like a good time for a short story. I said, "I don't know how many of you know the name Peggy Payne. She's a contemporary writer, who is anthologized in one of our textbooks, although I haven't assigned this story. Anyway, it's fairly short and I think a good follow-up to our discussion on epiphanies. The author later expanded this story into her first novel, *Revelation*. It's a really good read, too, but for now just consider the short story. Grab some more pita bread and hummus if you like, but as Nafisi would remind us, 'Breathe in the experience.' We'll talk about it afterwards." I passed out copies and sat down to read it again myself.

"The Pure in Heart"
By Peggy Payne

He would not have said that he was ever "called" to the ministry. It wasn't like that. Instead, he grew up knowing that it would be so. The church was Swain Hammond's future—unofficially. He got his doctorate at Yale. Then, after one brief stint as an associate minister, he became the pastor at Westside, a good choice for—as he had become—a man of rational, ethical orientation.

The church in Chapel Hill, North Carolina, is Presbyterian. It is fairly conventional, though influenced, certainly, by the university community. Swain is happy here. Westside suits him. But it is clearly not the best place to hold the pastorate if you're the sort who's inclined to hear the actual voice of God. Up until recently, this would not have been a problem for Swain. But about eight weeks ago, the situation changed. At that time, Swain did indeed hear God.

He and his wife Julie were grilling skewers of pork and green peppers on the back patio of the stone house they chose themselves as the manse. They have no children. Julie works. She is a medical librarian at the hospital, though if you met her you would never think of libraries. You might think of Hayley Mills in some of those movies from her teenage years. She has the same full features and thick red hair. On this particular night, Julie is turning a shish ke-bab, which seems to be falling apart. Swain, bare-footed—it is June—is drinking a beer and squinting up the slight hill of their backyard, which they have kept wooded.

"Isn't that a lady slipper?" he says. "Was that out yesterday?" But Julie is busy; she doesn't look. Swain, his long white feet still bare, carefully picks his way up the hill to examine the flower. It is then, as he stops yards away from the plant—clearly not a lady slipper—that he hears God for the first time.

The sound comes up and over the hill. One quick cut. Like a hugely amplified PA system, blocks away, switched on for a moment by mistake. "Know that there is truth. Know this." The last vowel, the "i" of this, lies quivering on the air like a note struck on a wineglass.

The voice is unmistakable. At the first intonation, the first rolling syllable, Swain wakes, feeling the murmuring life of each of a million cells. Each of them all at once. He feels the line where his two lips touch, the fingers of his left hand pressed against his leg, the spears of wet grass against the soles of his feet, the gleaming half-circles of tears that stand in his eyes. His own bone marrow hums inside him like colonies of bees. He feels the breath pouring in and out of him, through the damp red passages of his skull. Then in the slow way that fireworks die, the knowledge fades. He is left again with his surfaces and the usual vague darkness within. He turns back around to see if Julie has heard.

She has not. Her back turned to him, she is serving the two plates that he has set on the patio table. A breeze is moving the edge of the outdoor tablecloth. She turns back around toward him, looking up the hill. "Soup's on," she says, smiling. "Come eat." She stands and waits for him, as he walks, careful still of his feet and the nettles, back down to her. Straight to her. He takes her in his arm, ignoring her surprise, the half-second of her resistance. He pulls her close, tight against him, one hand laced now in her hair, one arm around her hips. He is as close as he can get. He has gathered all of her to him that he can hold.

He puts the side of his face against her cheek, so he will not have to see her eyes when he says: "Julie, over there on the grass, I heard something. A voice."

She pulls back from him, forcing him to see her. She raises her eyebrows, half-smiling, searching his face for the signs of a joke. "A voice?" she says. There is laughter ready in her voice.

"God," he says. His mouth is dry. "God's voice."

She watches him carefully now, her eyes scanning his eyes, ever-so-slightly moving. The trace of a smile is gone. "What do you mean?"

"Standing up there on the hill," he says, almost irritably. "I heard God. That's what I mean." He watches her, his own face blank. Hers is struggling. Let her question it if she wants to. He doesn't know how to explain.

"So what happened?" she says. "Tell me some more." She pauses. "What did it—what did the voice sound like?"

Swain repeats the words he heard. He does not say then what happened to him: that hearing the voice, he had felt the mortality of his every cell.

They stand apart from each other now. She reaches over and touches his hair, strokes it. If one of us was to hear God, it should have been Julie, he thinks. But a different God—the one he has believed in until today.

She is looking at him steadily. "I don't think you're crazy if that's what you're worried about." Her uncertainty has left her. "It's all right," she says. "It is."

"For you it would be," he says. He means it as a compliment. He has envied her imaginings, felt left behind sometimes by the unfocused look of her eyes. Though she will tell him where she is: that she goes back, years back, to the particular days with particular weathers. That she plays in the backyard of her grandparents' house, shirtless, in seer-sucker shorts, breathing the heavy summer air, near the blue hydrangeas. Swain wants to be with her then. He wants to go: "Except ye become as little children, ye shall not enter . . ." He wants, and yet he doesn't want.

She glances at the food on the plates. They move toward the table. The sweat that soaked his shirt has started to chill him.

"I'm going to get a sweater," he says. "Do you want anything?" She shakes her head no. She sits, begins to eat her cooling dinner.

There are no lights on inside the house, only the yellowish glow of the patio light through the window, shining on one patch of floor in the hall. He goes to the hall closet, looking for something to put on. He finds a light windbreaker. He has his hand in the closet, reaching for the jacket, when he hears the voice again. One syllable. "Son." The sound unfurls down the long hall toward him. He feels the sounds and its thousand echoes hit him all at once. He holds onto the wooden bar where the coat hangs, while the shock washes over his back.

He stays where he is, his back and neck bent, his hand bracing him, waiting. Nothing else happens. Again, it is over. Again he is wet with sweat. He straightens, painfully, as if he had held the position for hours. He walks again out onto the patio. Julie, at the table, squints to see his face against the light beside the door.

"Are you alright?" she says.

He sits, looks down at his plate. He holds the jacket, lays it across his lap like a napkin. He shakes his head. A sob is starting low in his chest, dry like a cough. He feels it coming, without tears. He has not cried since he tore a ligament playing school soccer. He has had no reason. Now he is crying, his own voice tearing and breaking through him. Inside him, walls are falling. Interior walls cave like old plaster, fall away to dust. He feels it like the breaking of living bones. In the last cool retreat of his reason, he thinks: I am seeing my own destruction. Then that cool place is invaded too. He feels the violent tide of whatever is in him flooding his last safe ground. He holds himself with both arms; Julie, on her knees beside his chair, holds him. God has done this to him. This is God. Tears drip from his face and trickle down his neck.

Two days later Swain sits alone in his office at the church. He has a sermon to write. Should he tell the congregation what happened to him? His notepad is blank. He has put down his pen. It is an afternoon with all the qualities of a sleepless night: hot, restless, unending. There are no distractions from what he is unable to do. The secretary is holding his calls. The couple who were to come in with marital difficulties cancelled. The window behind his desk is open; he stares out into the shimmery heat and listens to the churning of a lawn mower. He has already been through the literature and found nothing to reassure him.

Son. He keeps coming back to that one word in his mind. It was not Swain's own father talking. That was clear. His father would never have been so definite, so terse. The elder Dr. Hammond would have interspersed his words, and there would have been more of them, with long moments of musing and probably the discreet small noises of his dyspepsia. He would have asked Swain to consider whether there was indeed 'a truth.' Swain would have considered this, as he was asked. And possibly at some later time they would have discussed it, without conclusion.

Swain, twisting in his chair, resettling his legs, knows he did not create the voice. He did not broadcast that sound out through the pines of his own backyard. He sees again the reddish gold light of the late sun on the bark of those backyard trees. He did not imagine it. His mind does not play tricks.

Though the whole thing seems like a bad trick, a bad dream—divine revelation, coming now. He imagines himself in the pulpit, staring out at the congregation, telling them. He sees the horror waking on their faces, as they understand him. He sees them exchanging glances, glances that cut diagonally across the pews. He would be out. It would cost him the church. Leaders of the congregation would gradually, lovingly ease him out, help him make 'other arrangements.' He tries to imagine those other arrangements: churches with marquees that tally up the number saved on a Sunday, churches with buses and all-white congregations. Appalling. It makes him shudder.

He turns his chair away from the window, back to his desk. It is too soon. He has nothing to say. Know that there is truth? A half-sentence? He at least needs some time to think about it. Then perhaps he can make some sense out of it. Of course he will make public confession finally. He will witness. He has to. "Whoever shall confess me before men, him shall the Son of Man also confess before the angels of God." There is no question. ". . . He that denieth me before men . . ." It is his mission—to speak. A man could not remain a minister with such a secret.

On Saturday, he has a wedding. He has already put on his robe. His black shoes gleam. He sits at his desk, ready early, signing letters left here in his box by the secretary. Routine business. His sermon for Sunday is written, typed in capital letters. It makes no direct reference to hearing the voice of God.

He does like marrying couples, thinks of it, in fact, as an important part of his ministry. When a couple gets together within the church, it always seems to him a sort of personal victory. As the boy said two weeks ago at the junior high retreat, "Human relations is where it's at."

The pair this afternoon is interesting to him in a more particular way. He has been counseling them since Louise, the bride-to-be, found out she was pregnant. She is thirty-eight, roughly his own age. She and Alphonse, a Colombian, have lived together for about three years. They have planned for today, a fairly traditional, almost formal ceremony. She is not yet showing. He remembers her when she was alone. He could see her on Sunday mornings canvassing the congregation with her eyes, picking out the occasional male visitor holding his hymnbook alone. Watching her in those years, he wondered what his own life would be like, without Julie. Whether he would show that same hunger so plainly on his face. He is glad for Louise, pregnant as she is. He caps his pen and stands. It's time to go.

The feeling is different now in the sanctuary, more relaxed than the eleven o'clock. Maybe it's only the afternoon light, filtered as it is by stained glass. He stands at the chancel steps, the ceremony begins. Alphonse comes to stand beside him. They face the aisle where Louise is to enter on the arm of her sister's husband. Swain tests the sound of their names, rehearses them in silence—Louise Elizabeth Berryman, Alphonse Martinez Vasconcellos. The twang and the beat of the Spanish—he has resolved to get it right, not to anglicize. He runs through the name again—and a scene unwinds like a scroll inside him. Gerona.

Louise, coming down the aisle now, slowly, slowly, moves in her long pale dress behind the clear shapes of his sudden unsought memory. He is twenty years old, standing in a stone-walled room in Spain. The straps of his backpack pull at his shoulders. It is quiet here, blocks away from the narrow river and the arched bridges. In this room—he read it in his guide-book—there was a revelation. He stands, with his two friends, in a medieval landmark of the kabbalah. It is the moment, unplanned, when all three become quiet, when he can only hear the muted traffic from the street. He is looking for something in this room. He lays his hand on the grainy stone of the wall. Standing now in the sanctuary, he feels the damp grit of rock against the flat of his palm. He can't escape it, he can't shake it off. He wears it—this slight tingling pressure—like a glove. A wet glove that clings to his skin. Louise is now at the front before him.

The couple turns to him. They wait. "Dearly beloved," he hears himself say. Faces stretch in a blur to the back of the church. He hears his voice—it must be his—float out to those faces, saying, "We are gathered here today . . ."

He has told Julie everything, about hearing the voice. Not just the words, but how it felt. He has told her about the intrusion of the scene from Spain at the wedding this afternoon. "That was the last thing I needed," he says. "For that to happen while I'm actually standing at the front." They are sitting at the kitchen table. It's late.

She shrugs. The look on her face is the one he tries to cultivate in counseling. She is not shocked. Yet she does not diminish what has happened to him. The look is one of sympathy and respect at once. She does it, he knows, without thinking.

She nods toward the typewriter, his old one, standing in its case near the bookshelves. They both use it for letters, neither one of them has a legible handwriting. "You've always set the margins so narrow," she says. "On yourself, on what's real. You don't give yourself much room."

She waits. He thinks about it.

"True," he says, nodding, looking away from her. "And you give yourself that kind of—'room' you're talking about." He looks at her, her chin propped on one hand, her face pushed slightly out of shape. "But do you actually believe in it," he says, "in what you see and hear, in the things you imagine? You don't. Of course you don't."

She puts her hand down, on the table, away from her face. She takes a breath and holds it a second before she speaks. The look she has had, of authority, is gone. "In a way," she says. She searches his face. "I don't think too much about it. But—yes, in a way, I do."

There is no joy in it. That's what bothers him. He is lying on the living room floor, still thinking about it, though he hasn't mentioned any of it, even to Julie, for almost a week. Julie is in the armchair reading, her feet in old white tennis shoes, her ankles crossed near his head. He watches her feet move, very slightly, in a rhythm, as if she were listening to music instead of reading. Maybe she hears music and never mentions it. She likes music. Maybe she's hearing Smetana's *Moldau*, close enough to the orchestra to hear between the movements the creakings of musicians' chairs. She would do this and think nothing of it. She has been patient with his days of silent turmoil.

As a kid, he wanted something like this to happen. Some sign. He did imagine though that it would bring with it pleasure— great happiness, in fact. He had a daydream of how it would be, set in the halls and classrooms of his elementary school, where he first imagined it. A column of warm pink light would pour over him, overpowering him with a sensation so intensely sweet it was unimaginable. He tried and tried to feel how it would feel. The warmth would wrap around his heart inside his chest, like two hands cradling him there. He would be full of happiness, completely at peace. The notion stayed with him past childhood, though, certainly in his earlier years, he didn't talk about it.

But he did what he could to have that experience. Divine revelation. He wanted it. He lay on the floor of his bedroom at home, later his dorm room at Brown, and waited. He stared at rippling creeks and wind-blown leaves and the deep chalky green of blackboards until his mind was lulled into receptive quiet. The quietness always passed, though, without interruption, at least by anything divine.

The search must have ended finally. Only now does his realize it, lying here with the front door standing open and moths batting against the screen. He doesn't recall any such preoccupation during divinity school, though there was that one thing that happened in his last year. It hardly qualified him as a mystic, though it was reassuring at the time.

He was sitting out on the balcony of his apartment, a second-floor place he shared with two other students. He and Julie, not married then, were in one of their off times. He was feeling bad. The concordance, the notepad has slid off his lap. His legs were sprawled, completely motionless, in front of him, hanging off the end of the butt-sagged recliner. He had lost Julie; he was bone-tired of school, he wouldn't have cared if he died.

He was staring at the scrubby woods behind the apartment complex, behind the parking lot and a weedy patch of mud and three dumpsters. Nothing mattered. Nothing at all. Then while he watched, everything—without motion or shift of light—everything he saw changed. He stared at the painted stripes on the asphalt, at water standing on the yellowish mud. It was all alive. Alive and sharing one life. The parking lot, the bare ground had become the varied skin of one living being. In the stillness, he waited for the huge creature to move, to take a breath. Nothing stirred. Yet he felt the benevolence of the animal, its power, rising off the surface before him like waves of heat.

When he felt then was a lightness, a sort of happiness. This was so important. It was at least a hint of what he had once imagined.

That afternoon he was buoyed. He finished the work he had sat with the whole afternoon. He fried himself a hamburger and ate it and was still hungry. He watched a few minutes of the news. He did not die or think further of dying that day, other than for the purposes of sermons, counseling, and facing the inevitable facts.

Facts. He is lying on the floor of his living room. Julie is reading in the chair. God has spoken to him, in English, clearly, in an unmistakable voice. He is not glad.

"What would you do, Julie?" he says. He is looking at the ceiling, he does not turn his head. "Would you stand up in that pulpit and tell them, 'I have heard the voice of God'? Would you do it?" He rolls over on his side and looks at her. Her foot has stopped moving. She has put her book down.

"I've been thinking about that," she says.

"What did you decide?"

"Probably," she says. "I think I would." She is not smiling. She looks at him steadily. Her eyes are tired.

"Oh?" he says. There is an edge in his voice. "What else would you say? How would you explain it? Explain to me, if you understand so well." He pauses, waits.

"Say as much as you know," she says.

"What is that? One piece of a sentence: know that there is truth. It isn't enough. I have nothing to say."

"It's your job, isn't it?" she says. "To tell them. Isn't it?" He sees the fear flickering across her face now. She needs to say it, but she's scared. It's the way he would be, standing before his incredulous congregation. Fearing the cost. What could it cost her to say this?

"You're afraid to tell me," he says. His voice is weary, dull.

She nods.

"Why?"

She swallows, looks away from him. "Because I'm saying you need to do something that may turn out bad. It would be the most incredible irony—but it could happen. They might decide you're losing your marbles. They might call it that, when really they don't want a minister who says this kind of stuff—about hearing God. It's not that kind of church. You know?"

He ignores the question. "We could have to move," he says. "We could wind up somewhere we would hate. Is that what you're worried about?"

"Some," she says. "But mostly that you would blame me, if it happened—that you would always feel like I pushed you into it."

"And then the marriage would fall apart," he says.

"Yeah," she says. Her voice shakes. Her mouth has the soft forgotten look it gets when all of her is concentrated elsewhere. In this case, on fear. He is not in the mood to reassure her.

"And what if I don't?" he says. "What if I never say a word and you spend the rest of your life thinking I'm a shit—a minister who denies God? What happens to us then?"

She shakes her head. She is close to tears. "I don't think that will happen," she says. It comes out in an uneven whisper.

Swain stands, straightens his pants legs. He looks at her once without sympathy, but her face is averted, she doesn't see. He leaves the room, goes into the kitchen. He gets out a small tub of Häagen-Dazs and a spoon, stands near the fridge, eating from the container. There is no sound from her in the other room. Pink light—what a joke. "Suppose ye that I am come to give peace on earth? I tell you, Nay; but rather division." The voice didn't warn him, didn't remind him. He shakes his head. He digs and scrapes at the ice cream.

He is turning his car into the church parking lot when it happens again. He hears God. His window is open. The car is lurched upward onto the incline of the pavement. The radio is on, but low. From the hedge, a few feet from his elbow on the window frame, a sound emerges. It clearly comes from there: a burst, a jumble of phrases, scripture, distortions of scripture: "He that heareth and doeth not . . . for there is nothing hid . . . the word is sown on stony ground . . . why reason ye . . . seeketh his own glory . . . he that hath ears . . . he that hath . . ." A nightmare. A nightmare after a night of too much reading. A spilling of accusation, reproach. Swain is staring straight ahead. A hot weight presses into him, into the soft vee beneath the joining of his ribs. It hurts, it pins him to the seat. It passes like cramp, leaving only a shadow, a distrust of those muscles.

Another car is waiting behind him, easing toward his fender. He pulls into the parking lot, into a space. He does it automatically. His face feels as hot as the sun-baked plastic car seat. He looks at the hedge, running between the sidewalk and the street. Tear it out—that's what he wants to do. Pull it up, plant by plant, with his hands. He is a pastor. Not a prophet. Not a radio evangelist. He does not believe in gods that quote King James version out of bushes and trees.

He gets out of the car, goes into the church, into his office. He kicks the door shut behind him. He tosses a new yellow legal pad onto the bare center of his desk. There has to be something in this room to smash. He looks around: at the small panes of the window; at the veneer on the side of his desk; at the cluster of family pictures, framed; at the bud vase Julie gave him, that now holds two wilting daisies and a home-grown rose. Something to break. He grabs the vase by the neck and slings it, overarm, dingy water spilling, into a pillow of the sofa. A soft thump, and the stain of water spreads on the dark upholstery. He looks away from it, looks at the yellow pad on his desk. His career. That's what he'll smash. That ought to be enough. He walks around behind the desk, red-faced, breathing audibly through parted lips. He stares at the lined paper with the pen in his hand. Say as much as you know. He begins to write. Beyond writing it down, he tells himself, he has made no decision.

On the following Sunday, he walks forward into the pulpit. He has received the offering. He has performed the preliminary duties with a detached methodical calm. Now he stands with his hands on the wooden rail, his fingers finding their familiar places along the tiered wood. "Friends," he says. He looks at no one in particular. "I have struggled with what I have to say to you today." They are waiting, with no more than their routine interest. "I have come to say to you that I have heard the voice of God." He says it to the rosette of stained glass at the back of the sanctuary. He cannot look at Julie in the third row. He cannot look at the McDougalls or Sam Bagdikian or Mary Elgar, as he says it. In the ensuing silence, his eyes sweep forward again, from the window back across three hundred faces. They are blank, waiting still, mildly interested. No one is alarmed. They have not understood.

He begins again. As much as he knows. "I think you know that I believe in an immanent God. I think you know that I believe in the presence and power of God in all our lives. I have come to tell you today that something has happened to me in recent days which I do not understand.

"A voice has spoken to me. I know that it is God. A voice has spoken to me that was a chorus of voices. I know that they are God." He pauses. "My wife Julie and I were cooking dinner on the grill on our back patio . . ." The faces grow taut with attention. Sudden stillness falls over the church to the back pews of the balcony. There is no flutter of church bulletins. There are no averted faces. It is not a metaphor, not a parable he is telling. His wife Julie, the back patio—they are listening. He proceeds, with a trembling deep in his gut. He begins with the lady slipper and voice that came over the hill.

He tells them about the word "son" and the windbreaker and his own tears. "I asked myself whether I should bring this to you on a Sunday morning," he says. He looks from face to face in the rows in front of him. What are they thinking? It's impossible to tell. The shaking inside him has moved outward, to his hands. He feels them damp against the wood of the pulpit rail. He does not trust his voice.

"I asked myself how you, the members of the congregation, would react. Would you think that I've—" he tries to say this lightly, with a wry laugh—"that maybe I've been under too much stress lately." The laugh is not convincing. He hears himself its false ring. "But I will tell you," he says, "that that is not what happened. I have not taken leave of my senses."

He looks at Julie. He can see her wrists, before the back of the pew breaks his vision. He knows her hands are knotted together, moving one against the other. He pulls his eyes away.

"I asked myself whether you would want a pastor who hears voices. Or even whether some of you might come to expect

wisdom from me, because of what happened, that I do not have."
He pauses. "I don't know what to expect," he says, "from you
or—" he hesitates—"from God. But I will tell you that my heart
is now open. I will listen." He steps back, hearing as he does
so the first note of the organ; reliable Miss Bateman is playing.
The congregation stands, hymnbooks in hands. The service
ends without incident. Swain stands as usual at the front steps
afterwards to shakes hands and greet people. Three of all those
who file past tell him that the Lord works in wondrous ways, or
something to that effect. Miss Frances Eastwood squeezes his
elbow and tells him to trust. Ed Fitzgerald lays one hand on his
shoulder, close to his collar, and says, "I like what you did here
today." The rest make no mention of what has occurred. The line
moves quickly past him, handshakes, heartiness, veiled eyes.

It is not over, of course. Julie keeps her hand on his knee as
he drives home, though they say little. During the afternoon,
he receives several phone calls at home, of an encouraging and
congratulatory nature. Coming back into the kitchen, where
Julie is cleaning out drawers to keep busy, he says, "It's the ones
who don't call, who are calling each other . . ."

What does occur happens gradually. Swain is given no answer, no sense of having-got-it-over on that Sunday afternoon.
First, as he surmises, conversations buzz back and forth, on the
telephone, at get-togethers, in chance meetings on the street.
People inside and outside the church talk about what happened,
about Swain Hammond's sermon.

The night the church operations committee meets, Swain
and Julie stay home and play Scrabble. Swain can't concentrate,
but Julie protests every time he wants to quit. The call comes at
11:15. It's Joe Morris. "Between you and me," Joe reminds him,
"this is an unofficial . . ."

The upshot of it is that the committee voted five-to-four to
privately recommend that Swain get professional help. The
chairman, Bill Bartholomew, who made the motion, comes to
Swain's office to tell him. "Of course," he says, "this is something
which is not easy to say. But we all go through times when we
need . . ."

"Thank you for your prayers and concern," Swain says. He is
accustomed to assuming a look of gratitude when it is called for.
It only fails him in the last minutes of the conversation.

"Are you sure I'm crazy, Bill?" he says. The two of them are
standing now in the office doorway, there is no one in the hall.
"Doesn't it seem contradictory?" Swain says. Bill is watching

him carefully. "It's okay to believe in God, but only if God is distant. A presence in history. Is that the idea?"

"I'm sure I don't want to debate this with you," Bill says. "It's only the will of the committee—"

"I understand your position," Swain says. He does not seek counseling.

When news of the committee's action leaks, a petition circulates and the members take sides. This time the vote is with Swain. The letter, signed by the majority of the members, affirms that Dr. Swain Hammond is in his right mind and will continue to be welcome as minister. These are not the exact words, but this is the meaning.

Swain mentions this decision from the pulpit, but only as a brief comment among the day's other announcements. "Thank you for your love and support," he says. Unexpectedly, as he says it, he feels a tightness in his throat. He looks from face to face. He won't be leaving. If he thinks about it, he'll lose his composure. He summons a bit of the anger that has sustained him through the last few weeks. It works, he manages to keep the wave of love at bay.

"Besides," he tells Julie later that day, "I don't completely trust it." They are taking a late afternoon walk through the neighborhood around their house. "I feel like all this could change, if the balance shifted just a little. I'm reasonably secure for the moment," he says. "I suppose that will have to do."

She doesn't say anything. She has said her part several times already: that she is proud of him, that she is proud of what he did.

"I'm also disappointed," he says. They stop for a moment to avoid the arc of spray from a sprinkler cutting across the sidewalk. "I thought maybe a few people would be curious about what actually happened. Would want to hear more." He shakes his head. "They don't." It makes him mad to think about it. They've decided to put up with him—that's what they've made of all this. They're being broad-minded and tolerant, that's all.

Swain does hear the voice of God again. This time—last Tuesday morning—it is as a note of music, as he is just waking up. Julie lies beside him asleep. It is early, still twenty minutes before the alarm is set to go off. He knows before it happens that it's coming. He does not move. He waits, while the note emerges from a sound too deep to be heard. Then it is audible, filling the room, hugging against his bare stomach, like the live warm touch of a hand. In the same moment, it begins to diminish, a dwindling vibration on piano strings.

Swain lies still. He does not cry this time, or soak the sheets with his sweat. He does not wake Julie, whose breath he can feel on the curve of his shoulder. He looks at the morning light on the far wall, shifting with the shadows of tree branches. He watches the triangles and splinters of light, forming and re-forming, and feels the slow rise and fall of his own chest. Everything is quiet: the room, the yard beneath the window, the street out front. He can see it all in his mind now, one surface, connected, breathing with his same slow breath. What he feels then, flooding the whole space of his being, is joy, undeniably joy, though it has not come as he would have expected. It is not what he looked for at all.

One by one they finished the story, some of them smirking like they'd just been dealt four aces, others with furrowed faces like they'd been dealt four jokers. I knew this would be a different experience than reading Alice Walker's "The Welcome Table," and that later stories would push them even more. "Okay," I said, "what did you think? It's different, huh?"

Carlos jumped in, "I don't get it. I mean the story is okay, sort of interesting and all. But I don't see how this relates to preaching." He hesitated, and then continued, "I'm sorry, but I just don't get it."

I didn't see any reason to comment on his confession or his apology. He didn't say anything about "hearing the voice of God." I waited for others to join the conversation. Rosa looked at Carlos and said, "I can see why you say that. In our context it's hard to imagine including something like this in a sermon. But at the same time, it's a powerful story that I think most ministers can relate to in some way or another. I've never heard God speak, not out loud. But the tension Rev. Hammond feels about telling the truth God has laid on his heart or keeping quiet, that's something we all know."

Alesha said, "Sure, there is that tension he feels, but my mind went another direction altogether. I kept thinking about Moses and the burning bush. Swain hears God out of a flower in the backyard. And if that's not enough of a clue, the author lets him hear God out of a bush. I don't know how I would do it, but seems like a good sermon pairing to me, this story and Exodus 3." Several of them liked that idea, although it was hard to say who had seen the connection prior to her pointing it out.

We talked at some length about the particulars of the story, other texts that might work, and the idea of how ministers are supposed to tell the truth even when it's hard to hear it. Then I added, "I shared this story in class because it's shorter than most, but also because of how it touches upon the idea of God breaking into our fleshly lives. A minister and his wife grilling out, a beer in hand, and suddenly God shows up. Good preaching deals with our fleshly lives. Remember that hymn at Christmas, 'O Come, All Ye Faithful': the line about the Christ, 'now in flesh appearing.'"

We talked for a long while about the story and some different sermon ideas. I said, "But there's something else for us to remember about narrative preaching, apart from the particulars of this one story. Narrative preaching isn't powerful just because it takes the form of a plot or evokes an experience, important as those things are. And it's not powerful just because we tell stories, as vital as that is to good preaching. Narrative preaching needs stories that resonate with the depths and complexities of our lives, and stories like this one deal with real life. Even if it's fiction, the story feels real. And so should our sermons."

I thought about how the world's literature is defined in terms of fiction. Everything else we call *non*fiction. Judging how some people feel about novels and short stories, a person might think it would have been the other way around.

I wanted to stress how stories are about more than the ideas they convey. I said, "What if after you read Walker's story, I had asked what it's about? Or what if I asked you now, 'What is Payne's story about?' I'm not sure what you would say, but my answer would be 'oh, about four pages,' or 'about twelve pages.'" Several of them chuckled. I said, "I know, it sounds silly; but it's also profound in another way. Here's what I mean. Literary critics note the absurdity of naming in a few words what anything is about: a short story, a movie, and so forth. A person has to experience a story to get it, enter into its pathos. Summarizing it in a phrase won't do. This is what the literary critic Cleanth Brooks referred to as 'the heresy of paraphrase.'" They shook their heads up and down in agreement. I continued, "And yet, people talk about the movies they see, the stories they read. They seek to put the experience into words. That is precisely how I feel about narrative preaching, that we need our listeners to experience these stories, but also to hear something of an explanation or exposition that grows from reflecting upon the story." I paused, and then added, "Experience and exposition. That's the idea."

I waited a few moments. "Go in peace. See you next week."

CHAPTER EIGHT

Inside the Green Gate

S eminary students who are juggling lots of balls need to set them down from time to time, before they come crashing down. It's amazing the loads many of them carry—school, family, ministry, the list is long. So on this restless Thursday of the semester, I waited for all the backpacks to be put down, for everyone to catch their breath and get quiet.

I began, "This evening's excerpt from *Reading Lolita in Tehran* is about the green gate through which they entered the university."

> I passed through it at least twice a day on weekdays for a number of years, but I still can't quite conjure it properly. In my memory the iron gate acquires an elastic quality and becomes a magic door, unsupported by walls, guarding the university grounds. Yet I do remember its boundaries. It opened on one side to a wide street that appeared to lead straight into the mountains. On the other side it faced a small garden.

> Next to the green gate there was a small opening with a curtain hanging from it. It was an aberration that attracted attention, because it did not belong there: it gaped with the arrogant authority of an intruder. Through this opening all the female students, including my girls, went into a small, dark room to be inspected. Yassi would describe later, long after that first session, what was done to her in this room: "I would first be checked to see if I have the right clothes: the color of my coat, the length of my uniform, the thickness of my scarf, the form of my shoes, the objects in my bag, the visible traces of even the mildest makeup,

the size of my rings and their level of attractiveness, all would be checked before I could enter the campus of the university, the same university in which men also study. And to them the main door, with its immense portals and emblems and flags, is generously open.

I led us in a time of prayer, reading lines from one of the Lenten psalms, interspersed with silence. Afterwards, Joey said, "Would it be okay to share a prayer request with the class? I should have said something before now."

"Of course," I said. "What's on your mind?"

He told us about his girlfriend's mom, who had recently been diagnosed with breast cancer. He said the prognosis was fairly positive but the family would still appreciate prayers. Alesha offered to lead us in prayer since her mom had battled the same thing years earlier.

Joey also brought the treat for the evening. I asked, "So, Joey, what did you bring?"

He said, "Good question, dude. My girlfriend made it. I think they're some kind of brownies with caramel swirls." He removed the foil from the pan and we all had a religious moment right then and there.

Cassandra said, "Chocolate! Nothing Gnostic about that."

We passed the pan and napkins around, removing squares of brownies with a plastic knife. I said, "I want us to get in two groups again this evening, one dealing with the readings from Neil Postman's *Amusing Ourselves to Death*, and the other Richard Jensen's *Thinking in Story*. But before we do the group thing, I want you to take out a piece of paper and number it 1 and 2."

Brock wiped some chocolate crumbs from his mouth. "Please don't tell me we're having a pop quiz. I hate pop quizzes. Come to think of it, I hate quizzes, period."

I said, "No, not a pop quiz. But I want you to write down your reflections to these two questions, not just think about them vaguely." A few borrowed pen and paper from others, then I said, "Okay, first question: What is your Christology? In other words, if you were writing your summative credo paper for the MDiv, what would you say about the Christ? What do you believe? Second question, and I don't care to elaborate on this one: What brand of tires do you think is best? Take a few minutes."

Brock looked at me like I had lost my marbles, and he was not alone. Carlos, however, was already busy with the first question, so he didn't seem to be intrigued by the second question at all even though I expected him to flip out over such trivial matters. After a few minutes, I said, "We will get to your responses in awhile, but for now let's break into two groups. Cassandra and Alesha, I'd like for each of you to convene one of the groups. Cassandra, you take Postman, and Alesha, you take Jensen." This was a deliberate choice. I did not give them any specific instructions for discussion other than to think about the main point and how they might interact with it.

Cassandra, Lisa, and Joey sat at one end of the room; Alesha, Brock, Carlos, and Rosa at the other. But the discussions were loud, so Cassandra's group asked if they could meet somewhere else. I said sure, and they found one of the informal study areas in a nearby lounge.

When we were all together again I shared how sometimes I have said to preachers in a retreat setting that Postman's book is one of the "most important books some preachers never read." I'm not sure why it went unnoticed by so many folks, especially given his treatment not just of culture but religion as well. The subtitle is *Public Discourse in the Age of Show Business*, and on the cover is a drawing of a family watching TV, only none of them have any heads. I asked, "So what did you come up with?"

Cassandra looked at the others, probably so as not to do all the talking. Joey said, "The dude's not a big fan of TV, that's for sure."

I said, "Okay, but why not? What is his critique of TV?"

Lisa said, "Well, it's not so much about *what's on* TV but *what it does* to us when it's on."

"Yes," I said, "very well put. Postman is concerned with 'media epistemology,' how TV affects the way we know things, or don't."

Joey added, "I loved the part about the debates with Lincoln and, who was that other dude?"

A chorus of folks chimed in, "Douglas."

"Yeah," said Joey, "the Lincoln-Douglas debates. I can't believe that people could sit still for seven-hour debates. Is that true?"

I said, "As far as I know," which was meant as an epistemological joke, although no one seemed to get it.

Cassandra said, "And the part where Lincoln actually told the audience he didn't really want applause but thoughtful reflection on their part. What a contrast with our political debates."

I said, "Okay, but let's go back to 'media epistemology,' the way TV (and this is larger than TV) and cultural trends like it affect the way we receive our world. What does Postman say about that?" While Cassandra flipped through some pages, I continued, "Look at his statement on page 27, near the middle: 'My argument is limited to saying that a major new medium changes the structure of discourse. . . . I believe the epistemology created by television not only is inferior to a print-based epistemology but is dangerous and absurdist.' Does that seem like Chicken Little crying out about a sky called literacy falling in on us? Is it fair?"

People in the other group wanted to respond, but for now I wanted to hear from this one group. Cassandra said, "I do think it's fair. He is not passing judgment on the content of television, too much sex and violence, that sort of thing. He is simply noting that *how* one receives material, *how* we come to know certain things through a particular medium, affects us."

I said, "Yes, good."

Besides Postman's work, I had recently read David Gordon's *Why Johnny Can't Preach*. The title is a takeoff from the much older books, *Why Johnny Can't Read* and *Why Johnny Can't Write*. Gordon believes the lack of critical reading and writing skills among preachers has greatly contributed to the demise of much preaching. It's no longer thoughtful. The masculine gender is part of his theology when it comes to preaching, so while that's troublesome, I do appreciate the work for another reason. Gordon wrote the book when he learned he had terminal cancer. Turns out, it wasn't terminal, but it's refreshing that he thought if he was going to die, something needed to be said about the poor quality of preaching in the churches. For Gordon, somewhat like Postman, it's due to a lack of intellectual rigor.

Continuing our discussion of Postman, I said, "Looking at chapter 4 and the material about the Lincoln-Douglas debates, how does Postman distinguish exposition from entertainment? What is his main concern? And he's obviously very concerned."

Lisa answered, "Exposition wouldn't be what we usually mean by it in preaching lingo. Although I guess it's somewhat related. But to me, it's his way of talking about serious critical thinking rather than the shallowness of so much programming."

I said, "Okay, good. And I think in some ways he does use exposition the way I'm using it, although I'm expanding on it just a bit. He later describes exposition as 'a sophisticated ability to think conceptually,' and a 'high valuation of reason and order.' I think many sermons could use some of those things. But why does he care about critical thinking? What's that to him?"

Cassandra said, "He is—or was?—a university professor. He's worried about the level of thinking in the generations to come, afraid that fewer and fewer of us will know the difference between the Great Depression and depression. Which is really depressing."

"Good," I responded. "Let's stop right there. What about Jensen? How might he wrestle with these same issues? How does he understand the difference between oral and literate cultures?"

Alesha said, "Well, I think his references to Marshall McLuhan go along nicely with Postman, the line about 'the medium is the message.' Media, like TV, touch us in certain ways."

I asked, "How many of you have read Marshall McLuhan before, maybe in college? No one? He is not an easy read, that's for sure." Then I told a story that a guest lecturer shared with the seminary some years back, about when McLuhan was a university professor in Toronto. One day he discovered a student's car parked in his faculty space, so he wrote a note and placed it on the windshield. The student got the note, and made an appointment to see the professor since he had taken a class with McLuhan before. He said, "Professor McLuhan, I just wanted to apologize for parking in your space, but also to thank you for the note. This is the first thing you've ever written that I actually understand." We all laughed.

I said, "It is true that McLuhan is sometimes hard to understand. By the way, he really did conceive of the Internet back before the technology was even available. He was a true pioneer in these circles. And that line about 'the medium is the message' is accurate, although the title of his infamous book is *The Medium Is the Massage*. His point was about how different media massage us, or touch us. Some forms massage the brain, others more the gut. This would be another interesting topic for us to explore, McLuhan's theory of 'hot' and 'cool' media, especially in relation to the use of Power-Point in much preaching these days. But for now, let's stick with what we have read."

Alesha said, "To me, the amazing thing about Jensen is that he's not upset with the new storytelling media like TV. I think he celebrates it."

Brock added, "Yeah, he believes that the early oral culture in which the Bible was born is not that much different from the electronic one in which we now live. It's radically different from the print culture in which I was educated, but I know that my grandkids are hardwired differently from me."

Carlos said, "I don't know if this is what you're looking for, but this author Jensen even quotes Postman."

I said, "Yes, he does. And what does he say?"

Carlos flipped over his book. He said, "On the bottom of page 36 he says, 'I am more optimistic than Postman that the public discourse of preaching can adapt itself to this new technology.'"

I said, "Good, thank you. In some ways Jensen's book is a homiletical response to Postman's lament. But it is only one homiletical response. We will consider others. So let me ask a similar question I asked the other group about Postman. Why does Jensen celebrate the power of story? Why is he optimistic?"

Cassandra, although not in this group, raised her hand. "I think it's because he's a practitioner of the New Homiletic. He believes in experiencing the sermon."

"Exactly," I said. "Jensen as preacher celebrates what Postman as educator laments. So what about you? Not just you, Cassandra, but all of you. What are your hopes for preaching? Are you more concerned with what people learn when you preach? With what they experience? What?"

Carlos said, "The Apostle Paul warns against a kind of preaching in which people have their ears tickled, where they get what they want. I think teaching the Bible and the ways of God is the most important thing we can do."

Brock said, "I get where you're coming from, brother, I do. And I agree, at least in part. But I'm wondering why we can't have both in our sermons. My daddy used to say there are ditches on both sides of the road. As someone who drove a truck for umpteen years, I can testify to that."

I said, "Okay, before we pursue the idea of sermons doing both, let's go back to the first two questions you wrestled with. 'What is your Christology?' Anyone?"

Joey said, "I have no clue why we answered these two really strange questions, one about Jesus and the other about tires."

I said, "That's okay. I'll explain. What did you write about the Christ?"

He said, "I remember how Christology is usually divided into the person and work of Christ. The person of Christ is what all those councils were about, his divinity and humanity, all that stuff."

I said, "Okay. Someone else?" Several of them commented on the Chalcedonian formula popular in Western Christianity, Jesus as completely divine and human, sacrificing neither. Others noted his relationship to the Trinity, even perichoretic understandings, the Three-in-One divine dance. I said, "Very good. But notice how your thinking focused almost exclusively on his person, his nature. Elaine Pagels and other scholars note how academic notions have influenced these categories as opposed to what the Gospels show in story. They don't speculate about his nature and the like; the Gospels tell stories of his feeding people, healing the sick, speaking in parables. This is what he did. Focusing on his person is an epistemological frame, as is focusing on his work.

"So now for the oddest question you'll ever be asked in seminary, 'What kind of tires do you think are best?' Anyone? In fact, let's see if there's something of a consensus."

As a former truck driver, Brock waited. Lisa said, "Goodyear?"

Joey said, "I don't think it's Goodyear. Maybe Firestone."

Several others responded, then Brock said with a tone of finality, "Michelin. No question." So no one dared question him.

Except me. "Okay, Michelin. What do you know about how Michelin manufactures tires? And how do you know that?"

Brock said, "Same way I know most things in life. Experience."

I said, "Well, I guess we could discuss the merits of Wesley's quadrilateral on that one. But here's my real point, and I take this from Postman's work. We don't know much about tires, not really. Remember that early ad by Paul Revere for false teeth that Postman quotes at length?" I flipped through some pages. "Here it is":

> Whereas many persons are so unfortunate as to lose their Fore-Teeth by Accident, and otherways, to their great Detriment, not only in Looks, but Speaking both in Public and Private:—This is to inform all such, that they may have them re-placed with false Ones, that look as well as the Natural, and Answers the End of Speaking to all Intents, by Paul Revere, Goldsmith, near the Head of Dr. Clarke's Wharf, Boston.

"What a long way from that to 'Michelin, because so much is riding on your tires,' or whatever their latest slogan happens to be. But here's the point, in the early centuries of Christianity the church moved from story to logic, councils wrestling with creeds and centuries later the Enlightenment focusing on critical thinking. Christianity has largely been a way of thinking. But more recently our culture, and in some ways, Christianity with it, has moved from logic and discourse to anecdotes—stories and even slogans. These days, Americans do their theologizing on bumper stickers and Twitter. And we'll have more to say about the mystical movement among some church folks. We'll also want to think about different ways of knowing, even in sermons. There's an intellectual knowing, but also a bodily kind of knowing, experiential.

"But for now, let me ask you a question. Maybe you remember that collection of essays published a few years back, *What's the Matter with Preaching Today?* It was a takeoff from an article by Harry Emerson Fosdick who had his own assessment of preaching. In the collection, a group of scholars answered the question from their viewpoints. But my question is for you: What do *you* think is the matter with preaching today? Too boring? Too shallow? For now, I'm too thirsty. Let's take a break and we'll continue the discussion afterwards."

CHAPTER NINE

Hyphenated

W hile we waited for a few stragglers to return from break, we discussed the latest movies we'd seen. In addition to *The Help*, Joey said that new baseball movie *Moneyball* was "awesome." Someone else said *The Debt* was not your typical spy movie, that it was worth seeing too, a kind of commentary on guilt and grace. I told them a little about the narrative preaching course I offer using movies, even if it probably wouldn't come around again until after most of them graduated. "Of course," I said, "you can always come back after graduation and take a course."

Lisa heard that as she entered the room. "Did I hear the word 'graduation'? Do we know someone who's graduating?" Several of them protested out of envy.

After a few more squares of brownies were served, I said, "So the question we left with was this: 'What's the matter with preaching today? Is it too boring? Too shallow?' What do you think?"

Brock cleared his throat and said, "Is 'yes' a sufficient answer?"

I said, "I think so, Brock. Couldn't have said it better myself, although maybe 'boring' isn't the right word. Still, give that man another brownie." He said he would pass, but he had made a really valid point. I said, "Preaching needs to have substance, or else what's the point. It also needs to create interest, or the substance might not be heard. Remember, we talked about this before. Preachers should have something to say, and they should say it well. In fact, in some ways this is another lens through which to look at the history of preaching."

Joey said, "I was thinking about what you said about history earlier this semester. I do think I might be allergic to it. The second church history course is killing me, dude."

Several of us laughed. I said, "We'll keep an eye on you. If a rash breaks out, you can be excused." Joey just smiled. I said, "When we looked at the history of preaching we started with 1958 and H. Grady Davis's work on organic preaching forms. Remember? Well, obviously the history of preaching is older than that. The church's first professor of homiletics was none other than Saint Augustine. In 427 he wrote a book called *On Christian Doctrine* or sometimes translated *On Christian Teaching*. It had four books, or parts; and Book IV was on preaching."

I continued, "What you need to remember about Augustine was his life prior to becoming a Christian. He was a trained rhetorician, which in that day usually meant either an educator or lawyer. Educators helped students to think clearly and formulate their thoughts. Lawyers were among the learned who helped illiterate folks with legal matters. But what is most telling about rhetoricians back then was the way many Christian thinkers viewed them with suspicion.

"Jerome, who was roughly a contemporary of Augustine's, is a classic example of how rhetoric was viewed with more than suspicion, with something like contempt. One story is about a dream Jerome had, in which he appears before the judgment seat of God. He is asked to confess his identity. He says he is a Christian, only to hear God say, 'You lie. You are a Ciceronian.' Cicero, if you don't know, was a highly influential teacher of rhetoric. Jerome says he struggled all the time with keeping a stash of rhetoric handbooks around. He would repent of his wicked ways and swear never to look at that stuff again, only to slip back into reading it."

Alesha said, "I'd like to have seen this guy's MMPI, his psychological profile. He sounds messed up."

Brock said, "He clearly had issues, but his description of giving up rhetoric sounds like someone battling an addiction to porn. What's the deal?"

I said, "The deal is that Christians regarded rhetoric as shallow at the very least, perhaps even evil. They associated it with heresy and philosophical schools of thought. So when Augustine experienced his conversion from Manichean philosophy to Christianity, one of the pressing questions was what could he bring with him and what would need to be jettisoned. And this brings us to Book IV of his work. In the first three sections he deals with the interpretation of Scripture, but Book IV focuses primarily on preaching.

"Augustine justified this focus on what we might call 'homiletical rhetoric' on the grounds that while the false religions and philosophies were just that, false, they spoke so eloquently as to win over followers. Meanwhile, Christians who had the truth often bumbled about in their proclamations. So Augustine penned this famous line about how the purposes of preaching are threefold: to teach, to delight, and to move."

Joey said, "Could you repeat that? To teach, to delight, and what?"

I said, "To teach, to delight, and to move." I wrote these terms on the board. "Actually, Augustine was quoting an even earlier source. He said, 'A certain eloquent speaker has said, the purposes of preaching are to teach, to delight, and to move.' That certain eloquent speaker was none other than Cicero, the rhetorician. Of course Cicero wasn't interested in preaching per se, but Augustine was."

I told them that some scholars believe that that third phrase, "to move," was just another way of combining the first two; others like George Kennedy believe it related to persuasion, which Augustine viewed as the work of God as well as the preacher. Either way, the preacher is still left with a twofold task: teaching and delighting.

I continued, "But here's what interests me about the need for teaching and delighting. In some ways it's the history of preaching in a nutshell. Ever since Augustine, preachers have gravitated toward one of those over the other, sometimes teaching at the expense of delight, other times delighting at the expense of teaching. Think about the preachers you know here in Kansas City, or where you grew up. Were their sermons primarily focused on teaching or delight?"

Cassandra said, "That word 'delight' bothers me for some reason. What are we talking about?"

"Good point," I said. "I remember years ago when Willimon wrote an article pitting exposition over against *entertainment*. That is not at all what homileticians have in mind. Maybe a better term would be *interesting* or better yet, *engaging*. Ideally, all preachers want to be both, *substantive-and-engaging*." I wrote this hyphenated phrase on the board.

"The history of preaching shows that most preachers have a default switch that leans toward one of those over the other. Think about a few different periods in the church's history. In the centuries leading up to the Reformation, for example, the monastic preaching orders gravitated toward ornamentation. Sure, they cared about teaching, but their sermons were as intricate as the flying buttresses of the time. Some so-called scholastic sermons had points, sub-points, and sub-sub-points. A person could get lost in all of that—the buildings and the sermons—but in the case of the latter it was a form of engagement at the time.

"Then along came the Reformers, with an intense interest in teaching. Luther's own style, sometimes called the 'heroic' method, was a no-nonsense approach to preaching. It was not ornamental so much as task-oriented. But flash forward just a hundred years or so, and in France we find court preachers. You've heard of court jesters and jugglers; what about court preachers? King Louis XVI employed court preachers."

Joey said, "You're making this up, dude, right?"

I said, "No, seriously. And it wasn't meant as mere entertainment; it was a spiritual part of the evening. But the form such preaching took had to be entertaining. So picture this: the juggler and the jester have done their thing. Enter the court preacher. These preachers were quick-witted, but also extremely eloquent. They could turn a phrase with attention to beautiful language. In fact, several times during their sermons, the audience—not really a congregation—would interrupt with polite applause.

"Fast forward again a few hundred years and preachers like Barth stress teaching over delight. Barth not only viewed illustrative stories with disdain, as we noted before, but the whole idea of introductions that would hook listeners was absurd to him. Human preachers, claimed Barth, can't make the preaching connection happen, no matter how talented or eloquent. God makes preaching happen when the preacher speaks the truth of Scripture."

Cassandra said, "Okay, so teaching and engaging are the two pulls, or exposition and experience as you've said before. And I can hear the voices of preachers I've known, some of them leaning toward the one, others toward a different stress. What I'm wondering is how am I predisposed?"

Brock said, "I'm with you, sister. I think my good friend, Carlos, here is clearly concerned with teaching. And I get that. I respect that. And I think I agree. But I also understand the need for engagement, creating interest. Why should people be bored with sermons?"

I said, "Ah, the word *boring*. In some ways it all comes down to what you think the cardinal sin in preaching is. Is boring the big sin, or having nothing much to say?" I pointed to the white board. "Note the hyphenated term *substantive-and-engaging*. We don't have to choose. We've talked a lot in here thus far about 'entering into an experience.' Entering into an experience of the text. Entering into an experience of the short story. That's great. Really great, and not just because stories are interesting; they testify to what God is doing in our day. But the best narrative preaching is both, experience and exposition, what Tom Troeger calls 'reason and rhapsody.' That's why I said the first night of class that narrative preaching is theologically thoughtful in content and in terms of texture, a storied experience. Honestly, I can't for the life of me figure out why we keep choosing between the two pulls rather than embracing both."

I said, "Here's another way to think about it. During the break some of us were talking about movies we've seen lately. That reminds me of something Walter Murch talks about in his textbook on film editing techniques. Yeah, I know, this isn't film class, but it is fascinating. Murch's little book *In the Blink of an Eye* is a classic in the field. He developed what he calls 'the rule of six.' It's his six rules for making a cut from one scene to another." I listed his rules on the board.

1) Emotion	51%
2) Story	23%
3) Rhythm	10%
4) Eye-Trace	7%
5) Two-dimensional plane of screen	5%
6) Three-dimensional plane of action	4%

I said, "As you might guess, some of this doesn't apply to us and we don't have to get bogged down in most of it. But there's something interesting near the top of his list, and I think it does apply to preaching. He argues that the *emotion* of a movie and the *story* being told are worth more than all the others. Do you see that? They add up to 74 percent, according to him. But notice how *emotion* is worth more than all the others combined, including the *story* told." I asked, "So what's my point?"

Joey said, "Good question. I like movies, but I don't get what you're saying."

I said, "Okay, so here's the point. According to Murch, and most every other moviemaker for that matter, the single most important thing is the experience of the film. His use of *story* would be the message he hopes to convey. Not surprisingly, movies are more about experience than exposition. I'm arguing that in terms of preaching both should be equal and add up to 100 percent. Or maybe both are 100 percent, sermons that are fully human, fully divine."

The biblical scholar Walter Brueggemann talks about "normative" and "imaginatively playful" ways of reading texts. He says if we use only the latter, there won't be enough substance, enough calories so to speak; and if only the former, such readings could be repressive, failing to address new situations.

I continued, "I really like the analogy Gene Lowry uses, and not just because he taught here for 130 years or something like that. Lowry uses the image of an envelope and Aristotle's terms *rhetoric* and *poetics*. We could just as easily substitute *teaching* and *delighting*. He said that in traditional homiletics the envelope was teaching. Sermons were all about teaching the lessons of the text. But they weren't just teaching, so preachers put stories and the like inside the envelope. The New Homiletic is like that, only reversed, says Lowry. The envelope, or the shape of the sermon, is narrative or delight, but it's not like the envelope is empty. Or at least it doesn't have to be.

"One of the critiques of narrative preaching worth pondering is whether we fell in love with stories and how they work to the neglect of what they were about. Not always, of course. But it can happen. David Bartlett, who helped put together the *Feasting on the Word* commentary series, said that after listening to narrative sermon after narrative sermon in preaching class, he wondered whatever happened to propositions. And Bartlett is a proponent of narrative preaching.

"But narrative preaching without substance is not really narrative preaching. It might be *narrative*, that is storylike, plotted, and full of stories for that matter; but it's not *preaching* in the fullest sense of the word. We want both. Think about it this way: When we read Jensen and his stress on 'thinking in story,' how did he build his case for that in an electronic world? He gave us a whole rationale. And when we read Postman, who was lamenting the lack of rational discourse, how did he build his case? He used rational discourse, true, but he also told the story of the Lincoln-Douglas debates. Rational discourse and story. Substantive-and-engaging."

We talked about embracing tensions rather than making choices, and the conversation was heated, even if abstract. Then Joey said, "This reminds me of those new Ford commercials, the ones about how 'and is better than or.' Y'all have seen them, this couple driving along, and the guy driving brags about how their new car has technology *and* good gas mileage. He says that's better than *or*, because that would be like sweet *or* sour chicken. And it shows them gagging on sour chicken at a Chinese restaurant." Several of us laughed.

Joey pulled up a YouTube of another one where a dad has put together an above-ground pool, only he asks, "I wonder what all these nuts are for?" The pool falls apart with water gushing everywhere. *And* is better than *or*.

I said, "That's a great illustration of embracing the tension. So as we continue to think about the 'and' of preaching, exposition *and* experience, let's do this. Get in groups of two and think about the preaching you've heard over the years. Can you see how preachers typically gravitate toward either teaching or engagement? And perhaps more importantly, how would you identify your own tendency? Is your biggest fear having nothing of substance? Boring folks? What? Take a few minutes and we'll discuss it together after that."

There was a surprising amount of energy in the room given that they had mostly been listening to me all evening. And then I interrupted the growing buzz. "Sorry to interrupt. One more thing, remember that assignment from the intro class, the one where you had to complete a sentence? 'To me, preaching a sermon is like . . .' What was your answer back then? What's your answer now?"

Even though the seating arrangement in the room had become a habit, new pairings happened this time. Carlos shared with Lisa, "I guess it's fairly obvious that I'm a biblical preacher. To me, teaching the Scriptures is everything." I didn't hear all of Lisa's response, but she said something about how even the Scriptures give attention to engagement, something we've learned from literary criticism. Good for her, I thought. I heard them discussing the parables of Jesus. Other conversations focused on the comparisons, "I remember in the intro class, I said preaching is like writing a song." Someone else, "To me, it's like cooking a fancy meal." One person, I think it was Joey, said he wanted to be a court preacher when he grows up.

After a while, I stood by the white board with marker in hand. Rosa raised her hand. She said, "To me, preaching a sermon is like making tortillas." Several of them loved the analogy, although maybe the idea of eating her fresh tortillas more so than what she meant by it. She continued, "Whenever I make tortillas, I care about how they look. I don't want them to be perfectly round because then they would look store-bought, but I also don't want them to look like the shape of Australia either. I care about the shape, the color too. I want them to have some dark spots where the skillet has warmed them to a golden brown. So I care about delight. But I also want to feed my family. We don't sit around looking at tortillas. We eat them."

Brock said, "I don't think Carlos has been going hungry." He patted his own bulging belly and added, "I know. Me neither."

Alesha said, "Rosa, what a great metaphor, making tortillas. I love it."

Cassandra said, "To me, preaching a sermon is like art. I love the two Van Gogh prints on the wall, but I was thinking more about the poster on the far wall." We all turned to look. She said, "It celebrates the Saint John's Bible, which is obviously the Bible but also illuminated. It wouldn't have to be illuminated, but because it is the piece celebrates both substance and engagement. I really have trouble with the word 'delight,' though. Substantive-and-engaging. Seems like the term 'hyphenated' might be important in preaching."

After everyone had had a turn, Cassandra asked me, "So what's your metaphor? What is preaching like for you?"

I said, "Good question, and a fair one, too. My answer has changed over the years, and I suspect that's true for most ministers. Sermons are

what scholars call *sui generis*, its own genre. They're unique, totally different even if like some other forms. I mean, they're like Bible studies but not
exactly. They're a speech, of course, but not exactly. And they are at least
related to certain art forms."

At one point, I might have said, "To me preaching a sermon is like
directing a movie." I even wrote a short article about that for a preaching
journal, something that other homileticians have noted as well, David Buttrick and Paul Scott Wilson for instance. In the article I pointed out how
we are the producer, director, editor, cast, everything. And in many ways,
putting a narrative sermon together is like putting a movie together.

But now I said, "Lately, I've been thinking about two possible comparisons. The first would be that preaching is like listening to National Public
Radio. Not all the time, of course, but you know how there are stories that
are equal parts head and heart? One minute it's an interview from Story-
Corps, the next some detailed analysis of military spending. And sometimes
with just the right piece of music in between. Equal parts head and heart."

Alesha said, "I remember how you required us to listen to NPR in the
introductory class. I thought that was the craziest thing I ever heard for a
class assignment. Now I think it's the best assignment ever. NPR keeps me
alive." I smiled. Professors live for moments like that.

I said, "That's the first image. But more recently I've been thinking
about the Jewish genre midrash. Okay, so everybody share your best line
about rashes."

Joey said, "Is a midrash what I get from being allergic to history?"

Brock said, "Only if you're allergic to the middle ages." A few boos and
hisses went up.

I said, "Honestly, Jewish midrash is hard to pin down. Even among
the rabbinic scholars they note how the term can mean lots of things, from
a form of exegesis to the resulting sermons. I'm interested in midrash as
a kind of commentary or sermon on Scripture. Rabbinic homiletics cares
about midrash. And the rabbis note two forms: *haggadah* and *halakah*." I
wrote both terms on the board.

I continued, "Like most Jewish vocabulary, it's hard to get a handle
on a precise meaning. Let's start with the term *midrash* itself, which most
likely comes from the verb *darash*, meaning 'to seek' or 'to inquire.' So the
sermon is an inquiry, a seeking. That's a nice image for preaching. *Halakah*
comes from the verb 'to walk.' We would call it application or the ethical
claims of the sermon, the way one lives. In Jewish midrash, *halakah* is about
the legal codes and decisions. *Haggadah* is pretty much everything else, and
especially the stories of Scripture and the rabbinic stories they use to retell
Scripture and picture it anew. It comes from the verb 'to tell' or 'to relate.'

I'm not trained in Jewish homiletics, but in some ways the two terms correspond nicely to our hyphenated 'teaching-and-delighting.' Jewish sermons often include running commentary on the biblical passage; but Jewish sermons also value storytelling as a way of making sense."

I glanced at my watch as well as the windows. There were predictions of freezing rain later in the evening, and no one wanted to get caught in that mess. I said, "So what are your thoughts about hyphenated homiletics?"

Lisa said, "I keep thinking this would relate to those two poems you cited in the intro course. Is that accurate?" Several of them nodded. Evidently, it had made an impact on them.

I said, "Yes, William Blake was the poet's name. Remember, I shared two of his poems with the class, 'The Garden of Love' and 'A Poison Tree.' In fact, 'The Garden of Love' is one of the few poems I have memorized." So I recited it again for the class, "'I went to the garden of love and saw what I never had seen. . . .'" In the introductory course I recite the poem with no commentary, just a recitation of that incredible piece. Then I tried to recall the kind of commentary I share about the other poem, about its four stanzas, each with four lines. I said something about the rhyming scheme, the syllables of meter. And I noted how it's about a fractured relationship, using the metaphor of an apple that turns out to be as poisonous as the friendship gone awry.

I use the two poems in the introductory course to demonstrate the difference between "experiencing" a poem or text and "talking about" a poem or text. In the first example we may not know much about it, but we have encountered it. In the second we know a lot about it, even if we haven't really experienced it. I never do read the second poem to the class; I just comment on it. The contrast is always palpable. Now I said, "Of course, why not both? In the best discussions of poetry, people hear the poem and discuss it. Hyphenated, that's the key."

Then I remembered something I hadn't thought of in years, something I knew Joey would appreciate. I said, "Joey, this was before your time but in the history of the NFL there was an experiment in broadcasting the game on TV years ago. I don't remember the year, although I do remember the game. It was between the Dolphins and the Jets. NBC decided that viewers wanted a realistic experience of the game, to feel like they were there. So instead of a play-by-play announcer and color commentator, they simply showed the game. No words other than those of the stadium announcer. Well, Bryant Gumbel came on during the pregame, and reminded viewers about what would happen. That was hardly necessary, since fans had been talking about the publicity stunt all week. After his introduction, he put his microphone down and went silently into the stadium. As you might imagine, it was a disaster, pure and simple. No one has ever tried it since. But here's what I love about how games are called: play-by-play *and* color commentary. Hyphenated. Fans want to see the game, and they want help making sense of it, even if they disagree with the commentary."

Joey said, "That really happened?"

I said, "Sure did. You can look it up online. There's more to the story. But you get the point about preaching." I added, "It's almost time to go, but there is one other image that strikes me. It comes from our devotional reading in Nafisi, the one about the green gate whereby women entered. The university was not only to be a place of reading stories uncensored but a place of critical inquiry. How refreshing it would be if education could be creativity-and-critical thinking. You know, hyphenated. See you next week. Go in peace."

CHAPTER TEN

Revelation

Like a lot of seminaries these days, the Saint Paul School of Theology uses web-based technologies to supplement what happens in the classroom. Some of my colleagues are in love with technology; and others, well, let's just say others are allergic. I'm probably somewhere in the middle. The one thing I really like goes by the name Moodle. I like what Moodle does; I don't like the name. It's another version of Blackboard, if you're familiar with that service. But Moodle? Who dreamed up a name like that? Maybe the seminary food service should serve chicken moodle soup sometime.

In theory, Moodle is where I can upload articles on reserve for students to read outside of class. It is also where I had posted the short stories we would be reading, except this week we were having trouble with Moodle. Who has ever heard of trouble with technology? It reminded me of the on-line course that I was invited to partake in a few years back. A group of preaching professors was asked to take part, to see what they thought about teaching preaching online. I was very reluctant but agreed to give it a try. We were given passwords to websites and told what time to log in for the synchronous course on preaching. But it never worked. They never could get it to work. Homileticians by nature value incarnation. Are there online courses available on incarnation?

With Moodle down, several students emailed me about the Flannery O'Connor short story for this week. So I replied with an attachment. I was tempted to warn them how this might be offensive to some, but figured they could determine that for themselves.

"Revelation"
By Flannery O'Connor

The Doctor's waiting room, which was very small, was almost full when the Turpins entered and Mrs. Turpin, who was very large, made it look even smaller by her presence. She stood looming at the head of the magazine table set in the center of it, a living demonstration that the room was inadequate and ridiculous. Her little bright black eyes took in all the patients as she sized up the seating situation. There was one vacant chair and a place on the sofa occupied by a blond child in a dirty blue romper who should have been told to move over and make room for the lady. He was five or six, but Mrs. Turpin saw at once that no one was going to tell him to move over. He was slumped down in the seat, his arms idle at his sides and his eyes idle in his head; his nose ran unchecked.

Mrs. Turpin put a firm hand on Claud's shoulder and said in a voice that included anyone who wanted to listen, "Claud, you sit in that chair there," and gave him a push down into the vacant one. Claud was florid and bald and sturdy, somewhat shorter than Mrs. Turpin, but he sat down as if he were accustomed to doing what she told him to.

Mrs. Turpin remained standing. The only man in the room besides Claud was a lean stringy old fellow with a rusty hand spread out on each knee, whose eyes were closed as if he were asleep or dead or pretending to be so as not to get up and offer her his seat. Her gaze settled agreeably on a well-dressed grey-haired lady whose eyes met hers and whose expression said: if that child belonged to me, he would have some manners and move over—there's plenty of room there for you and him too.

Claud looked up with a sigh and made as if to rise.

"Sit down," Mrs. Turpin said. "You know you're not supposed to stand on that leg. He has an ulcer on his leg," she explained.

Claud lifted his foot onto the magazine table and rolled his trouser leg up to reveal a purple swelling on a plump marble white calf.

"My!" the pleasant lady said. "How did you do that?"

"A cow kicked him," Mrs. Turpin said.

"Goodness!" said the lady.

Claud rolled his trouser leg down.

"Maybe the little boy would move over," the lady suggested, but the child did not stir.

"Somebody will be leaving in a minute," Mrs. Turpin said. She could not understand why a doctor—with as much money as they made charging five dollars a day to just stick their head in the hospital door and look at you—couldn't afford a decent-sized waiting room. This one was hardly bigger than a garage. The table was cluttered with limp-looking magazines and at one end of it there was a big green glass ashtray full of cigarette butts and cotton wads with little blood spots on them. If she had had anything to do with the running of the place, that would have been emptied every so often. There were no chairs against the wall at the head of the room. It had a rectangular-shaped panel in it that permitted a view of the office where the nurse came and went and the secretary listened to the radio. A plastic fern in a gold pot sat in the opening and trailed its fronds down almost to the floor. The radio was softly playing gospel music.

Just then the inner door opened and a nurse with the highest stack of yellow hair Mrs. Turpin had ever seen put her face in the crack and called for the next patient. The woman sitting beside Claud grasped the two arms of her chair and hoisted herself up; she pulled her dress free from her legs and lumbered through the door where the nurse had disappeared.

Mrs. Turpin eased into the vacant chair, which held her tight as a corset. "I wish I could reduce," she said, and rolled her eyes and gave a comic sigh.

"Oh, you aren't fat," the stylish lady said.

"Ooooo I am too," Mrs. Turpin said. "Claud he eats all he wants to and never weighs over one hundred and seventy-five pounds, but me I just look at something good to eat and I gain some weight," and her stomach and shoulders shook with laughter. "You can eat all you want to, can't you, Claud?" she asked, turning to him.

Claud only grinned.

"Well, as long as you have such a good disposition," the stylish lady said, "I don't think it makes a bit of difference what size you are. You just can't beat a good disposition."

Next to her was a fat girl of eighteen or nineteen, scowling into a thick blue book which Mrs. Turpin saw was entitled *Human Development*. The girl raised her head and directed her scowl at Mrs. Turpin as if she did not like her looks. She appeared annoyed that anyone should speak while she tried to read. The poor girl's face was blue with acne and Mrs. Turpin thought how pitiful it was to have a face like that at that age. She gave the girl a friendly smile but the girl only scowled the harder. Mrs. Turpin herself was fat but she had always had good skin, and, though she was forty-seven years old, there was not a wrinkle in her face except around her eyes from laughing too much.

Next to the ugly girl was the child, still in exactly the same position, and next to him was a thin leathery old woman in a cotton print dress. She and Claud had three sacks of chicken feed in their pump house that was in the same print. She had seen from the first that the child belonged with the old woman. She could tell by the way they sat—kind of vacant and white-trashy, as if they would sit there until Doomsday if nobody called and told them to get up. And at right angles but next to the well-dressed pleasant lady was a lank-faced woman who was certainly the child's mother. She had on a yellow sweatshirt and wine-colored slacks, both gritty-looking, and the rims of her lips were stained with snuff. Her dirty yellow hair was tied behind with a little piece of red paper ribbon. Worse than niggers any day, Mrs. Turpin thought.

The gospel hymn playing was "When I looked up and He looked down," and Mrs. Turpin, who knew it, supplied the last line mentally, "And wona these days I know I'll we-eara crown."

Without appearing to, Mrs. Turpin always noticed people's feet. The well-dressed lady had on red and grey suede shoes to match her dress. Mrs. Turpin had on her good black patent -leather pumps. The ugly girl had on Girl Scout shoes and heavy socks. The old woman had on tennis shoes and the white-trashy mother had on what appeared to be bedroom slippers, black straw with gold braid threaded through them—exactly what you would have expected her to have on.

Sometimes at night when she couldn't go to sleep, Mrs. Turpin would occupy herself with the question of who she would have chosen to be if she couldn't have been herself. If Jesus had said to her before he made her, "There's only two places available for you. You can either be a nigger or white trash," what would she have said? "Please, Jesus, please," she would have said, "Just let me wait until there's another place available," and he would have said, "No, you have to go right now and I have only those two places so make up your mind." She would have wiggled and squirmed and begged and pleaded but it would have been no use and finally she would have said, "All right, make me a nigger then—but that don't mean a trashy one." And he would have made her a near clean respectable Negro woman, herself but black.

Next to the child's mother was a redheaded youngish woman, reading one of the magazines and working a piece of chewing gum, hell for leather, as Claud would say. Mrs. Turpin could not see the woman's feet. She was not white trash, just common. Sometimes Mrs. Turpin occupied herself at night naming the classes of people. On the bottom of the heap were most colored people, not the kind she would have been if she had been one, but most of them; then next to them—not above, just away from—were the white-trash; then above them were the home-owners, and above them the home-and-land owners, to which she and Claud belonged. Above she and Claud were people with a lot of money and much bigger houses and much more land. But here the complexity of it would begin to bear in on her, for some of the people with a lot of money were common and ought to be below she and Claud and some of the people who had good blood had lost their money and had to rent and then there some colored people who owned their homes and land as well. There was a colored dentist in town who had two red Lincolns and a swimming pool and a farm with registered whiteface cattle on it. Usually by the time she had fallen asleep all the classes of people were moiling and roiling around in her head, and she would dream they were all crammed in together in a box car, being ridden off to be put in a gas oven.

"That's a beautiful clock," she said and nodded to her right. It was a big wall clock, the face encased in a brass sunburst.

"Yes, it's very pretty," the stylish lady said agreeably. "And right on the dot too," she added, glancing at her watch.

The ugly girl beside her cast an eye upward at the clock, smirked, then looked directly at Mrs. Turpin and smirked again. Then she returned her eyes to her book. She was obviously the lady's daughter because, although they didn't look anything alike as to disposition, they both had the same shape of face and the same blue eyes. On the lady they sparkled pleasantly but in the girl's seared face they appeared alternately to smolder and to blaze.

What if Jesus had said, "All right, you can be white-trash or a nigger or ugly"!

Mrs. Turpin felt an awful pity for the girl, though she thought it was one thing to be ugly and another to act ugly.

The woman with the snuff-stained lips turned around in her chair and looked up at the clock. Then she turned back and appeared to look a little to the side of Mrs. Turpin. There was a cast in one of her eyes. "You want to know where you can get you one of them there clocks?" she asked in a loud voice.

"No, I already have a nice clock," Mrs. Turpin said. Once somebody like her got a leg in the conversation, she would be all over it. "You can get you one with green stamps," the woman said. "That's most likely where he got hisn. Save you up enough, you can get you most anythang. I got me some joo'ry."

Ought to have got you a wash rag and some soap, Mrs. Turpin thought.

"I get contour sheets with mine," the pleasant lady said.

The daughter slammed her book shut. She looked straight in front of her, directly through Mrs. Turpin and on through the yellow curtain and the plate glass window which made the wall behind her. The girl's eyes seemed lit all of a sudden with a peculiar light, an unnatural light like night road signs give. Mrs. Turpin turned her head to see if there was anything going on outside that she should see, but she could not see anything. Figures passing cast only a pale shadow through the curtain. There was no reason the girl should single her out for her ugly looks.

"Miss Finley," the nurse said, cracking the door. The gum-chewing woman got up and passed in front of her and Claud and went into the office. She had on red high-heeled shoes.

Directly across the table, the ugly girl's eyes were fixed on Mrs. Turpin as if she had some very special reason for disliking her.

"This is wonderful weather, isn't it?" the girl's mother said.

"It's good weather for cotton if you can get the niggers to pick it," Mrs. Turpin said, "but niggers don't want to pick cotton any more. You can't get the white folks to pick it and now you can't get the niggers because they got to be right up there with the white folks."

"They gonna try anyways," the white-trash woman said, leaning forward.

"Do you have one of those cotton-picking machines?" the pleasant lady asked.

"No," Mrs. Turpin said, "they leave half the cotton in the field. We don't have much cotton anyway. If you want to make it farming now, you have to have a little of everything. We got a couple of acres of cotton and a few hogs and chickens and just enough white-face that Claud can look after them himself."

"One thang I don't want," the white-trash woman said, wiping her mouth with the back of her hand. "Hogs. Nasty stinking things, a-gruntin and a-rootin all over the place."

Mrs. Turpin gave her the merest edge of her attention. "Our hogs are not dirty and they don't stink," she said. "They're cleaner than some children I've seen. Their feet never touch the ground. We have a pig-parlor—that's where you raise them on concrete," she explained to the pleasant lady, "and Claud scoots them down with the hose every afternoon and washes off the floor." Cleaner by far than that child right there, she thought.

Poor nasty little thing. He had not moved except to put the thumb of his dirty hand into his mouth.

The woman turned her face away from Mrs. Turpin. "I know I wouldn't scoot down no hog with no hose," she said to the wall.

You wouldn't have no hog to scoot down, Mrs. Turpin said to herself.

"A-gruntin and a-rootin and a-groanin," the woman muttered.

"We got a little of everything," Mrs. Turpin said to the pleasant lady. "It's no use in having more than you can handle yourself with help like it is. We found enough niggers to pick our cotton this year, but Claud he has to go after them and take them home again in the evening. They can't walk that half a mile. No they can't. I tell you," she said and laughed merrily. "I sure am tired of buttering up niggers, but you got to love em if you want em to work for you. When they come in the morning, I run out and I say, 'How yawl this morning?' and when Claud drives them off to the field I just wave to beat the band and they just wave back." And she waved her hand rapidly to illustrate.

"Like you read out of the same book," the lady said, showing she understood perfectly.

"Child, yes," Mrs. Turpin said. "And when they come in from the field, I run out with a bucket of ice water. That's the way it's going to be from now on," she said. "You may as well face it."

"One thang I know," the white-trash woman said. "Two thangs I ain't going to do: love no niggers or scoot down no hog with no hose." And she let out a bark of contempt.

The look that Mrs. Turpin and the pleasant lady exchanged indicated they both understood that you had to have certain things before you could know certain things. But every time Mrs. Turpin exchanged a look with the lady, she was aware that the ugly girl's peculiar eyes were still on her, and she had trouble bringing her attention back to the conversation.

"When you got something," she said, "you got to look after it." And when you ain't got a thing but breath and britches, she added to herself, you can afford to come to town every morning and just sit on the Court House coping and spit.

A grotesque revolving shadow passed across the curtain behind her and was thrown palely on the opposite wall. Then a bicycle clattered down against the outside of the building. The door opened and a colored boy glided in with a tray from the drug store. It had two large red and white paper cups on it with tops on them. He was a tall, very black boy in discolored white pants and a green nylon shirt. He was chewing gum slowly, as if to music. He set the tray down in the office opening next to the fern and stuck his head through to look for the secretary. She was not in there. He rested his arms on the ledge and waited, his narrow bottom stuck out, swaying slowly to the left and right. He raised a hand over his head and scratched the base of his skull.

"You see that button there, boy?" Mrs. Turpin said. "You can punch that and she'll come. She's probably in the back somewhere."

"Is that right?" the boy said agreeably, as if he had never seen the button before. He leaned to the right and put his finger on it. "She sometime out," he said and twisted around to face his audience, his elbows behind him on the counter. The nurse appeared and he twisted back again. She handed him a dollar and he rooted in his pocket and made the change and counted it out to her. She gave him fifteen cents for a tip and he went out with the empty tray. The heavy door swung too slowly and closed at length with the sound of suction. For a moment no one spoke.

"They ought to send all them niggers back to Africa," the white trash woman said. "That's wher they come from in first place."

"Oh, I couldn't do without my good colored friends," the pleasant lady said.

"There's a heap of things worse than a nigger," Mrs. Turpin agreed. "It's all kinds of them just like it's all kinds of us."

"Yes, and it takes all kinds to make the world go round," the lady said in her musical voice.

As she said it, the raw-complexioned girl snapped her teeth together. Her lower lip turned downwards and inside out, revealing the pale pink inside of her mouth. After a second it rolled back up. It was the ugliest face Mrs. Turpin had ever seen anyone make and for a moment she was certain that the girl had made it at her. She was looking at her as if she had known and disliked her all her life—all of Mrs. Turpin's life, it seemed too, not just all the girl's life. Why, girl, I don't even know you, Mrs. Turpin said silently.

She forced her attention back to the discussion. "It wouldn't be practical to send them back to Africa," she said. "They wouldn't want to go. They got it too good here."

"Wouldn't be what they wanted—if I had anythang to do with it," the woman said.

"It wouldn't be a way in the world you could get all the niggers back over there," Mrs. Turpin said. "They'd be hiding out and lying down and turning sick on you and wailing and hollering and raring and pitching. It wouldn't be a way in the world to get them over there."

"They got over here," the trashy woman said. "Get back like they got over."

"It wasn't so many of them then," Mrs. Turpin explained.

The woman looked at Mrs. Turpin as if here was an idiot indeed but Mrs. Turpin was not bothered by the look, considering where it came from.

"Nooo," she said, "they're going to stay here where they can go to New York and marry white folks and improve their color. That's what they all want to do, every one of them, improve their color."

"You know what comes of that, don't you?" Claud asked.

"No, Claud, what?" Mrs. Turpin said.

Claud's eyes twinkled. "White-faced niggers," he said with never a smile. Everybody in the office laughed except the white-trash and the ugly girl. The girl gripped the book in her lap with white fingers. The trashy woman looked around her from face to face as if she thought they were all idiots. The old woman in the feed sack dress continued to gaze expressionless across the floor at the high-top shoes of the man opposite her, the one who had been pretending to be asleep when the Turpins came in. He was laughing heartily, his hands still spread out on his knees. The child had fallen to the side and was lying now almost face down in the old woman's lap.

While they recovered from their laughter, the nasal chorus on the radio kept the room from silence.

"You go to blank blank And I'll go to mine But we'll all blank along To-geth-ther, And all along the blank We'll help each-other out Smile-ling in any kind of Weath-ther!"

Mrs. Turpin didn't catch every word but she caught enough to agree with the spirit of the song and it turned her thoughts sober. To help anybody out that needed it was her philosophy of life. She never spared herself when she found somebody in need, whether they were white or black, trash or decent. And of all she had to be thankful for, she was most thankful that this was so. If Jesus had said, "You can be high society and have all the money you want and be thin and svelte-like, but you can't be a good woman with it," she would have had to say, "Well don't make me that then. Make me a good woman and it don't matter what else, how fat or how ugly or how poor!" Her heart rose. He had not made her a nigger or white-trash or ugly! He had made her herself and given her a little of everything. Jesus, thank you! she said. Thank you thank you! Whenever she counted her blessings

she felt as buoyant as if she weighed one hundred and twenty-
five pounds instead of one hundred and eighty.

"What's wrong with your little boy?" the pleasant lady asked
the white-trashy woman.

"He has a ulcer," the woman said proudly. "He ain't give me
a minute's peace since he was born. Him and her are just alike,"
she said, nodding at the old woman, who was running her leathery fingers through the child's pale hair. "Look like I can't get
nothing down them two but Co' Cola and candy."

That's all you try to get down em, Mrs. Turpin said to herself.
Too lazy to light the fire. There was nothing you could tell her
about people like them that she didn't know already. And it was
not just that they didn't have anything. Because if you gave them
everything, in two weeks it would all be broken or filthy or they
would have chopped it up for lightwood. She knew all this from
her own experience. Help them you must, but help them you
couldn't.

All at once the ugly girl turned her lips inside out again. Her
eyes were fixed like two drills on Mrs. Turpin. This time there
was no mistaking that there was something urgent behind them.

Girl, Mrs. Turpin exclaimed silently, I haven't done a thing to
you! The girl might be confusing her with somebody else. There
was no need to sit by and let herself be intimidated.

"You must be in college," she said boldly, looking directly at
the girl. "I see you reading a book there."

The girl continued to stare and pointedly did not answer.

Her mother blushed at this rudeness. "The lady asked you a
question, Mary Grace," she said under her breath.

"I have ears," Mary Grace said.

The poor mother blushed again. "Mary Grace goes to
Wellesley College," she explained. She twisted one of the buttons on her dress. "In Massachusetts," she added with a grimace.
"And in the summer she just keeps right on studying. Just reads
all the time, a real book worm. She's done real well at Wellesley;
she's taking English and Math and History and Psychology and
Social Studies," she rattled on "and I think it's too much. I think
she ought to get out and have fun."

The girl looked as if she would like to hurl them all through
the plate glass window.

"Way up north," Mrs. Turpin murmured and thought, well, it
hasn't done much for her manners.

"I'd almost rather to have him sick," the white-trash woman
said, wrenching the attention back to herself. "He's so mean when
he ain't. Look like some children just take natural to meanness.

It's some gets bad when they get sick but he was the opposite. Took sick and turned good. He don't give me no trouble now. It's me waitin to see the doctor," she said.

If I was going to send anybody back to Africa, Mrs. Turpin thought, it would be your kind, woman. "Yes, indeed," she said aloud, but looking up at the ceiling, "It's a heap of things worse than a nigger." And dirtier than a hog, she added to herself.

"I think people with bad dispositions are more to be pitied than anyone on earth," the pleasant lady said in a voice that was decidedly thin.

"I thank the Lord he has blessed me with a good one," Mrs. Turpin said. "The day has never dawned that I couldn't find something to laugh at."

"Not since she married me anyways," Claud said with a comical straight face.

Everybody laughed except the girl and the white trash.

Mrs. Turpin's stomach shook. "He's such a caution," she said, "that I can't help but laugh at him."

The girl made a loud ugly noise through her teeth.

Her mother's mouth grew thin and tight. "I think the worst thing in the world," she said, "is an ungrateful person. To have everything and not appreciate it. I know a girl," she said, "who has parents who would give her anything, a little brother who loves her dearly, who is getting a good education, who wears the best clothes, but who can never say a kind word to anyone, who never smiles, who just criticizes and complains all day long."

"Is she too old to paddle?" Claud asked.

The girl's face was almost purple.

"Yes," the lady said, "I'm afraid there's nothing to do but leave her to her folly. Some day she'll wake up and it'll be too late."

"It never hurt anyone to smile," Mrs. Turpin said. "It just makes you feel better all over."

"Of course," the lady said sadly, "but there are just some people you can't tell anything to. They can't take criticism."

"If it's one thing I am," Mrs. Turpin said with feeling, "It's grateful. When I think who all I could have been besides myself and what all I got, a little of everything, and a good disposition besides, I just feel like shouting, 'Thank you, Jesus, for making everything the way it is!' It could have been different!" For one thing, somebody else could have got Claud. At the thought of this, she was flooded with gratitude and a terrible pang of joy ran through her. "Oh thank you, Jesus, Jesus, thank you!" she cried aloud.

The book struck her directly, over her left eye. It struck almost at the same instant that she realized the girl was about to hurl it. Before she could utter a sound, the raw face came crashing across the table toward her, howling. The girl's fingers sank like clamps into the soft flesh of her neck. She heard the mother cry out and Claud shout, "Whoa!" There was an instant when she was certain that she was about to be in an earthquake.

All at once her vision narrowed and she saw everything as if it were happening in a small room far away, or as if she were looking at it through the wrong end of a telescope. Claud's face crumpled and fell out of sight. The nurse ran in, then out, then in again. Then the gangling figure of the doctor rushed out of the inner door. Magazines flew this way and that as the table turned over. The girl fell with a thud and Mrs. Turpin's vision suddenly reversed itself and she saw everything large instead of small. The eyes of the white-trashy woman were staring hugely at the floor. There the girl, held down on one side by the nurse and on the other by her mother, was wrenching and turning in their grasp. The doctor was kneeling astride her, trying to hold her arm down. He managed after a second to sink a long needle into it.

Mrs. Turpin felt entirely hollow except for her heart which swung from side to side as if it were agitated in a great empty drum of flesh.

"Somebody that's not busy call for the ambulance," the doctor said in the off-hand voice young doctors adopt for terrible occasions.

Mrs. Turpin could not have moved a finger. The old man who had been sitting next to her skipped nimbly into the office and made the call, for the secretary still seemed to be gone.

"Claud!" Mrs. Turpin called.

He was not in his chair. She knew she must jump up and find him but she felt like someone trying to catch a train in a dream, when everything moves in slow motion and the faster you try to run the slower you go.

"Here I am," a suffocated voice, very unlike Claud's, said.

He was doubled up in the corner on the floor, pale as paper, holding his leg. She wanted to get up and go to him but she could not move. Instead, her gaze was drawn slowly downward to the churning face on the floor, which she could see over the doctor's shoulder.

The girl's eyes stopped rolling and focused on her. They seemed a much lighter blue than before, as if a door that had been tightly closed behind them was now open to admit light and air.

Mrs. Turpin's head cleared and her power of motion returned. She leaned forward until she was looking directly into the fierce brilliant eyes. There was no doubt in her mind that the girl did know her, know her in some intense and personal way, beyond time and place and condition. "What you got to say to me?" she asked hoarsely and held her breath, waiting, as for a revelation.

The girl raised her head. Her gaze locked with Mrs. Turpin's. "Go back to hell where you came from, you old wart hog," she whispered. Her voice was low but clear. Her eyes burned for a moment as if she saw with pleasure that her message had struck its target.

Mrs. Turpin sank back in her chair.

After a moment the girl's eyes closed and she turned her head wearily to the side.

The doctor rose and handed the nurse the empty syringe. He leaned over and put both hands for a moment on the mother's shoulders, which were shaking. She was sitting on the floor, her lips pressed together, holding Mary Grace's hand in her lap. The girl's fingers were gripped like a baby's around her thumb. "Go on to the hospital," he said. "I'll call and make the arrangements."

"Now let's see that neck," he said in a jovial voice to Mrs. Turpin.

He began to inspect her neck with his first two fingers. Two little moon-shaped lines like pink fish bones were indented over her windpipe. There was the beginning of an angry red swelling above her eye. His fingers passed over this also.

"Lea' me be," she said thickly and shook him off. "See about Claud. She kicked him."

"I'll see about him in a minute," he said and felt her pulse. He was a thin grey-haired man, given to pleasantries. "Go home and have yourself a vacation the rest of the day," he said and patted her on the shoulder.

Quit your pattin me, Mrs. Turpin growled to herself.

"And put an ice pack over that eye," he said. Then he went and squatted down beside Claud and looked at his leg. After a moment he pulled him up and Claud limped after him into the office.

Until the ambulance came, the only sounds in the room were the tremulous moans of the girl's mother, who continued to sit on the floor. The white-trash woman did not take her eyes off the girl. Mrs. Turpin looked straight ahead at nothing. Presently the ambulance drew up, a long dark shadow, behind the curtain. The attendants came in and set the stretcher down beside the girl and lifted her expertly onto it and carried her out. The nurse helped the mother gather up her things. The shadow of the ambulance moved silently away and the nurse came back in the office.

"That there girl is going to be a lunatic, ain't she?" the white-trash woman asked the nurse, but the nurse kept on to the back and never answered her.

"Yes, she's going to be a lunatic," the white-trash woman said to the rest of them.

"Po' critter," the old woman murmured. The child's face was still in her lap. His eyes looked idly out over her knees. He had not moved during the disturbance except to draw one leg up under him.

"I thank Gawd," the white-trash woman said fervently, "I ain't a lunatic."

Claud came limping out and the Turpins went home.

As their pick-up truck turned into their own dirt road and made the crest of the hill, Mrs. Turpin gripped the window ledge and looked out suspiciously. The land sloped gracefully down through a field dotted with lavender weeds and at the start of the rise their small yellow frame house, with its little flower beds spread out around it like a fancy apron, sat primly in its accustomed place between two giant hickory trees. She would not have been startled to see a burnt wound between two blackened chimneys.

Neither of them felt like eating so they put on their house clothes and lowered the shade in the bedroom and lay down, Claud with his leg on a pillow and herself with a damp wash-cloth over her eye. The instant she was flat on her back, the image of a razor-backed hog with warts on its face and horns coming out behind its ears snorted into her head. She moaned, a low quiet moan.

"I am not," she said tearfully, "a wart hog. From hell." But the denial had no force. The girl's eyes and her words, even the tone of her voice, low but clear, directed only to her, brooked no repudiation. She had been singled out for the message, though there was trash in the room to whom it might justly have been applied. The full force of this fact struck her only now. There was a woman there who was neglecting her own child but she had been overlooked. The message had been given to Ruby Turpin, a respectable, hardworking, church-going woman. The tears dried. Her eyes began to burn instead with wrath.

She rose on her elbow and the washcloth fell into her hand. Claud was lying on his back, snoring. She wanted to tell him what the girl had said. At the same time, she did not wish to put the image of herself as a wart hog from hell into his mind.

"Hey, Claud," she muttered and pushed his shoulder.

Claud opened one pale baby blue eye.

She looked into it warily. He did not think about anything. He just went his way.

"Wha, whasit?" he said and closed the eye again.

"Nothing," she said. "Does your leg pain you?"

"Hurts like hell," Claud said.

"It'll quit terreckly," she said and lay back down. In a moment Claud was snoring again. For the rest of the afternoon they lay there. Claud slept. She scowled at the ceiling. Occasionally she raised her fist and made a small stabbing motion over her chest as if she was defending her innocence to invisible guests who were like the comforters of Job, reasonable-seeming but wrong.

About five-thirty Claud stirred. "Got to go after those niggers," he sighed, not moving.

She was looking straight up as if there were unintelligible hand writing on the ceiling. The protuberance over her eye had turned a greenish-blue. "Listen here," she said.

"What?"

"Kiss me."

Claud leaned over and kissed her loudly on the mouth. He pinched her side and their hands interlocked. Her expression of ferocious concentration did not change. Claud got up, groaning and growling, and limped off. She continued to study the ceiling.

She did not get up until she heard the pick-up truck coming back with the Negroes. Then she rose and thrust her feet in her brown oxfords, which she did not bother to lace, and stumped out onto the back porch and got her red plastic bucket. She emptied a tray of ice cubes into it and filled it half full of water and went out into the back yard. Every afternoon after Claud brought the hands in, one of the boys helped him put out hay and the rest waited in the back of the truck until he was ready to take them home. The truck was parked in the shade under one of the hickory trees.

"Hi yawl this evening?" Mrs. Turpin asked grimly, appearing with the bucket and the dipper. There were three women and a boy in the truck.

"Us doin nicely," the oldest woman said. "Hi you doin?" and her gaze stuck immediately on the dark lump on Mrs. Turpin's forehead. "You done fell down, ain't you?" she asked in a solicitous voice. The old woman was dark and almost toothless. She had on an old felt hat of Claud's set back on her head. The other two women were younger and lighter and they both had new bright green sun hats. One of them had hers on her head; the other had taken hers off and the boy was grinning beneath it.

Mrs. Turpin set the bucket down on the floor of the truck. "Yawl hep yourselves," she said. She looked around to make sure Claud had gone. "No. I didn't fall down," she said, folding her arms. "It was something worse than that."

"Ain't nothing bad happen to you!" the old woman said. She said it as if they all knew that Mrs. Turpin was protected in some special way by Divine Providence. "You just had you a little fall."

"We were in town at the doctor's office for where the cow kicked Mr. Turpin," Mrs. Turpin said in a flat tone that indicated they could leave off their foolishness. "And there was this girl there. A big fat girl with her face all broke out. I could look at that girl and tell she was peculiar but I couldn't tell how. And me and her mama were just talking and going along and all of a sudden WHAM! She throws this big book she was reading at me and . . ."

"Naw!" the old woman cried out.

"And then she jumps over the table and commences to choke me."

"Naw!" they all exclaimed, "naw!"

"Hi come she do that?" the old woman asked. "What ail her?"

Mrs. Turpin only glared in front of her.

"Somethin ail her," the old woman said

"They carried her off in an ambulance," Mrs. Turpin continued, "but before she went she was rolling on the floor and they were trying to hold her down to give her a shot and she said something to me." She paused. "You know what she said to me?"

"What she say?" they asked.

"She said," Mrs. Turpin began, and stopped, her face very dark and heavy. The sun was getting whiter and whiter, blanching the sky overhead so that the leaves of the hickory tree were black in the face of it. She could not bring forth the words. "Something real ugly," she muttered.

"She sho shouldn't said nothin ugly to you," the old woman said.

"You so sweet. You the sweetest lady I know."

"She pretty too," the one with the hat on said.

"And stout," the other one said. "I never knowed no sweeter white lady."

"That's the truth befo' Jesus," the old woman said. "Amen! You des as sweet and pretty as you can be."

Mrs. Turpin knew just exactly how much Negro flattery was worth and it added to her rage. "She said," she began again and finished this time with a fierce rush of breath, "that I was an old wart hog from hell."

There was an astounded silence.

"Where she at?" the youngest woman cried in a piercing voice.

"Lemme see her. I'll kill her!"

"I'll kill her with you!" the other one cried.

"She b'long in the sylum," the old woman said emphatically. "You the sweetest white lady I know."

"She pretty too," the other two said. "Stout as she can be and sweet. Jesus satisfied with her!"

"Deed he is," the old woman declared.

Idiots! Mrs. Turpin growled to herself. You could never say anything intelligent to a nigger. You could talk at them but not with them. "Yawl ain't drunk your water," she said shortly. "Leave the bucket in the truck when you're finished with it. I got more to do than just stand around and pass the time of day," and she moved off and into the house.

She stood for a moment in the middle of the kitchen. The dark protuberance over her eye looked like a miniature tornado cloud which might any moment sweep across the horizon of her brow. Her lower lip protruded dangerously. She squared her massive shoulders. Then she marched into the front of the house and out the side door and started down the road to the pig parlor. She had the look of a woman going single-handedly, weaponless, into battle.

The sun was a deep yellow now like a harvest moon and was riding westward very fast over the far tree line as if it meant to reach the hogs before she did. The road was rutted and she kicked several good-sized stones out of her path as she strode along. The pig parlor was on a little knoll at the end of a lane that ran off from the side of the barn. It was a square of concrete as large as a small room, with a board fence about four feet high around it. The concrete floor sloped slightly so that the hog wash could drain off into a trench where it was carried to the field for fertilizer. Claud was standing on the outside, on the edge of the concrete, hanging onto the top board, hosing down the floor inside. The hose was connected to the faucet of a water trough nearby.

Mrs. Turpin climbed up beside him and glowered down at the hogs inside. There were seven long-snouted bristly shoats in it—tan with liver-colored spots—and an old sow a few weeks off from farrowing. She was lying on her side grunting. The shoats were running about shaking themselves like idiot children, their little slit pig eyes searching the floor for anything left. She had read that pigs were the most intelligent animal. She doubted it. They were supposed to be smarter than dogs. There had even been a pig astronaut. He had performed his assignment perfectly but died of a heart attack afterwards because they left him in his electric suit, sitting upright throughout his examination when naturally, a hog should be on all fours.

A-gruntin and a-rootin and a-groanin.

"Gimme that hose," she said, yanking it away from Claud. "Go on and carry them niggers home and then get off that leg."

"You look like you might have swallowed a mad dog," Claud observed, but he got down and limped off. He paid no attention to her humors.

Until he was out of earshot, Mrs. Turpin stood on the side of the pen, holding the hose and pointing the stream of water at the hind quarters of any shoat that looked as if it might try to lie down.

When he had had time to get over the hill, she turned her head slightly and her wrathful eyes scanned the path. He was nowhere in sight. She turned back again and seemed to gather herself up. Her shoulders rose and she drew in her breath.

"What do you send me a message like that for?" she said in a low fierce voice, barely above a whisper but with the force of a shout in its concentrated fury. "How am I a hog and me both? How am I saved and from hell too?" Her free fist was knotted and with the other she gripped the hose, blindly pointing the stream of water in and out of the eye of the old sow whose outraged squeal she did not hear.

The pig parlor commanded a view of the back pasture where their twenty beef cows were gathered around the hay-bales Claud and the boy had put out. The freshly cut pasture sloped down to the highway. Across it was their cotton field and beyond that a dark green dusty wood which they owned as well. The sun was behind the wood, very red, looking over the paling of trees like a farmer inspecting his own hogs.

"Why me?" she rumbled. "It's no trash around here, black or white, that I haven't given to. And break my back to the bone every day working. And do for the church."

She appeared to be the right size woman to command the arena before her. "How am I a hog?" she demanded. "Exactly how am I like them?" and she jabbed the stream of water at the shoats. "There was plenty of trash there. It didn't have to be me.

"If you like trash better, go get yourself some trash then," she railed. "You could have made me trash. Or a nigger. If trash is what you wanted, why didn't you make me trash?" She shook her fist with the hose in it and a watery snake appeared momentarily in the air. "I could quit working and take it easy and be filthy," she growled. "Lounge about the sidewalks all day drinking root beer. Dip snuff and spit in every puddle and have it all over my face. I could be nasty.

"Or you could have made me a nigger. It's too late for me to be a nigger," she said with deep sarcasm, "but I could act like one. Lay down in the middle of the road and stop traffic. Roll on the ground."

In the deepening light everything was taking on a mysterious hue. The pasture was growing a peculiar glassy green and the streak of the highway had turned lavender. She braced herself for a final assault and this time her voice rolled out over the pasture. "Go on," she yelled, "call me a hog! Call me a hog again. From hell. Call me a wart hog from hell. Put that bottom rail on top. There'll still be a top and bottom!"

A garbled echo returned to her.

A final surge of fury shook her and she roared, "Who do you think you are?"

The color of everything, field and crimson sky, burned for a moment with a transparent intensity. The question carried over the pasture and across the highway and the cotton field and returned to her clearly, like an answer from beyond the wood.

She opened her mouth but no sound came out of it.

A tiny truck, Claud's, appeared on the highway, heading rapidly out of sight. Its gears scraped thinly. It looked like a child's toy. At any moment a bigger truck might smash into it and scatter Claud's and the niggers' brains all over the road.

Mrs. Turpin stood there, her gaze fixed on the highway, all her muscles rigid, until in five or six minutes the truck reappeared, returning. She waited until it had had time to turn into their own road. Then like a monumental statue coming to life, she bent her head slowly and gazed, as if through the very heart of mystery, down into the pig parlor at the hogs. They had settled all in one corner around the old sow who was grunting softly. A red glow suffused them. They appeared to pant with a secret life.

Until the sun slipped finally behind the tree line, Mrs. Turpin remained there with her gaze bent to them as if she were absorbing some abysmal life-giving knowledge. At last she lifted her head. There was only a purple streak in the sky, cutting through a field of crimson and leading, like an extension of the highway, into the descending dusk. She raised her hands from the side of the pen in a gesture hieratic and profound. A visionary light settled in her eyes. She saw the streak as a vast swinging bridge extending upward from the earth through a field of living fire. Upon it a vast horde of souls were tumbling toward heaven. There were whole companies of white trash, clean for the first time in their lives, and bands of black niggers in white robes, and battalions of freaks and lunatics shouting and clapping and leaping like frogs. And bringing up the end of the procession was a tribe of people whom she recognized at once as those who, like herself and Claud, had always had a little of everything and the God-given wit to use it right. She leaned forward to observe them closer. They were marching behind the others with great dignity, accountable as they had always been for good order and common sense and respectable behavior. They alone were on key. Yet she could see by their shocked and altered faces even their virtues were being burned away. She lowered her hands and gripped the rail of the hog pen, her eyes small but fixed unblinkingly on what lay ahead. In a moment the vision faded but she remained where she was, immobile.

At length she got down and turned off the faucet and made her slow way on the darkening path to the house. In the woods around her the invisible cricket choruses had struck up, but what she heard were the voices of the souls climbing upward into the starry field and shouting hallelujah.

CHAPTER ELEVEN

Echoes of Eden

I was running a little late for class, having been on the phone with Andrew, a colleague from another seminary with whom I usually shared a room at conferences. The Academy of Homiletics is always in the fall, but in the spring there are other opportunities to meet and discuss projects we're working on. The "Preacher's Festival" was coming up in Ann Arbor, Michigan, and both of us were presenters. Ann Arbor was also one of the sites for regional games in the NCAA men's basketball tournament, March Madness. Getting out of town to talk preaching, eat good food, and watch basketball sounded great. But that was still a week away.

I apologized to the class for running behind, but stopped midsentence when I spied the sopapillas Rosa had made. They weren't the flaky kind, warm and puffy, the kind you fill with honey, but the crispy ones, drizzled with honey and brown sugar. Several were already enjoying the treat, and the room almost sounded like that scene in *When Harry Met Sally*—"I'll have what she's having." Oh, my God, the sopapillas were amazing!

I thought the night's readings from Nafisi's memoir were amazing, too. I said, "This is yet another reference to those veils the women were required to wear, and what they represented. Listen:

> Several months into the class, my girls and I discovered that almost every one of us had had at least one nightmare in some form or another in which we either had forgotten to wear our veil or had not worn it, and always in these dreams the dreamer was running, running away. In one, perhaps my own, the dreamer wanted to run but she couldn't; she was rooted to the

ground, right outside her front door. She could not turn around, open the door and hide inside.

In all great works of fiction, regardless of the grim reality they present, there is an affirmation of life against the transience of that life, an essential defiance. This affirmation lies in the way the author takes control of reality by retelling it in his own way, thus creating a new world. Every great work of art, I would declare pompously, is a celebration, an act of insubordination against the betrayals, horrors and infidelities of life.

We read Scripture and prayed. The only housekeeping matter I recall for sure was a reminder I would be gone next week, and even though we weren't meeting, there were two short stories on Moodle they were to read for pleasure—"A Father's Story" by Andre Dubus and "See the Other Side" by Tatyana Tolstaya—both powerful stories that had touched me but which I had not yet figured out how to use in a sermon.

Brock said, "Speaking of Moodle, that thing drives me crazy. When it works, great. But it drives me crazy."

I said, "Amen. But at least the email worked. I assume everyone received the O'Connor story?" They all said yes. I couldn't tell if any of them were upset. If anyone had cause to be, it was Alesha. O'Connor's story uses the 'N' word, after all. It's painful for me to read, having grown up with a father like Ruby Turpin. I couldn't imagine what Alesha was feeling.

I said, "Normally, we talk about the articles and textbook readings the first half of class, then the short story for that week. Let's reverse that this evening. I would think you are bursting at the seams to discuss this one. Anybody?"

There was a slight pause. Alesha broke in, "I'll start. The story hurt me as I read, but it wasn't so much the language. I've been called that more than once, by the way." Several of us winced. She continued, "It just hurt to see Ruby Turpin's hypocrisy. She 'does for the church' and all, but what a bitch. Pardon my French. Actually, I thought she was a bitch at first. Then I felt some sympathy for her." She paused. "After all, it happens in a doctor's office, a place where sick people go. Everyone is broken in one way or another in the story. And most importantly, I have hope that she is changed by the vision at the end."

Several of us thanked Alesha for her candid reflections. Joey said, "Is this the end of the story?" He flipped over the last page. "I mean, is there another chapter or something? What happens after this?"

"Good question," I said. "There is no more of the story according to O'Connor, but there is more for the reader. The writer E. M. Forster claimed that the merit of any story is compelling listeners to ask 'What happened next?' on every page. And the good ones even end that way. We get to decide if Ruby has been changed, and we get to decide how we will live as well in a world like this." I said, "How many of you were physically upset by the story, you could feel your stomach churning or whatever?"

Three or four raised their hands, shook their heads up and down. Cassandra said, "But I think that's the point. O'Connor has held up a mirror to the South she lived in, and as readers we are not supposed to like what we see. Not one bit."

I said, "Exactly. I've shared some quotes from her book on writing throughout the semester. You may recall the title is *Mystery and Manners*. When she uses the term *manners* she means the customs and ways of the South, a South she said was 'Christ-haunted.' When you read this story, you see a South that was, or is, real."

Brock said, "You won't believe this, or maybe you will, but I remember driving across rural Georgia one time and stopping for lunch at a truck stop. The image of this is vivid in my mind. I was refilling my traveling mug with iced tea, when I noticed the T-shirts on this couple there with their kids. It read, 'The south was right in 1861 because America was right in 1776.' I mean, I know it was a statement about states' rights, but in support of slavery?"

Alesha, who grew up in Georgia, said, "I believe it."

I said, "What O'Connor does is tell what she has seen. Only she doesn't describe a T-shirt visible for all the world to see, but rather a sentiment underneath Ruby Turpin's respectable ways. That's the *manners* part. And she wants us as readers to be upset. Physically."

Joey said, "I'm not proud of this, but Ruby sounds a lot like my grandmother. I love Mimi to death, I do. But Ruby is my grandmother."

Lisa said, "Is it possible for a story to be too powerful? Too graphic? I can't imagine a sermon with a story like this in it."

I said, "Well, I've brought a sample sermon with me that uses this story, which we'll look at after the break. So you can tell me what you think then. And week after next we'll wrestle in more detail with your question about a story being too much. Although I do think it's worth noting how many sermons have been preached over the years on race relations, civil rights, prejudice, the list goes on and on, sermons *about* such things but that didn't come close to the pathos of a story like this one. Maybe our sermons could use some more *manners*. Not the polite kind where we avoid the tough subjects but the kind O'Connor intends by the term, holding up a mirror to behold the world's ugliness. Remember, one of the hallmarks of good narrative preaching is tapping into experience. That's what O'Connor does so well."

I said, "But there's also O'Connor's emphasis on *mystery,* which is about the grace of God breaking in among us in a world like that. And I guess that's a good play on words, since the grace comes in the form of Mary Grace and the breaking in is a book upside Ruby's head. But the grace does come. By the way, her terms *mystery* and *manners* correspond nicely with Dodd's definition of parables. If you've studied the parables in detail, perhaps you recall C. H. Dodd's classic description. He says parables are 'drawn from nature or common life,' which would be what O'Connor calls *manners,* but according to Dodd, the parables arrest hearers by their 'vividness or strangeness.' That's the *mystery* part. In many ways, these short stories are modern-day parables." I mentioned how pairing these stories with some of the parables of Jesus is often a good fit, though certainly not the only viable option.

I said, "And with parables, a key question is whether listeners get them or not. What about this short story? Do you think Ruby got the vision?"

Alesha said, "Well, according to one of the authors we read, she did."

Cassandra said, "Yeah, that was John Holbert's article from the *Journal for Preachers.* I love that piece."

I said, "Yes, it's an excellent article. Look back at it if you have it with you. Holbert begins with a quote from a letter Flannery O'Connor wrote to a friend. She said Ruby gets the vision, and then adds, 'Wouldn't have been any point in that story if she hadn't.' That's a crucial thought here. O'Connor, while avoiding moralism, does have a point in mind. She doesn't just want to hold up mirrors. She wants to shatter them as well. That's how many of the parables work. This story should bother us, just like Alice Walker's story in which a black woman is thrown out of the church. But these stories should also lift us up, to see Jesus coming down the road or to behold Ruby's vision in the sky."

Joey continued to read the first part of Holbert's article. He said, "O'Connor also says in that same letter that Ruby is a 'country female Jacob.' That totally blew me away. I liked the story, well, I didn't *like* it; you know what I mean. But I didn't see how this had any connection with Jacob's story in Genesis. I wouldn't have made that connection in a million years."

I said, "That's okay. And this is what Holbert means by *intertextuality* versus *allusion.* Did you get that?" A few of them shook their heads. I explained, "Holbert shows how *intertextuality* is setting two different things side by side—he jokingly suggests Dr. Suess' *Horton Hears a Who* next to George Eliot's *Middlemarch.* The two have nothing to do with each other, but that's okay. That's an example of intertextuality, maybe an absurd one, but still. *Allusion,* however, is more controlled, when an author purposefully echoes an earlier work. The New Testament does that with its use of

Old Testament images and stories all the time. So we'd be tempted to call O'Connor's use of the Jacob story an *allusion*. Only Holbert says it's probably somewhere in between, what he calls *evocation*. All right, so what's the point of all this?" The class sat still, waiting for me to answer that question. "Well, for starters, as preachers we can use short stories in combination with Scriptures no one else would have imagined. We hope the connections are good ones, since not all juxtapositions are created equal. But we can use unusual combinations. Although let's be honest, some pairings are better than others.

"And when authors formally allude to a biblical image, in this case, Jacob's story, we don't have to use that but we certainly should consider it. The author has thrown us a homiletical bone, as far as I'm concerned."

Cassandra said, "I'm trying to reconcile this with the other pages we read in Foster's *How to Read Literature Like a Professor*."

I said, "Okay, so long as you remember he means 'like an English professor,' not a preaching professor."

She smiled. "Sure. But in those pages we read about how authors can't always be clear themselves on what echoes they are invoking. He says there's only one story anyway, what he calls the 'us-in-the-world' story."

I said, "Do you agree? Not just you, Cassandra, but others? What do you think of that?"

Lisa said, "I've heard different takes on how many kinds of stories or plots there are in the world. Some folks say there are only two, others that there are variations on four types. I don't remember any of them off the top of my head. Well, there is the adventure story. Oh, and boy-meets-girl variety."

I said, "Obviously, no one can be *the* definitive voice for a taxonomy on story types. One critic wrote a book called *The Seven Basic Plots*. Seven, three, four; like I said, no one can be the definitive voice on this. But I like Foster's 'one story,' that no matter what happens, it's about the human condition, 'us-in-the-world.' Imagine that, another hyphenated phrase. What else does Foster discuss?"

Rosa said, "Well, he mentions intertextuality as well."

I said, "Yes, what does he say about it? It's on page 189, near the top."

Rosa flipped through the pages. "He says, 'The basic premise of intertextuality is really pretty simple: everything's connected.'"

I said, "Yes, thank you. It's funny he says it's simple, especially in light of his use of Mikhail Bakhtin, a Russian critic whose works are anything but simple. But Foster's point is that reading literature is logging on to a 'World Wide Web of writing.' There are echoes in everything we read. And I would add that some of those echoes are of Eden. Remember that line I printed on the first page of the syllabus? It's by the novelist John Irving." I flipped the pages over and read, 'God doesn't care at all what we write, but when we get it right, [God] can use it.' That's one of my favorite lines." I said, "Foster also talks about *archetype*. What's that all about?"

Joey said, "Well, he says it's a 'five-dollar word for "pattern."' I like this guy Foster. He takes five-dollar words and gives me some change back."

I said, "Okay, it's a fancy word for pattern. But what's his point about patterns? What do you think, Joey?"

He said, "I think it's kind of the same idea of everything being connected."

I said, "I think you're right. Foster is reminding us with terms like *intertextuality* and *archetype* about the interconnectedness of stories, the printed variety as well as the ones we tell each other." I saw several of them yawning, looked at my watch and said, "So let's take a break and we'll discuss this further afterwards."

When everyone was back in the conference room, I reminded them I would be gone next week but to read the two stories and submit a reading report anyway. I said, "We've been talking about patterns and plots, the ways that all stories in one way or another are about the human condition and our struggles to be human in this world. And most importantly, because this isn't an English lit course but a preaching one, we need to focus on how to preach narrative sermons using these stories. I think I admitted that if it weren't for the O'Connor letter in which she says Ruby is a female Jacob, I never would have seen that connection. But because I did read that, and because of the influence of Holbert's article, that's the way I tried to preach it."

Alesha said, "Is the sample sermon we're going to look at yours?"

I said, "Yes, it is. I'm of two minds in doing this. I mean, I do like what I've written or else I wouldn't have preached it. But it's also risky putting one's sermons out there. Then I thought, well, that's what you're going to be doing in here. So, me too. I'm not going to preach it for you this evening, but let me hand out copies and after you've read it, we can talk about it."

"The Face in the Mirror"
Genesis 32:22–32

Once upon a time, long, long ago—before there were any videos (that long ago), before there were televisions, before there were radios, even before there were books—there were stories. At first, these stories floated around in the cosmos, God sending them out into the cold air to bounce about.

Eventually storytellers discovered some of the tales. These tellers would hold on to them as best they could, then release them back into the air as the people gathered around to listen. There were two kinds of stories—day stories and night stories. Day stories were told while the sun shone. A caravan of travelers stopping for food and water might hear a day story, perhaps the comical tale of Jonah and the whale. That's a day story. But night stories were told only in the dark. Camped by a river, with a fire burning, night stories spoke of mystery. Of all the stories in Genesis, most of them night stories, this one about Jacob at the river Jabbok is undoubtedly one of the darkest of them all. And even though it is daylight at this retelling of it, I invite you to gather around the fire to hear this stunning night story. Who knows, you might see yourself in it.

It is late at night. The moon and the stars shine overhead, reflected in the river's waters where Jacob bends down to wash. Repeatedly he splashes water on his face, an attempt to clean more than just his face but perhaps his conscience as well. Or perhaps he wants to keep from looking at his reflection. You see, there is more than just a river to cross that keeps him from God's promised land of peace and rest. Jacob still has to face his angry brother Esau. For that matter, Jacob still has to face himself. And these are not the only things he must face.

You probably remember the story of Jacob from Sunday school—you know, the trickster, the conniver, the heel-grabber. That's what Jacob means in Hebrew, and he always lived up to his reputation. As a young man he tricked his older brother out of the rights of the first born. Later, when their father Isaac's eyesight was failing, Jacob tricked his old blind dad out of the family blessing as well. Jacob fled for his life, afraid that Esau might try to kill him. Jacob only knew two ways of getting along in the world—either he made a bargain with people or he tricked them. Often, he did both.

He married the daughters of Laban, Leah then Rachel, learning what it's like to be tricked himself. But Jacob prospered. Now much older, he, along with his family and all of his possessions, is about to enter the promised land. He sends word to Esau, offering him a bribe if he will forgive the past. All Jacob learns is that Esau is coming to meet him, along with 400 men. Jacob is afraid for his life.

He sends all of his servants and family ahead of him, and there at the river Jabbok (a term that means "to wrestle"), Jacob wrestles within himself. He tries to get some rest, when suddenly someone jumps him.

Everything is dark. Jacob can't see, but it must be Esau or one of his strong men. The man is huge, with arms like tree trunks, yet agile. Strong, yet under control. And in the dark, wet mud they wrestle throughout the night. The man's breath is hot on Jacob's neck. The stranger prevails, then Jacob, back and forth in the dark.

Seeing the first rays of dawn, the stranger decides that the time has come to end it. With a fierce thrust, he pulls Jacob down across his knees and Jacob's thigh comes out of its socket. Over Jacob's screams, the stranger demands to be let go. Ever the one to bargain, Jacob says, "Not unless you bless me." Jacob, the conniving one.

"What is your name?" the man asks, although you get the idea he already knows.

With a mouthful of mud, he sputters, "Jacob."

"Not any more. Your name is now Israel."

Ever wanting to be in control, Jacob wants to know the stranger's name and demands a blessing as well. The name of the man is withheld, but Jacob receives the blessing. The story ends not at sunset but sunrise. A new day is dawning for this man called Israel and the people of God who will inherit his name.

That's the story we heard in Sunday School, and unless I miss my guess, we also heard something else with it—the moral. What a shame! Unfortunately, most of us learned how to turn the mysterious night stories of Genesis into Aesop's Fables. You know, the moral of the story is . . . as a well-known author of children's books once quipped, ask a child what she learned in Sunday School and she's apt to reply, "Jesus loves me. Sit down! Sit Down! SIT DOWN!"

We have a tendency to turn these puzzling tales into neat little lessons. But Old Testament texts are not about morals, not primarily. They are mirrors. You don't read the Abraham narratives only to be told at one point, "Be like Abraham," and the next week, "Don't be like Abraham." No, you read the Abraham narratives because we are just like Abraham. In these tales we see ourselves, and we learn about the God of surprises who comes to us in ways we never could have fathomed.

This story is not neat and clear. The reflection in the river is hazy. It's like looking through a piece of opaque glass. There are several ambiguities in the text. For instance, scholars aren't sure if the name Israel means "one who strives with God" or "the God who strives with us." It is God, after all, who jumps Jacob; not the other way around. Then again, they aren't sure who the stranger is either. The storyteller calls him a man, but Jacob who sees him face-to-face swears it was God. Who can say? This is a night story, after all. It's hard to see in the dark.

One thing is certain, scholars agree that Jacob's encounter with the stranger mirrors his meeting with Esau in the next chapter. When finally Jacob meets up with his brother, he sees in Esau's face the very face of God. Somehow, you get the impression Jacob speaks the truth in that moment, perhaps for the first time in his life. He declares that in the face of the brother he cheated, who now chooses to be forgiving, he has seen the face of God. What is it John writes: "Whoever says, 'I am in the light,' while hating a brother or sister, is still in the darkness" (1 John 2:9)?

Flannery O'Connor, the great southern writer, tells a different version of the Jacob story in a piece called "Revelation." It's the story of Ruby Turpin, a large woman in whose presence everyone seems smaller. Ruby has become good at sizing up other people. She has practiced all her life, it seems. In the story, she and her husband Claud make a trip to the doctor. The waiting room is where most of the story takes place.

Ruby looks around the room and notes only one other stylish lady, besides herself of course. The rest are what she calls white-trash. Sometimes at night she drifts off to sleep while naming the classes of people in this world: on the bottom are most of the colored people, except for the kind she would have been if she had been born black; then the white-trash; followed by home-owners; and above them the home-and-land owners, to which she and Claud belong. Above them, however, are the people with even more land and bigger houses. There is a problem in her system though, one that bugs her greatly. Some of those with more money than she and Claud are common folks, and some of the black families in town are wealthy.

So while Mr. and Mrs. Turpin are waiting for the doctor, Ruby strikes up a conversation with the other stylish lady there. The two of them exchange pleasantries, but all the while Ruby Turpin is bothered by this other lady's daughter, who keeps giving Ruby the evil eye. The girl is disgusted with Mrs. Turpin's social arrogance, so just after Ruby Turpin finishes a speech about how she thanks Jesus that she wasn't born into a lower class like some other people, the girl hurls her college textbook into Mrs. Turpin's forehead. In the ensuing mayhem the girl locks her gaze with Mrs. Turpin and declares, "Go back to hell where you came from, you old wart hog."

Later in the day, after having a little rest time at home, Ruby Turpin takes a walk out toward the hog pen. All alone, she whispers aloud, "What do you send me a message like that for? How am I a hog and me both? How am I saved and from hell too?" She looks into the pen and asks again, "How am I like these dirty pigs? I do for the church and all."

Ruby Turpin stands out there among the pigs wondering about life and who she is. A few moments later the purple sky is intersected with clouds, one of which has the look of a ramp leading up to heaven. Then Ruby Turpin has a vision. On this swinging bridge, this ramp, all sorts of souls are rumbling toward heaven. White-trash, blacks in white robes, freaks, and lunatics. And bringing up the rear is a procession of good folks like herself. And it is these good folks who are marching behind the others, with "even their virtues . . . being burned away."

The sun sets, and the vision fades, but Ruby Turpin cannot move. She is changed. In the woods around her the invisible crickets strike up what sounds to her like some kind of hallelujah chorus.

Ruby gets the vision. She sees herself like never before, and others, too. And as for Jacob, we can only hope he gets it. It's hard to say, because Esua suggests that they travel on together, and while Jacob agrees, he departs by another way. Still, the sun comes up, and Jacob is off on a new day with the very blessings of God upon his life.

Of course, he is limping. And so are we. We are all of us limping in the spirit of Jacob . . . and in the spirit of Jesus who staggered out of the tomb as the sun came up, limping toward the resurrection. We are on a journey called Lent, a journey with Easter blessings awaiting us. But in the meanwhile, we are limping. Together, as brothers and sisters in Christ, we are limping toward Easter. Amen.

The following resources were especially helpful in the preparation of this sermon: Walter Brueggemann, *Genesis* (Louisville: Westminster John Knox, 1982); Frederick Buechner, *The Magnificent Defeat* (New York: Harper and Row, 1966); Frederick Buechner, *The Son of Laughter* (New York: Harper, 1993); Terrence Fretheim, *Genesis* (Nashville: Abingdon, 1994); John Holbert, "Revelation According to Jacob and Mrs. Turpin," *Journal for Preachers* 1 (1993), 11–21; Flannery O'Connor, "Revelation" in *The Complete Stories* (New York: Farrar, Straus and Giroux, 1971), 488–509; and Michael Williams, ed., *Genesis* in *Storyteller's Companion to the Bible* (Nashville: Abingdon, 1991).

While they read the sermon, I reread it, paying attention to things I might point out, but also a bit self-conscious about sharing it with the class. I've passed out copies of my own sermons before, but not usually. It can shut down honest conversation when the sermon in question is the professor's.

In a class on preaching the parables, for instance, there are so many examples out there to choose from. But with sermons using short stories, the pickings are slim.

When the last folks finished, I said, "Okay, part of any preaching class is being mature enough to commend each other's sermons but also critique them. And the preacher has to be able to listen. So I'm listening, just listening for now. What would you like to say?"

Carlos started us off. "I had serious doubts about this story stuff, you all know that. And I'm not saying this one sermon has changed my mind, but what I like best is the amount of attention given to the biblical text. I have always liked that story, although I have never preached on it. And while I might have done more with the text and theology, I appreciated that."

I didn't say a word, and even used my best poker face. Although I've been told I don't have much of a poker face. Over the years of listening to sermons in chapels, many of them wonderful but some of them atrocious, students have come up to me afterwards and said, "I could see how uncomfortable you were. It was written all over your face." The worst one was probably the time a pastor told us he'd written the sermon in the car during the five-hour trip to Kansas City. He said all this as he tried to hold his four-year old daughter in his arms during the message. I'm not making this up.

Brock said, "I like the attention to the text, like Carlos here, but I also like the way you use the short story. I wondered how we were supposed to do this. It's helpful to see an example." Several others noted that an example made a big difference. I wondered if I should have done that much earlier in the semester. Better late than never, I guess.

A few more commented on different aspects: word choice, the opening idea of night stories, "limping toward Easter," that sort of thing. I finally said, "As is the case with any sermon, there are lots of homiletical categories we might discuss. But given this is a course on narrative preaching, and one that uses short stories, let me say just a few things about that. I don't have any formulas in mind. I don't like formulas. Still, I do want you to note how this roughly eighteen-minute sermon is about one-third biblical story, one-third short story, and one-third exegetical/theological reflection. It's not the proportions so much, but the things included. I'm interested in the short stories making more than a cameo appearance. I'm interested in the biblical story making more than a cameo appearance. And besides the telling of these two stories as an experience that listeners are drawn into, I want to offer theological reflection. In fact, one of the most disappointing things in teaching preaching is when students prepare sermons without using critical commentaries and the like. They would never do that for an exegesis paper.

We seem to have a divide when it comes to moving from scholarship to pulpit. Sermons need experience but also exposition."

Joey said, "So, one-third is the ideal for each?"

I said, "Nope. That's just a ballpark figure. Don't worry about how many paragraphs each takes up. Do justice to a narrative treatment of the text and the short story, and do justice to exegetical/theological reflection as well. That's what I'm saying. Maybe these three things are the primary colors of preaching. And you need all three to get all those variations in the paint department at the Home Depot. Imagine a world without color combinations."

I continued, "One other thing, I want to imagine that if Walter Brueggemann and Flannery O'Connor were in the congregation, afterwards both would give us a thumbs-up, maybe Neil Postman too. They would appreciate our respect for the integrity of the text-and-story. That's hyphenated, by the way."

After a few more questions and some discussion, it was time to go. I said, "I'll see you in two weeks. Go in peace."

CHAPTER TWELVE

The Sacred Sandwich

At the "Preacher's Festival" in Ann Arbor, Andrew and I both finished our presentations on the first evening and went to a sports bar to catch the late game. We had tickets for the next afternoon's game. On TV, Wisconsin was playing Michigan State, which was something of a home game for the latter, even in Wolverine territory. The waitress brought us two beers, and convinced us that the onion rings were to die for. She was right.

A few minutes later, some other colleagues arrived, many of them graduates of Princeton Seminary, where Andrew had earned his doctorate as well. Most every year I ended up at a restaurant with the Princeton gang; they had made me an honorary member. They ordered drinks, and more onion rings, too. At half time, Andrew said to me, "Tell them about the book you're working on."

I said, "Some of you may remember how Craddock compared sermons to short stories, even calling them cousins. Well, I've taken that to heart, and the book is about narrative preaching and short stories."

Allison, who teaches at a seminary out west, said, "I'm guessing Flannery O'Connor and John Updike are on your list?"

I said, "Yep, you bet; and a bunch of others: Raymond Carver, Andre Dubus, the usual suspects. Originally I thought the book would just be about the creative use of short stories by authors like those. But my thinking has evolved. Now it's more about narrative preaching in general than the use of short stories in particular, although the short stories serve as a lens for thinking about narrative." I paused. "I'm not describing this very well, am I? What I'm really trying to do is two things: one, remind preachers about the power of narrative experience, which is narrative preaching's big thing. That's where the short stories come in. Second, I'm trying to offer a corrective to the kind of narrative preaching in which exposition and reflection have gone the way of the dinosaur. That's the basics."

A few nodded some encouragement. Andrew said, "And?"

I said, "And what?"

He said, "You know. And what shape is this book taking?"

I said, "Yeah, well, in addition to being a book *on* narrative preaching, the book *is* a narrative itself. I'm telling a story about a class of students learning to preach narratively."

Allison said, "Wow, that's cool." And she asked lots of good questions to prove her enthusiasm.

Andrew said, "Yeah, it's like that *Seinfeld* episode, the one where Kramer invents a coffee table book that can function as a small coffee table."

A few remembered the episode, others didn't. And some of the others were not impressed with a narrative book on narrative preaching. One of them, who shall remain nameless, said, "That's the craziest thing I've ever heard. Someone's actually going to publish this? I don't get it. You do realize some of your colleagues in the guild will write you off?"

I could tell he was one of them, that maybe even my honorary status among the Princeton grads was slipping away, at least in his eyes. That was pretty much the thing I remember from the conference. And that the Badgers won that night.

Back in Kansas City, several of the students asked about the conference. Others were commenting on one of the stories they read last week when I was gone. I knew which story it was. "A Father's Story," by Andre Dubus, is one of the most amazing stories ever, especially the ending with the protagonist Luke Ripley accusing God of loving an only child too much, and the difference between that child being a boy or girl. And Luke should know. Some folks think that story is too powerful for preaching. I get that but usually respond, "And what about a story where the Son of God dies?" We obviously have worn smooth the rough edges of Scripture's stories.

I picked up my copy of *Reading Lolita in Tehran* and opened it to page 94:

> That first day I asked my students what they thought fiction should accomplish, why one should bother to read fiction at all. It was an odd way to start, but I did succeed in getting their attention. I explained that we would in the course of the semester read and discuss many different authors, but that one thing these authors all had in common was their subversiveness. . . .

I wrote on the board one of my favorite lines from the German thinker Theodor Adorno: "The highest form of morality is not to feel at home in one's own home." I explained that most great works of the imagination were meant to make you feel like a stranger in your own home. The best fiction always forced us to question what we took for granted. It questioned traditions and expectations when they seemed too immutable. I told my students I wanted them in their readings to consider in what ways these works unsettled them, made them a little uneasy, made them look around and consider the world, like Alice in Wonderland, through different eyes.

After we prayed, I said, "We talked a few weeks back about the Gnosticism so prevalent in Christian thinking these days. People may not know that term, but a fear of the flesh is very real. More than that, the messiness of life is something they avoid like the plague. Somehow God's 'very good' in Genesis becomes 'very bad' in the thinking of Gnostics. As far as I'm concerned, the antidote for that approach is a healthy dose of sacramental theology, the notion that God's presence fills this good world in which we live. Of course, not all Christian traditions use the term *sacrament* in the same way, so some clarity might be helpful."

I told them about a retreat I did for some American Baptist ministers in Kansas a few years back, some of whom were clearly upset when I suggested that things as mundane as walking and reading could be viewed as sacraments in ministerial life. What I meant by it was that these things were gifts from God, ways in which God's grace is mediated to us. For them, there were only two sacraments (the Lord's Supper and baptism), and they weren't all that comfortable calling those things sacraments as opposed to ordinances. For them, *sacraments* sounded Roman Catholic, implying a kind of salvation apart from grace alone. I could have told them how the writer Andre Dubus says that in his Roman Catholic upbringing he was taught there were only seven sacraments, to which he scoffed, "There are seven times seventy sacraments, to infinity." But I didn't think they would be interested in quotes from Catholics.

I asked the class, "So how would you define *sacrament*?"

Cassandra said, "I seem to recall a definition something like 'an outward sign of an inward truth, an inward and spiritual truth.' Something like that."

I said, "Yeah, that's probably the most common definition, largely influenced by Augustine. The bread served in communion, therefore, would be a tangible (thus, *outward*) sign (that which signifies something else) of Christ's broken body by which Christians partake of forgiveness or any other number of spiritual understandings (thus, a spiritual truth). While that definition has proved helpful for many folks over the years, it also seems to be slightly Gnostic to my ears, making these tangible things of our lives into mere illustrations of something more important. Are inward, spiritual truths of more consequence than their outward manifestations? What if they are one and the same?"

Joey said, "So what are you saying?"

I said, "I'm saying since when is the *idea* of communion more sacred than the *act* of eating together? Since when is the *idea* of the sanctity of marriage more sacred than the *acts* of caring for each other in hard times, sharing stories over dinner, or making love?"

I added, "Andre Dubus, whose story you read last week, was also an essayist who drew upon his Roman Catholic theology. In one essay he writes: 'A sacrament is physical, and within it is God's love; as a sandwich is physical, and nutritious and pleasurable, and within it is love.' What a great image, the sacred sandwich. So while some might claim love is more spiritual than a sandwich, no one has ever tasted love. Sandwiches made in love, and sandwiches eaten in love—that's the real deal."

I paused. "Now what I'm going to say next will sound somewhat crazy, but here it is. While things like *peace*, *grace*, *mercy*, and *love* are all worthy topics to preach on, there are really no such things."

Brock said, "Well, you warned us. And yes, that's crazy."

Carlos said, "What do you mean, there's no such thing as *peace* or *love*? The Scriptures say 'God is love.'"

I said, "Okay, but hear me out. Of course there are such things as *grace* or *love*, but these are only names after all for tangible things in our lives. When a lover bends a straw and holds the glass of water for her hospitalized partner to get a drink that is love. That is real. *Love* is the word we use to describe that. Another Catholic thinker, Andrew Greeley, notes the inevitability of how biblical stories become doctrines over time. 'Bethlehem becomes the Incarnation. The empty tomb becomes the Resurrection. The final supper becomes the Eucharist.' But Greeley is not interested in a zero-sum game, whereby we must choose between doctrines and stories; and neither am I, as we've discussed. Greeley writes, 'None of the doctrines is less true than the stories. Indeed, they have the merit of being more precise, more carefully thought out, more ready for defense and explanation. But they are not where religion or religious faith starts, nor in truth where it ends.' That's a crucial insight.

"So this is one aspect of sacramental thought, celebrating the goodness of creation and incarnation. And stories do that. But there is another notion related to sacramental thought, and that is the concept of how a sacrament is a happening, an event. A sandwich actually feeds us. Baptism is not *just* a water bath. Communion is not *just* a piece of bread and wine. Watch out for folks fond of the word *just*. It's just wine, or just grape juice. A sacramental understanding of communion, or Eucharist, or the Lord's Supper—whatever your tradition prefers to call it—means something actually happens.

"I know Easter is still a few weeks away, but think about Luke's post-resurrection story on the road to Emmaus. As he tells the story, it's Easter Sunday, the first Easter Sunday, only these two disciples don't know it. They are shuffling along the road from Jerusalem back to Emmaus. We're told it was seven miles but it might as well have been seven million for these two travelers. Their slumped shoulders tell it all. The one whom they followed and believed in has been tragically killed, and while rumors of his resurrection are circulating, no one they know has seen him. The dead stay dead, that much they know.

"That's when the resurrected Jesus joins them. Only they don't know it's him. What follows is a kind of first-century version of one of those prank shows with the hidden camera and all. Jesus seems to be playing with them. Unrecognized, he says to them, 'So what are you two talking about?' (Luke 24:17). And I think I see him winking at the hidden camera. The two travelers are in shock. Hasn't this stranger heard the buzz around Jerusalem? Jesus even baits them into rehearsing the gospel story of how it was the Christ who was going to set things right and so forth. Jesus chastises them for their thickheadedness and preaches a brief sermon of sorts as they walk along. Still nothing on their part.

"Eventually they reach their home in Emmaus, with Jesus pretending that he's continuing on down the road. Another wink at the camera, maybe? They invite him in, an expected act of hospitality in the first century. Only instead of guest, he becomes host. Suddenly, with the language of the Passover meal he ate only a few days earlier in an upper room with his disciples—the same language Luke's readers would have rehearsed regularly in worship—Jesus takes bread, gives thanks, breaks it, and gives it to them. Luke writes, 'Then their eyes were opened' (Luke 24:31). I guess so! So in the eating of this sacred meal God opens our eyes.

"But if their eyes were opened at the breaking of the bread, we might wonder why the preaching of Jesus didn't register with these two followers on the road. What about a sacramental theology of preaching? If the preaching of the resurrected Christ doesn't work, what hope do we have?"

Joey said, "Good point. You'll take that into account when assigning grades in here, right?"

Cassandra said, "It feels like we're having church right now. Keep on preaching."

I said, "A closer reading of the whole chapter sheds some light on the dilemma. Luke's gospel ends with the ascension, just as his second volume, the book of Acts, will begin with the ascension. But before he is lifted up from their presence, Luke tells us that Jesus opened their minds to understand the Scriptures. In other words, the hearing of a sermon on the part of listeners is a work God does.

"We might also wonder what was wrong with these two that they didn't recognize their Lord in the first place. If he was the one who was going 'to redeem Israel,' shouldn't they be able to pick him out in a lineup or at the very least recognize him on the road? Lots of preachers have gone down that homiletical path: 'Why is it that we, like the disciples on the road to Emmaus, often miss the Christ who is right beside us?' Type 'Luke 24' or 'Emmaus Road' into Google, and look at all the sermons on how we are sometimes blind to the presence of Christ around us. Look at the sermons that quote Elizabeth Barrett Browning's line about every bush on fire with God's presence,

> But only he who sees takes off his shoes.
> The rest sit 'round it and pluck blackberries.

I said, "The only trouble is that a close reading of Luke's text won't allow such a reading because initially their eyes '*were kept* from recognizing him,' and when finally they do see him clearly it's because their eyes '*were* opened' (Luke 24:16, 31). Passive voice. For me, two things become apparent from Luke's story: 1) the so-called hidden Christ is all around us, in word and table on Sundays as well as life's conversations on the road and at supper tables any day of the week; and 2) the only way he is ever made known to us is by the grace of God. So Luke ends his story of Jesus with a stress on the One who will be made known to the church in the preached word and the sacred meal. That is a sacramental theology—something happens.

"But there is one other thing that fascinates me about this chapter. What is often overlooked is how we as readers/hearers of Luke's gospel are made aware of the divine presence through the hearing of this story. Word and table, sure. And story! What if stories are seen as sacramental themselves? Not all of them but some of them for sure. Do you know the old Jewish story about the power of storytelling? The Jewish scholar Martin Buber has collected lots of them. Here's one:

> My grandfather was paralyzed. One day he was asked to tell about something that happened with his teacher—the great Baalschem. Then he told how the saintly Baalschem used to leap about and dance while he was at prayers. As he went on with the

story my grandfather stood up; he was so carried away that he had to show how the master had done it, and started to caper about and dance. From that moment on he was cured. That is how stories should be told.

Brock said, "That's fantastic. I love it." Several others seemed to think it at least interesting, if some thought it quaint.

I said, "Although that comes from Buber, I was quoting it from one of the authors you read for today, albeit a different chapter than what you read. I'm sure you picked up on how Hilkert's work is Roman Catholic in perspective."

Several of them said, "Which reading was that? What book?"

They had all read it, but sometimes I've noticed students don't get the bigger picture, of which author said what and came from what perspective. I said, "That's the yellow-covered one from the reserve readings, *Naming Grace*. Mary Catherine Hilkert is writing about sacramental preaching."

Lisa said, "Oh, yeah. She draws on Karl Rahner in the chapter we read. I did a paper on him for something in my "Protestant and Catholic Theologies" course."

I said, "Right, Rahner is one of the theologians she draws from. Rahner, like Brunner in his debate with Barth, believed the goodness of creation was still intact in us, and that preaching. . . . Here, let me read the Rahner quote from page 33: 'Preaching is the awakening and making explicit of what is already there in the depths of [the person], not by nature but by grace.' Or from another chapter you didn't read, Hilkert says, 'Preachers do not simply retell a story from the past, not even the story of the death and resurrection of Jesus. Rather, preachers point to the power of the resurrection here and now in concrete human lives.'"

I said, "After the break I want us to think in more detail about how stories work, maybe even read another short story if we have time. I also want us to think about the performative nature of preaching and storytelling, how when we *say* things, something isn't just said but something *happens*. Like when I say, 'OK, let's take a break,' everyone takes a break."

CHAPTER THIRTEEN

A Narrative Species

As a few stragglers were filing in, Joey said, "So when you say 'let's take a break' and we do, does that mean if you say 'let's go home early tonight' that could also happen?"

I said, "Yeah, I guess it does. The power of the professor, awesome, huh?"

He said, "Can I have the power too?"

"I'm afraid that would be like Mickey Mouse wearing the sorcerer's cap: too much power. I don't think I can trust you with it."

"Dude, that's cruel."

I smiled. "Actually, Joey, you already have the power anyway, every time you preach. For that matter, you have it every time you speak. We all do." This would be another critique of narrative preaching that we would need to explore, power differentials. Everyone had returned from break, so I pushed on.

"One of the things at work when we tell stories and preach is the performative nature of language. In the West we're used to thinking of words as *saying* things, period. Candidates for political office make promises, and we think, 'Words are cheap.' But in a biblical framework, which is obviously an Eastern or Middle Eastern perspective, words don't just say things (there's that word *just* again); they do things. In Genesis 1 God says 'Light,' and there is light. God says 'cactus' and 'azaleas,' and parts of the world look like Arizona, others like Georgia. If God says "Golden Retriever," there it is, shaking its tail. God speaks and creation happens. And it's not just in the mouth of God that words do things. Even old blind Isaac's blessings on Jacob instead of Esau cannot be taken back. The word has already been spoken, the deed has already been done. Words *do* things.

"Some of you will remember the example I used in the introductory class, about the power of words and stories: Imagine a beautiful Saturday afternoon with friends and family over at the house, grilling burgers and enjoying each other's company. Suddenly one of the kids lets out a blood-curdling scream. There are screams, and then there are *screams*. This is one of the latter. A bolt on the swing set has become impaled in the temple of one of the children. The child is wrapped in a blanket and rushed to the emergency room. Almost like an offering, she is handed over. Everyone waits in that room where they have magazines and a TV playing, but no one cares about the articles on weight loss, or which Hollywood stars are rumored to be dating. The clock ticks, the hours pass. Prayers are offered, spoken and silent. Finally, the doctor comes out, removes that little mask, and says, 'I'm sorry; we did everything we could.'"

I waited a moment. "Did you feel that just now?" Several nodded yes. I said, "But why, it was only some words? We feel that because there's no such thing as only words. Words like that do something to our very existence. Thoreau said, 'Writing may be either the record of a deed or a deed.' He added, 'It is nobler when it is a deed.' I feel the same way about crafting a sermon.

And this, by the way, is similar to how gospel words work. Of the thirty-three different verbs the New Testament uses for *preaching*, the most frequently used is *kerrusein*. It could be translated 'to herald' or 'to proclaim.' Much like a town crier might herald a royal decree in the town square, the preacher announces the decree of God. And this decree changes reality for the folks listening. If the crier says that the war is over, that war which has perhaps actually been over for days, is now over for them. Their sons, husbands, and fathers can come home. There is peace in the land. A new reality!

"So imagine rushing to the emergency room, and after waiting all those hours, the doctor emerges and says instead, 'Everything's going to be fine.' Can you imagine feeling that? That is what those first women preachers said on the first Easter morning, 'Christ is risen, and everything's going to be fine.' Fine, indeed! Words *do* something! And so do stories." A few of them nodded, made some notes. Lisa said with Easter coming that would definitely preach.

I continued, "So how exactly do stories work? Let's consider at least one theory by Kenneth Burke, another name you need to know. In some ways, reading Burke is like reading McLuhan; they both use easy words but in very complicated ways. Only I think this concept from Burke is not that hard. And in fact, he uses theological language you'll be familiar with.

"Drawing on different theologies of the Eucharist, Burke uses the Lutheran term *consubstantiation*. Okay, so let's do a review. *Transubstantiation* is the Roman Catholic term that means what?"

Lisa said, "Ooh, let me; I loved that course on Protestant and Catholic Theologies. Transubstantiation is the notion that the bread and wine *become* the body and blood of Christ."

I said, "Okay, and at the other end of the spectrum, the symbolic view contends what?"

She said, "Well, for several Protestant traditions the elements do not *become* anything but instead *represent* or serve as *reminders* of Christ's body and blood. They are symbols, sometimes even called emblems, although that latter term leaves me cold."

I said, "Which leaves us with the Lutheran notion of consubstantiation. How would you describe that view?"

She hesitated slightly, acknowledging the difficulty of explaining it. She said, "It's somewhere in between. The elements are more than symbols but they do not become the body and blood either. Instead, Christ is somehow, I don't know, somehow present with these elements. Real presence, but *present with* is key."

We were all impressed. No wonder she had come through the ordaining boards with flying colors. I said, "Thanks, Lisa." I continued, "For Burke, that is how stories work. The characters on the pages of a short story do not become us, nor do we become them. But neither are the characters just characters, separate from us. Somehow we are present in their lives even as they become present in ours. As we hear the story, we have not rushed to the emergency room with our child in our arms; but neither is that child just a symbolic character. We are not in that pig pen with Ruby Turpin, and yet somehow we are."

I continued, "But—and this is an important 'but'—I don't think all stories are necessarily sacramental, not even all short stories for that matter. I was reading James Smith's recent work on worship the other day, *Desiring the Kingdom*, and I especially like the way one ethicist he quotes puts it: 'Although all of creation is sacramental, not all of creation is sacramental to the same degree.' Smith says that while we should regard all of life as sacrament, maybe there are such things as 'hot spots.' I really like that image. I think some short stories are 'hot spots.' Remember that line by John Irving, 'God doesn't care at all what we write, but when we get it right, [God] can use it.' I think he's correct on at least two counts. Getting it right happens when their stories echo with the truth of God, and God's using it can happen when we use it in our sermons.

Brock said, "A person starts to get the idea stories are the *real deal*, the very essence of preaching. I mean, I've always enjoyed them, and as I said before, my daddy said we're all story animals. But still, I don't know if I've recognized their importance overall." Even Carlos seemed to nod in agreement.

I said, "No doubt, stories are important, more so than most of us have ever realized. But to be clear, I'm on a twofold mission this evening: the first to convince the skeptics among us of the Superman power inherent in storytelling; and the second, to point out its kryptonite. Narrative preachers don't like to think about the weaknesses. But we need to examine the good, the bad, even the ugly in relation to storytelling and narrative preaching. So let's start with the good.

"Back in the early '90s I attended a meeting of the Religious Speech and Communication Association in Chicago. There were papers presented on a variety of topics, each meeting in breakout rooms. But there were also a few larger plenary sessions, one of which featured two professional storytellers.

"Donald Davis, a rather well-known storyteller and Methodist minister, was one of them. I don't recall the name of the other fellow, but the person who introduced them made a point of how Davis was this fellow's mentor in storytelling. So you have to picture this. We listened to the one fellow tell stories for about forty-five minutes, then Davis for another forty-five minutes. Time flew in their hands, by the way. They were captivating, entertaining but also inspiring.

"Now I just so happened to be sitting in the second row in this auditorium, right behind the two storytellers. After the first one finished and sat back down, Davis went up for his turn. But something was wrong. The first storyteller was evidently upset, who knows why. Maybe it was with how his presentation had gone or he was jealous of Davis, maybe mad at him for all I know. But his body language said, I'm not going to listen to your stories. And he turned sideways, even crossed his arms across his chest.

"As I listened to Davis spin his yarn, I also watched his former student try to resist. But he couldn't. Within a few minutes he was hooked like the rest of us. Stories have a pull on us, even when we don't want them to. No question. And I could give you example after example of their power.

"One more I'll share and then we'll reflect more critically on storytelling and narrativity. Isn't that something? Leave it to seminary to turn *storytelling* into *narrativity*."

Joey said, "That's for sure. We learn lots of words ending with *-ivity* and *-ology*."

I joked, "That's why you pay tuition, to learn fancy words. You wouldn't want to pay money for terms like *story*." Several of them laughed. "So here's my other evidence. A few years ago on faculty retreat we celebrated the fiftieth anniversary of the ordination of women in the United Methodist Church. Our dean at the time thought we should note the occasion, and rightly so. What she envisioned was a sort of reader's theater, various folks reading different parts of a transcript from the actual proceedings in which women were granted the right to ordination.

"Normally, reader's theater doesn't do much for me. Partly it's the less-than-theatrical readings by the performers, but also the distance between us and the event itself. Anyway, several of us were given parts, including me as the presiding bishop."

Joey said, "Cool, dude. Bishop Freeman."

I said, "Well, it's the closest I'll ever come, especially since I'm not United Methodist myself. Anyway, we started into reading the various parts, sometimes having to remind someone that it was their turn. Truth be told, it was sort of flat.

"But then something happened, the sort of epiphany so common in storytelling. Playing the part of presiding bishop, I spoke the lines about the path to ordination now being opened to women. And I could feel it. I think all of us felt it. It was a holy moment. That's the power of storytelling."

Cassandra and Alesha both noted how many times this semester the image of women being set free had popped up, a recurring theme related to storytelling. We knew that stories are about other things as well, but those readings from Nafisi's memoir certainly echoed that theme.

I said, "Okay, so that's a glimpse at the *good* inherent in storytelling. And we've been considering a lot of strengths along the way, and no doubt, we will consider other strengths as well. But what about the *bad*, even the *ugly* side of narrative preaching? As we read a few weeks ago, Neil Postman laments the lack of exposition in much preaching today. We must take that seriously. But there are other critiques as well. Let's consider some of their complaints.

"You read that chapter from Tom Long's *Preaching from Memory to Hope* in which he looks at some of the criticisms. How would you summarize his assessment? Let's do this together instead of in groups. I'll be the scribe and write on the board. What does he say?"

A few of them found their photocopies of the chapter, others flipped open laptops and iPads. They skimmed the chapter, but no one was saying anything. I said, "There are three categories he explores in relation to criticisms of narrative." Still nothing. "Okay, let me remind you. Although he doesn't use this terminology per se, the three categories could be labeled the three Es—evangelistic, educational, and ethical." I wrote the three words on the board. I said, "Look on page 12."

Alesha found the paragraph and read aloud for us. "The theological right zings most sharply at the level of churchly practice: the telling of stories may ease minds and entertain the choir, but it doesn't build churches and extend the body of Christ.'"

I said, "Thanks. And if you look ahead a few pages, this evangelistic critique is spelled out in more detail, how some evangelicals view narrative approaches as too soft, too ambiguous to save souls. What do you think about that? Is that a fair criticism? Do narrative preachers need to concern themselves with such things?"

Carlos said, "Absolutely. This is why we preach, to save souls. What other purpose really matters if people are not converted to the faith?"

Joey said, "I grew up with revivals in Oklahoma, and y'all may not know this, but that's how I came to be here. A revival preacher's sermon convicted me of my sins, and I became a Christian while I was in high school. So I get your point, Carlos. But while I was in college, the church I attended had a pastor who preached nothing but evangelistic messages. After a person becomes Christian, where is the teaching?"

I said, "Okay, before we get to the educational critique of narrative, let's stick with the evangelistic. Joey's testimony is that preaching led him to faith. And we appreciate hearing that, Joey. I have a similar story. But as Carlos rightly notes, evangelism matters. It is not the only thing, and we will discuss education, but it matters nonetheless. Is narrative preaching capable of that?"

Cassandra said, "I want to go back to another question you raised about narrative and evangelism, namely do narrative preachers have to concern themselves with such things? In my opinion, most definitely. I've been thinking about how we tend to restrict preaching to Sunday morning and the four walls of the church. What about preaching outside those walls?" Several of them appreciated this idea but wondered if we were talking about street preaching, or what.

I said, "It's funny you bring this up. Over the Christmas break, my wife and I went to Austin, Texas, for a weekend getaway. If you don't know, Austin considers itself the 'live music capital of the world.' You know how Texans are, a little over the top."

Cassandra said, "A little?"

"Okay, a lot. I'm a Texan, and it's true we exaggerate. But Austin does have an amazing amount of venues for live music any night of the week. So one evening before going out to eat and listen to some music, we had spent the afternoon in a coffee shop, reading and sipping on hot chocolate. I was reading something that triggered the same concerns Cassandra brought up about preaching outside the walls of the church. It was Diana Butler Bass's new book on trends in religious life among Americans, how more people consider themselves spiritual but not necessarily religious.

"I thought about the numbers of people for whom church was not on the radar even if they considered themselves spiritual persons. So that evening while we were listening to some music—some amazing music by the way—I looked around at the folks there and wondered how many of them are spiritual but not necessarily religious. It's an interesting thing to ponder. Then it hit me. Why does our culture have so many venues for live music, and almost none for live storytelling?

"Okay, so I'm fantasizing here, but humor me. What if those bars and restaurants and coffee shops featured storytellers sometimes? People love to listen to Garrison Keillor. What if a storyteller did a retelling of a certain Flannery O'Connor short story, about Ruby standing in a pig pen and coming to a different way of practicing her faith? That could be a form of evangelism even if there wasn't an altar call per se."

The students' reviews were mixed, although Brock thought it was brilliant. I said, "Y'all will probably think I'm crazy, but I may have a gig like that coming up." They looked surprised. "Well, not exactly, but something close. I don't know if you're familiar with the band 'The Wilders.' They've been on Keillor's *Prairie Home Companion* and performed around the world. Well, one of the band members is a friend who attends the same church I do. So one time, we were sitting around talking and I mentioned an idea I got from Fred Craddock. I told him about this really amazing narrative preacher who used to do a concert of sorts with a local symphony in the Atlanta area every Advent season. I told him I didn't know exactly how it went, but the orchestra would play a piece or two, then Fred would tell a story, then they would play, that sort of progression. So I said to my musician friend, 'What if we did something like that? And what if instead of just doing it for church folks, we opened it up to the wider community?' He was really excited, and we might actually give it a try. We're going to work at putting together a concert/storytelling kind of event in which we share the gospel in a kind of indirect way."

Several of them wanted to know the date and venue. Everyone was excited. Except Carlos. He said, "I think this is a great idea, I do. But you said, 'in a kind of indirect way.' That's what bothers me. Narrative is too indirect when it comes to saving people."

I said, "Great point. I appreciate your catching that. The concert/storytelling gig will probably be indirect. But narrative preaching doesn't have to be, even if some scholars believe indirect is more effective than direct, even when it comes to evangelism. But you're right, narrative sermons don't have to be indirect. We will look later at how the expositional voice is often silenced in narrative preaching, but unnecessarily. And for me, that expositional voice can be evangelistic, loud and clear. Or at least clear; I'm not really into loud preaching. We will consider that, Carlos. Great point.

"Okay, so there's the evangelistic critique. What about the educational? What does Long say about that? Look back at page 12. Someone care to read that?"

Lisa said, "I've got it. 'The middle has an educational complaint: the telling of stories may educe theological knowledge when it is already in place, but it doesn't supply it when it is not.'" She said, "I think we read something similar in Campbell's work earlier this semester."

I said, "Yes, we did. So what do you think about that? Anyone?"

Joey said, "Sorry, but what does the word *educe* mean?"

Lisa said, "I think it means to draw out the meaning of something. So narrative preaching works best when the people hearing the stories can make sense of them, have a biblical foundation upon which to make meaning of the preacher's sermon." She looked at me for confirmation.

I said, "I think you're right on target. Keep going."

She continued, "Looking ahead a few pages, I love what Long writes there about Kierkegaard and Craddock. She found the place. 'Kierkegaard in the nineteenth century and Craddock in the 1970s may have claimed that "there is no lack of information in a Christian land," but now there *is* a lack of information, and it *isn't* a Christian land.'"

I said, "Ah, yes, the teaching role of the sermon. And here my guilty past catches up with me. Let me explain. I've said more than once this semester that narrative preaching was a godsend to my own ministry and teaching, but that it occasionally lacks theological reflection, or exposition. Well, I didn't always see it that way. When I stumbled onto narrative ways of preaching, I mistakenly thought all those expository sermons needed to be thrown overboard. I'm ashamed to admit it, but in my early days of teaching narrative preaching I discouraged students from using exposition in their narrative sermons.

"It took me quite a few years to realize we could be experiential and expositional in narrative preaching. Not so for Tom Long. Years ago he wrote an article in the *Journal for Preachers* claiming that the New Homiletic and narrative preaching were born because we didn't want to bore listeners any longer. But as he rightly noted, we just never stopped to think that a strict diet of storytelling alone could eventually result in biblically illiterate congregations. And it's not just biblical illiteracy, but having a theological vocabulary by which to make sense of the Bible.

"But please notice my careful use of two different terms here—*storytelling* and *narrative preaching*. They are not the same. For me, narrative preaching is larger than just storytelling. I love that line Long writes in the chapter we read, 'Narrative is not just one arrow in the quiver but is, in a sense, the quiver that holds all of the other arrows.' He is talking there about the Scriptural canon itself. So let me say something about that.

"Think for a moment about how the New Testament is put together, and what it says about narrative. It's a kind of confusing history in some ways because of chronological and canonical order being different. The letters of Paul were the first written documents of the New Testament, penned more than a decade before the first complete Gospel was written down. But of course in our Bibles the Gospels come first because it's the story of Jesus upon which Paul's ministry to the churches rests. As I said, it's the difference between chronological and canonical ordering. What I like about the canonical arrangement is how the stories of Jesus are followed by theological reflection and application. In some ways, the New Testament canon models the need for story and reflection, or maybe better yet, story-and-reflection. Hyphenated. And that's not even accounting for the narrative nature of the epistles, too.

"Think about just one example, the resurrection. That's a fairly central story in the Scriptures, wouldn't you say? All four Gospels tell the story of Jesus' resurrection; well, okay, Mark only hints at it. But in the Pauline and Johannine epistles we are given theological reflections upon the meaning of the resurrection—conquering sin and death, first fruits among many who will be raised, eschatological hope, and so forth. Those first women preachers who proclaimed Jesus raised from the dead may have been narrative preachers of a sort, but in the Corinthians correspondence Paul comes pretty close to a three-point sermon. He says, 'If Christ be not raised . . .' and then lists three things (1 Cor 15). The canon models the need for story and reflection."

I said, "Okay, we're still thinking about the educational component of preaching in relation to narrative. So let me summarize some other pieces we did not read for this evening but which you might want to look at further some time. This educational critique is very important to me, since I keep stressing that narrative preaching at its best is both experiential and expositional.

"The writer Roger Rosenblatt says we are a 'narrative species,' a kind of play on the notion of us being a 'rational species.' I think he's right, even if we are really both. Brock, you said before how we are story animals. Same idea. I think that's true, and I think I've mentioned how to be alive is to be part of a story, that even squirrels are part of a story." Several of us looked out the window to see if any of them were playing. "But near as we know, squirrels don't reflect upon the meaning of their stories like we do. Hard to imagine a squirrel at the end of the day saying, 'Wow, that was a close call with that truck earlier this afternoon. Do you think acorns are really worth the effort if we could get run over?'"

Rosa laughed. Lisa said, "You never know. Maybe animals are smarter than we think."

I said, "I'm sure they are, but you get the idea. Humans not only are caught up in stories, but we try to make sense of those stories in one way or another. Joey mentioned earlier our tendency to make fancy words out of simple ideas here in seminary. That's true. But it's a worthwhile endeavor because we do try to make sense of things. A theological and philosophical vocabulary is a way to do just that."

I also told them about Stephen Prothero's book *Religious Literacy*, which I find very helpful on this very point. He wonders how it is that sincerity among religious folks became synonymous with ignorance. I asked, "How's that for a thesis? When did book learning, in other words, become the opposite of piety? His answer is that we in the religious community are to blame, not secularists. In some ways it was there at the First Great Awakening, but even more so with the Second Great Awakening, when religious discourse moved from rationalism to revivalism. Think especially about Charles Finney and his eccentric tactics, pragmatism valued over everything else. Prothero claims that that particular brand of revivalism made Christians out of us, but mostly forgetful ones. Preachers like Dwight Moody and Sam Jones bragged about it. They said things like, 'My theology! I didn't know I had any.' Or, 'If I had a creed, I would sell it to a museum.' They were interested in results, not critical thinking.

"In fact, Prothero notes several cultural and ecclesial shifts that took place, many of which sounded good at the time but which had unintended consequences. Things like: a shift from rational to emotional (an experience of Jesus and not just thoughts about him) or a shift from doctrine to storytelling. Most folks don't realize it now, but the WWJD bracelets made popular a few years back actually stem from a novel by Charles Sheldon called *In His Steps*. In the book, a preacher is working on his sermon and has written his first two points, when the doorbell rings. It's a guy down on his luck and so the rest of the story is about what Jesus would do about the poor and homeless among us. But as some scholars have noted, we never hear the preacher's third point. Some took this to signal a change in preaching that was underway, stories instead of doctrine. Harriett Beecher Stowe, the author of *Uncle Tom's Cabin* and daughter of the famed preacher Lyman Beecher, believed that before long preachers would be reading stories to their congregations each week instead of preaching sermons. Turns out, that's exactly what Charles Sheldon did. On Sunday evenings at his church in Topeka, Kansas, Sheldon read the chapters of his novel he was writing.

"One other trend Prothero highlights was a shift from theology to morality. The Social Gospel movement, for all its wonderful stress on justice, unfortunately was pitted against deep thinking. Caring for the poor was more important than memorizing the Apostles' Creed. The problem, of course, is that it's a false dichotomy, another unintended consequence."

I hesitated a few moments as the students took notes. A few commented on historical trends, how pendulums swing from one stress to another. It was a good discussion.

After a while, I said, "Prothero says that like the patriots of 1776, folks came to be opposed to authority and tradition, only in religious matters this time around. But think for a moment about recent political trends, when folks became suspicious of President Obama's appointing an Ivy League scholar to a post in economics. There remains a kind of anti-intellectualism in our country."

Several of the students weighed in on this one, some of their observations political and others more religious. In the end, however, we all agreed on the need for a kind of preaching that does more than spin a good yarn, a kind of proclamation that equips the saints to think theologically and biblically. It was a heated conversation, to say the least. I mentioned briefly an article by David Reynolds on the rise of storytelling in the history of preaching in which he notes how prior to the First Great Awakening and the influence of John Wesley, whose "heart" was "strangely warmed," Puritans believed that affections and the like should be invoked only after one had understood something. Understanding was key. We were a long way removed from that in much preaching today.

I said, "Okay, we have one more critique to consider, and it is probably the most crucial of all, the ethical, or the ugly as I said earlier. What does Long say about that?"

Lisa once again flipped to page 12, but Alesha beat her to it. She said, "Here we go. 'For the theological left, the challenge is ethical. Storytelling enforces through coercion a monochromatic world upon the multihued experiences of others.'"

I said, "Thanks, Alesha. So what does Long have to say about this critique? Anyone?"

Alesha said, "Allow me. This was the part I really wanted to talk about. I've appreciated all along the liberation theme of narrative, at least as we've explored it. But I've been doing some readings for my feminist/womanist studies, and this really hit home with me. Long cites John McClure and how stories can be a form of hegemony, demanding that what started out for the preacher as *a narrative* becomes *the metanarrative* for others."

She said, "I think there is some validity here, but not the whole truth. One of the authors I read for another class is Marcia Mount Shoop, *Let the Bones Dance.*" Alesha fetched her dog-eared copy from her backpack. She said, "It's subtitled *Embodiment and the Body of Christ.* I'm still working through it, but here's part of what she argues. She's interested in *feeling,* by which she doesn't mean our emotions but something even more primal. And she doesn't mean experience either. She's drawing on Schleiermacher and Whitehead to discuss *feeling.* And it's sort of hard to follow at times, except I get very much one of her emphases.

"Early on in the book she writes, 'There is no such thing as theology that does not touch us where we live and practice our faith.' Shoop is definitely not a Gnostic. As she is a survivor of rape, her book is about the stories of women that go untold, how silencing can be an act of violence. I think the criticisms of McClure and others are legitimate, forcing folks to fit into the narratives of others, I really do get that. But not letting a story be told can be a form of violence as well."

I thanked Alesha for her comments and her passion. We agreed that some forms of storytelling as well as silence could be oppressive. And we agreed that the best hermeneutic for reading Scripture as well as short stories was one of love, not hate. I briefly cited Robert Beck's *Nonviolent Story,* in which he shows how the Gospel of Mark tells the Jesus story as the antithesis of Louis L'Amour novels in which justice is always served up with a six-shooter.

Getting us back on track, I asked, "And what about Long's citing of the essay 'Against Narrativity' by Galen Strawson?" Nothing but silence. I understood this since it's a rather complicated piece, even if Long helps us out with his analysis. I said, "Let me get you started."

I went to the board and said, "Strawson says scholars in a whole range of fields, including theology, have tended to accept two theses as givens: 1) that we live our lives as part of some ongoing story and 2) that doing so is a healthy way to be in the world. He calls these the 'psychological Narrativity thesis' and the 'ethical Narrativity thesis.'" I wrote these terms down, and said, "Joey, you're going to get your money's worth today."

He said, "You can say that again. I really didn't follow this very well."

I said, "Okay, hang in there. As Long notes, Strawson believes there are Narrative and non-Narrative folks in the world. Is that better, Joey?"

He said, "Much better. Does the fact I'm struggling with these ideas make me a Narrative person?"

"Maybe so. But here's Strawson's point: not everyone is narratively wired. And for him, an exclusive diet of narrative forces a straitjacket on some persons who do not live their lives narratively, or at least don't make sense of their lives that way. And of course this fits very nicely with what we've been stressing about the ethics of narrative preaching. I love how Long stresses that narrative preachers do have to be mindful of the non-Narrative folks in our churches. Listen to what he writes on page 15, 'If we tell stories in sermons—biblical and otherwise—we will need also to step away from those stories and think them through in non-narrative ways, drawing out explicitly the ideas and ethical implications of the stories.' You can find scholars on both sides of the debate, no doubt about it. But narrative preaching need not choose between evangelism and nurture, between education and engagement. Of course we will want to avoid manipulation, but in doing so we don't have to avoid touching people at the deepest parts of their lives and teaching them in the process.

"Any questions? Thoughts? Reflections?" I took the silence to mean they were with me. I was about to cover some housekeeping matters, then recalled a lunch conversation I had earlier that week with a pastor new to the area. I told them how this minister had said that one of his mentors while in seminary had cautioned him against being too much of a teacher when preaching, practically chastised him for teaching in the sermon. Turns out, the mentor was a well-known preacher who in an attempt to champion storytelling as the real deal in narrative preaching, actually discouraged exposition. He told this young pastor that sermons shouldn't teach, or should be limited to one brief moment of teaching. I still shake my head at such counsel.

After some brief discussion on the balance of exposition and experience, I did wrap up some housekeeping matters. I reminded them that next week they would begin practicing the skill of retelling these short stories. They could choose between "The Welcome Table" and "Revelation." I reminded them these were not for a grade. I didn't want them to be crippled by grades, but to give themselves over to storytelling. So we discussed expectations related to the retellings and decided emails could also be used to ask further questions.

I thought about sharing one final story, of how E. B. White had repeatedly broken down crying when trying to record a audio version of his classic *Charlotte's Web*. But we'd shared a lot of stories and they were tired. Instead, I said, "Remember how words do things? Go in peace."

CHAPTER FOURTEEN

Knocking at Heaven's Door

The following Sunday afternoon I was playing golf, which is much better than a nap after a morning of preaching. It was chilly and windy, so I had the course to myself when I thought about my best friend and golfing buddy, Lane. His mother-in-law was dying, and for some reason I imagined it had happened. Sure enough, Lane called later that day to share the news. Lane and his family asked if I would be willing to do the funeral, which would not take place until Thursday. I knew that would mean missing class, but I assured them I would be glad to do it.

As any minister who's done funerals knows, listening to a family's stories about their loved ones is a sacred act. I sat in their living room, Lane and Charleé telling stories about Betty. Charleé said her mom had loved music. I had known Betty casually, but had never known this detail. Charleé said her mom grew up singing in the church choir and performing duets with her own mother nearly every Sunday. But then something happened, something I would not be sharing in the service, and yet the kind of thing that helps a minister to appreciate another person's journey more fully.

When Betty was still a teenager, she got pregnant out of wedlock. She married the boy shortly thereafter, but in those days and in that church, this was a cardinal sin. The minister said that Betty would not be able to take communion again, and she would not be allowed to sing in the choir or with her mother. I tried to absorb the weight of this. Charleé said that in her mom's last days, that memory continued to haunt her. More than sixty years later, her mom asked, "Do you think God will forgive me? Do you think God will let me in heaven?" I thanked Charleé for sharing such a private story with me, and silently reflected on the power of the stories ministers tell, the good ones and the bad ones.

I emailed the students that class was being canceled, and that we would reschedule their retellings. Since Moodle was down again, I also emailed them the short story for discussion the following week.

"The Garden Party"
By Katherine Mansfield

And after all the weather was ideal. They could not have had a more perfect day for a garden-party if they had ordered it. Windless, warm, the sky without a cloud. Only the blue was veiled with a haze of light gold, as it is sometimes in early summer. The gardener had been up since dawn, mowing the lawns and sweeping them, until the grass and the dark flat rosettes where the daisy plants had been seemed to shine. As for the roses, you could not help feeling they understood that roses are the only flowers that impress people at garden-parties; the only flowers that everybody is certain of knowing. Hundreds, yes, literally hundreds, had come out in a single night; the green bushes bowed down as though they had been visited by archangels.

Breakfast was not yet over before the men came to put up the marquee. "Where do you want the marquee put, Mother?"

"My dear child, it's no use asking me. I'm determined to leave everything to you children this year. Forget I am your mother. Treat me as an honoured guest." But Meg could not possibly go and supervise the men. She had washed her hair before breakfast, and she sat drinking her coffee in a green turban, with a dark wet curl stamped on each cheek. Jose, the butterfly, always came down in a silk petticoat and a kimono jacket.

"You'll have to go, Laura; you're the artistic one."

Away Laura flew, still holding her piece of bread-and-butter. It's so delicious to have an excuse for eating out of doors, and besides, she loved having to arrange things; she always felt she could do it so much better than anybody else.

Four men in their shirt-sleeves stood grouped together on the garden path. They carried staves covered with rolls of canvas, and they had big tool-bags slung on their backs. They looked impressive. Laura wished now that she was not holding that piece of bread-and-butter, but there was nowhere to put it, and she couldn't possibly throw it away. She blushed and tried to look severe and even a little bit short-sighted as she came up to them.

"Good morning," she said, copying her mother's voice. But that sounded so fearfully affected that she was ashamed, and stammered like a little girl, "Oh–er–have you come–is it about the marquee?"

"That's right, miss," said the tallest of the men, a lanky, freckled fellow, and he shifted his tool-bag, knocked back his straw hat and smiled down at her. "That's about it."

His smile was so easy, so friendly, that Laura recovered. What nice eyes he had, small, but such a dark blue! And now she looked at the others, they were smiling too. "Cheer up, we won't bite," their smile seemed to say. How very nice workmen were! And what a beautiful morning! She mustn't mention the morning; she must be business-like. The marquee.

"Well, what about the lily-lawn? Would that do?"

And she pointed to the lily-lawn with the hand that didn't hold the bread-and-butter. They turned, they stared in the direction. A little fat chap thrust out his under-lip, and the tall fellow frowned.

"I don't fancy it," said he. "Not conspicuous enough. You see, with a thing like a marquee," and he turned to Laura in his easy way, "you want to put it somewhere where it'll give you a bang slap in the eye, if you follow me."

Laura's upbringing made her wonder for a moment whether it was quite respectful of a workman to talk to her of bangs slap in the eye. But she did quite follow him.

"A corner of the tennis-court," she suggested. "But the band's going to be in one corner."

"H'm, going to have a band, are you?" said another of the workmen. He was pale. He had a haggard look as his dark eyes scanned the tennis-court. What was he thinking?

"Only a very small band," said Laura gently. Perhaps he wouldn't mind so much if the band was quite small. But the tall fellow interrupted.

"Look here, miss, that's the place. Against those trees. Over there. That'll do fine."

Against the karakas. Then the karaka-trees would be hidden. And they were so lovely, with their broad, gleaming leaves, and their clusters of yellow fruit. They were like trees you imagined growing on a desert island, proud, solitary, lifting their leaves and fruits to the sun in a kind of silent splendour. Must they be hidden by a marquee?

They must. Already the men had shouldered their staves and were making for the place. Only the tall fellow was left. He bent down, pinched a sprig of lavender, put his thumb and forefinger to his nose and snuffed up the smell. When Laura saw that gesture she forgot all about the karakas in her wonder at him caring for things like that—caring for the smell of lavender. How many men that she knew would have done such a thing? Oh, how extraordinarily nice workmen were, she thought. Why couldn't she have workmen for her friends rather than the silly boys she danced with and who came to Sunday night supper? She would get on much better with men like these.

It's all the fault, she decided, as the tall fellow drew something on the back of an envelope, something that was to be looped up or left to hang, of these absurd class distinctions. Well, for her part, she didn't feel them. Not a bit, not an atom . . . And now there came the chock-chock of wooden hammers. Someone whistled, someone sang out, "Are you right there, matey?" "Matey!" The friendliness of it, the–the–Just to prove how happy she was, just to show the tall fellow how at home she felt, and how she despised stupid conventions, Laura took a big bite of her bread-and-butter as she stared at the little drawing. She felt just like a work-girl.

"Laura, Laura, where are you? Telephone, Laura!" a voice cried from the house.

"Coming!" Away she skimmed, over the lawn, up the path, up the steps, across the veranda, and into the porch. In the hall her father and Laurie were brushing their hats ready to go to the office.

"I say, Laura," said Laurie very fast, "you might just give a squiz at my coat before this afternoon. See if it wants pressing."

"I will," said she. Suddenly she couldn't stop herself. She ran at Laurie and gave him a small, quick squeeze. "Oh, I do love parties, don't you?" gasped Laura.

"Ra-ther," said Laurie's warm, boyish voice, and he squeezed his sister too, and gave her a gentle push. "Dash off to the telephone, old girl."

The telephone. "Yes, yes; oh yes. Kitty? Good morning, dear. Come to lunch? Do, dear. Delighted of course. It will only be a very scratch meal—just the sandwich crusts and broken meringue-shells and what's left over. Yes, isn't it a perfect morning? Your white? Oh, I certainly should. One moment—hold the line. Mother's calling." And Laura sat back. "What, mother? Can't hear."

Mrs. Sheridan's voice floated down the stairs. "Tell her to wear that sweet hat she had on last Sunday."

"Mother says you're to wear that *sweet* hat you had on last Sunday. Good. One o'clock. Bye-bye."

Laura put back the receiver, flung her arms over her head, took a deep breath, stretched and let them fall. "Huh," she sighed, and the moment after the sigh she sat up quickly. She was still, listening. All the doors in the house seemed to be open. The house was alive with soft, quick steps and running voices. The green baize door that led to the kitchen regions swung open and shut with a muffled thud. And now there came a long, chuckling absurd sound. It was the heavy piano being moved on its stiff castors. But the air! If you stopped to notice, was the air always like this? Little faint winds were playing chase in at the tops of the windows, out at the doors. And there were two tiny spots of sun, one on the inkpot, one on a silver photograph frame, playing too. Darling little spots. Especially the one on the inkpot lid. It was quite warm. A warm little silver star. She could have kissed it.

The front door bell pealed, and there sounded the rustle of Sadie's print skirt on the stairs. A man's voice murmured; Sadie answered, careless, "I'm sure I don't know. Wait. I'll ask Mrs Sheridan."

"What is it, Sadie?" Laura came into the hall.

"It's the florist, Miss Laura."

It was, indeed. There, just inside the door, stood a wide, shallow tray full of pots of pink lilies. No other kind. Nothing but lilies—canna lilies, big pink flowers, wide open, radiant, almost frighteningly alive on bright crimson stems.

"O-oh, Sadie!" said Laura, and the sound was like a little moan. She crouched down as if to warm herself at that blaze of lilies; she felt they were in her fingers, on her lips, growing in her breast.

"It's some mistake," she said faintly. "Nobody ever ordered so many. Sadie, go and find mother."

But at that moment Mrs. Sheridan joined them.

"It's quite right," she said calmly. "Yes, I ordered them. Aren't they lovely?" She pressed Laura's arm. "I was passing the shop yesterday, and I saw them in the window. And I suddenly thought for once in my life I shall have enough canna lilies. The garden-party will be a good excuse."

"But I thought you said you didn't mean to interfere," said Laura. Sadie had gone. The florist's man was still outside at his van. She put her arm round her mother's neck and gently, very gently, she bit her mother's ear.

"My darling child, you wouldn't like a logical mother, would you? Don't do that. Here's the man."

He carried more lilies still, another whole tray.

"Bank them up, just inside the door, on both sides of the porch, please," said Mrs. Sheridan. "Don't you agree, Laura?"

"Oh, I *do*, mother."

In the drawing-room Meg, Jose and good little Hans had at last succeeded in moving the piano.

"Now, if we put this chesterfield against the wall and move everything out of the room except the chairs, don't you think?"

"Quite."

"Hans, move these tables into the smoking-room, and bring a sweeper to take these marks off the carpet and—one moment, Hans—" Jose loved giving orders to the servants, and they loved obeying her. She always made them feel they were taking part in some drama. "Tell mother and Miss Laura to come here at once."

"Very good, Miss Jose."

She turned to Meg. "I want to hear what the piano sounds like, just in case I'm asked to sing this afternoon. Let's try over 'This life is Weary.'"

Pom! Ta-ta-ta *Tee*-ta! The piano burst out so passionately that Jose's face changed. She clasped her hands. She looked mournfully and enigmatically at her mother and Laura as they came in.

"This life is Wee-ary,
A Tear—a Sigh.
A Love that Chan-ges,
This Life is Wee-ary,
A Tear—a Sigh.
A Love that Chan-ges,
And then . . . Good-bye!"

But at the word "Good-bye," and although the piano sounded more desperate than ever, her face broke into a brilliant, dreadfully unsympathetic smile.

"Aren't I in good voice, mummy?" she beamed.

"This life is *Wee*-ary
Hope comes to Die.
A Dream-a *Wa*-kening."

But now Sadie interrupted them. "What is it, Sadie?"

"If you please, m'm, cook says have you got the flags for the sandwiches?"

"The flags for the sandwiches, Sadie?" echoed Mrs. Sheridan dreamily. And the children knew by her face that she hadn't got them. "Let me see." And she said to Sadie firmly, "Tell cook I'll let her have them in ten minutes."

Sadie went.

"Now, Laura," said her mother quickly, "come with me into the smoking-room. I've got the names somewhere on the back of an envelope. You'll have to write them out for me. Meg, go upstairs this minute and take that wet thing off your head. Jose, run and finish dressing this instant. Do you hear me, children, or shall I have to tell your father when he comes home tonight? And—and, Jose, pacify cook if you do go into the kitchen, will you? I'm terrified of her this morning."

The envelope was found at last behind the dining-room clock, though how it had got there Mrs. Sheridan could not imagine.

"One of you children must have stolen it out of my bag, because I remember vividly—cream cheese and lemon-curd. Have you done that?"

"Yes."

"Egg and—" Mrs. Sheridan held the envelope away from her. "It looks like mice. It can't be mice, can it?"

"Olive, pet," said Laura, looking over her shoulder.

"Yes, of course, olive. What a horrible combination it sounds. Egg and olive."

They were finished at last, and Laura took them off to the kitchen. She found Jose there pacifying the cook, who did not look at all terrifying.

"I have never seen such exquisite sandwiches," said Jose's rapturous voice. "How many kinds did you say there were, cook? Fifteen?"

"Fifteen, Miss Jose."

"Well, cook, I congratulate you."

Cook swept up crusts with the long sandwich knife and smiled broadly.

"Godber's has come," announced Sadie, issuing out of the pantry. She had seen the man pass the window.

That meant the cream puffs had come. Godber's were famous for their cream puffs. Nobody ever thought of making them at home.

"Bring them in and put them on the table, my girl," ordered cook.

Sadie brought them in and went back to the door. Of course Laura and Jose were far too grown-up to really care about such things. All the same, they couldn't help agreeing that the puffs looked very attractive. Very. Cook began arranging them, shaking off the extra icing sugar.

"Don't they carry one back to all one's parties?" said Laura.

"I suppose they do," said practical Jose, who never liked to be carried back. "They look beautifully light and feathery, I must say."

"Have one each, my dears," said cook in her comfortable voice. "Yer ma won't know."

Oh, impossible. Fancy cream puffs so soon after breakfast. The very idea made one shudder. All the same, two minutes later Jose and Laura were licking their fingers with that absorbed inward look that only comes from whipped cream.

"Let's go into the garden, out by the back way," suggested Laura. "I want to see how the men are getting on with the marquee. They're such awfully nice men."

But the back door was blocked by cook, Sadie, Godber's man and Hans.

Something had happened.

"Tuk-tuk-tuk," clucked cook like an agitated hen. Sadie had her hand clapped to her cheek as though she had toothache. Hans's face was screwed up in the effort to understand. Only Godber's man seemed to be enjoying himself; it was his story.

"What's the matter? What's happened?"

"There's been a horrible accident," said cook. "A man killed."

"A man killed! Where? How? When?"

But Godber's man wasn't going to have his story snatched from under his nose.

"Know those little cottages just below here, miss?" Know them? Of course, she knew them. "Well, there's a young chap living there, name of Scott, a carter. His horse shied at a traction-engine, corner of Hawke Street this morning, and he was thrown out on the back of his head. Killed."

"Dead!" Laura stared at Godber's man.

"Dead when they picked him up," said Godber's man with relish. "They were taking the body home as I come up here." And he said to the cook, "He's left a wife and five little ones."

"Jose, come here." Laura caught hold of her sister's sleeve and dragged her through the kitchen to the other side of the green baize door. There she paused and leaned against it. "Jose!" she said, horrified, "however are we going to stop everything?"

"Stop everything, Laura!" cried Jose in astonishment. "What do you mean?"

"Stop the garden-party, of course." Why did Jose pretend?

But Jose was still more amazed. "Stop the garden-party? My dear Laura, don't be so absurd. Of course we can't do anything of the kind. Nobody expects us to. Don't be so extravagant."

"But we can't possibly have a garden-party with a man dead just outside the front gate."

That really was extravagant, for the little cottages were in a lane to themselves at the very bottom of a steep rise that led up to the house. A broad road ran between. True, they were far too near. They were the greatest possible eyesore, and they had no right to be in that neighbourhood at all. They were little mean dwellings painted a chocolate brown. In the garden patches there was nothing but cabbage stalks, sick hens and tomato cans. The very smoke coming out of their chimneys was poverty-stricken. Little rags and shreds of smoke, so unlike the great silvery plumes that uncurled from the Sheridans' chimneys. Washer-women lived in the lane and sweeps and a cobbler, and a man whose house-front was studded all over with minute bird-cages. Children swarmed. When the Sheridans were little they were forbidden to set foot there because of the revolting language and of what they might catch. But since they were grown up, Laura and Laurie on their prowls sometimes walked through. It was disgusting and sordid. They came out with a shudder. But still one must go everywhere; one must see everything. So through they went.

"And just think of what the band would sound like to that poor woman," said Laura.

"Oh, Laura!" Jose began to be seriously annoyed. "If you're going to stop a band playing every time someone has an accident, you'll lead a very strenuous life. I'm every bit as sorry about it as you. I feel just as sympathetic." Her eyes hardened. She looked at her sister just as she used to when they were little and fighting together. "You won't bring a drunken workman back to life by being sentimental," she said softly.

"Drunk! Who said he was drunk?" Laura turned furiously on Jose. She said just as they had used to say on those occasions, "I'm going straight up to tell mother."

"Do, dear," cooed Jose.

"Mother, can I come into your room?" Laura turned the big glass door-knob.

"Of course, child. Why, what's the matter? What's given you such a colour?" And Mrs. Sheridan turned round from her dressing-table. She was trying on a new hat.

"Mother, a man's been killed," began Laura.

"*Not* in the garden?" interrupted her mother.

"No, no!"

"Oh, what a fright you gave me!" Mrs. Sheridan sighed with relief, and took off the big hat and held it on her knees.

"But listen, mother," said Laura. Breathless, half-choking, she told the dreadful story. "Of course, we can't have our party, can we?" she pleaded. "The band and everybody arriving. They'd hear us, mother; they're nearly neighbours!"

To Laura's astonishment her mother behaved just like Jose; it was harder to bear because she seemed amused. She refused to take Laura seriously.

"But, dear child, use your common sense. It's only by accident we've heard of it. If someone had died there normally—and I can't understand how they keep alive in those poky little holes—we should still be having our party, shouldn't we?"

Laura had to say "yes" to that, but she felt it was all wrong. She sat down on her mother's sofa and pinched the cushion frill.

"Mother, isn't it terribly heartless of us?" she asked.

"Darling!" Mrs. Sheridan got up and came over to her, carrying the hat. Before Laura could stop her she had popped it on. "My child!" said her mother, "the hat is yours. It's made for you. It's much too young for me. I have never seen you look such a picture. Look at yourself!" And she held up her hand-mirror.

"But, mother," Laura began again. She couldn't look at herself; she turned aside.

This time Mrs. Sheridan lost patience just as Jose had done.

"You are being very absurd, Laura," she said coldly. "People like that don't expect sacrifices from us. And it's not very sympathetic to spoil everybody's enjoyment as you're doing now."

"I don't understand," said Laura, and she walked quickly out of the room into her own bedroom. There, quite by chance, the first thing she saw was this charming girl in the mirror, in her black hat trimmed with gold daisies, and a long black velvet ribbon. Never had she imagined she could look like that. Is mother right? she thought. And now she hoped her mother was right. Am I being extravagant? Perhaps it was extravagant. Just for a moment she had another glimpse of that poor woman and those little children, and the body being carried into the house. But it all seemed blurred, unreal, like a picture in the newspaper. I'll remember it again after the party's over, she decided. And somehow that seemed quite the best plan . . .

Lunch was over by half-past one. By half-past two they were all ready for the fray. The green-coated band had arrived and was established in a corner of the tennis-court.

"My dear!" trilled Kitty Maitland, "aren't they too like frogs for words? You ought to have arranged them round the pond with the conductor in the middle on a leaf."

Laurie arrived and hailed them on his way to dress. At the sight of him Laura remembered the accident again. She wanted to tell him. If Laurie agreed with the others, then it was bound to be all right. And she followed him into the hall.

"Laurie!"

"Hallo!" He was half-way upstairs, but when he turned round and saw Laura he suddenly puffed out his cheeks and goggled his eyes at her. "My word, Laura! You do look stunning," said Laurie. "What an absolutely topping hat!"

Laura said faintly "Is it?" and smiled up at Laurie, and didn't tell him after all.

Soon after that people began coming in streams. The band struck up; the hired waiters ran from the house to the marquee. Wherever you looked there were couples strolling, bending to the flowers, greeting, moving on over the lawn. They were like bright birds that had alighted in the Sheridans' garden for this one afternoon, on their way to—where? Ah, what happiness it is to be with people who all are happy, to press hands, press cheeks, smile into eyes.

"Darling Laura, how well you look!"

"What a becoming hat, child!"

"Laura, you look quite Spanish. I've never seen you look so striking."

And Laura, glowing, answered softly, "Have you had tea? Won't you have an ice? The passion-fruit ices really are rather special." She ran to her father and begged him. "Daddy darling, can't the band have something to drink?"

And the perfect afternoon slowly ripened, slowly faded, slowly its petals closed.

"Never a more delightful garden-party . . ." "The greatest success . . ." "Quite the most . . ."

Laura helped her mother with the good-byes. They stood side by side in the porch till it was all over.

"All over, all over, thank heaven," said Mrs. Sheridan. "Round up the others, Laura. Let's go and have some fresh coffee. I'm exhausted. Yes, it's been very successful. But oh, these parties, these parties! Why will you children insist on giving parties!" And they all of them sat down in the deserted marquee.

"Have a sandwich, daddy dear. I wrote the flag."

"Thanks." Mr. Sheridan took a bite and the sandwich was gone. He took another. "I suppose you didn't hear of a beastly accident that happened today?" he said.

"My dear," said Mrs. Sheridan, holding up her hand, "we did. It nearly ruined the party. Laura insisted we should put it off."

"Oh, mother!" Laura didn't want to be teased about it.

"It was a horrible affair all the same," said Mr. Sheridan. "The chap was married too. Lived just below in the lane, and leaves a wife and half a dozen kiddies, so they say."

An awkward little silence fell. Mrs. Sheridan fidgeted with her cup. Really, it was very tactless of father . . .

Suddenly she looked up. There on the table were all those sandwiches, cakes, puffs, all un-eaten, all going to be wasted. She had one of her brilliant ideas.

"I know," she said. "Let's make up a basket. Let's send that poor creature some of this perfectly good food. At any rate, it will be the greatest treat for the children. Don't you agree? And she's sure to have neighbours calling in and so on. What a point to have it all ready prepared. Laura!" She jumped up. "Get me the big basket out of the stairs cupboard."

"But, mother, do you really think it's a good idea?" said Laura.

Again, how curious, she seemed to be different from them all. To take scraps from their party. Would the poor woman really like that?

"Of course! What's the matter with you to-day? An hour or two ago you were insisting on us being sympathetic, and now—"

Oh well! Laura ran for the basket. It was filled, it was heaped by her mother.

"Take it yourself, darling," said she. "Run down just as you are. No, wait, take the arum lilies too. People of that class are so impressed by arum lilies."

"The stems will ruin her lace frock," said practical Jose.

So they would. Just in time. "Only the basket, then. And, Laura!"—her mother followed her out of the marquee—"don't on any account—"

"What mother?"

No, better not put such ideas into the child's head! "Nothing! Run along."

It was just growing dusky as Laura shut their garden gates. A big dog ran by like a shadow. The road gleamed white, and down below in the hollow the little cottages were in deep shade. How quiet it seemed after the afternoon. Here she was going down the hill to somewhere where a man lay dead, and she couldn't realize it. Why couldn't she? She stopped a minute. And it seemed to her that kisses, voices, tinkling spoons, laughter, the smell of crushed grass were somehow inside her. She had no room for anything else. How strange! She looked up at the pale sky, and all she thought was, "Yes, it was the most successful party."

Now the broad road was crossed. The lane began, smoky and dark. Women in shawls and men's tweed caps hurried by. Men hung over the palings; the children played in the doorways. A low hum came from the mean little cottages. In some of them there was a flicker of light, and a shadow, crab-like, moved across the window. Laura bent her head and hurried on. She wished now she had put on a coat. How her frock shone! And the big hat with the velvet streamer—if only it was another hat! Were the people looking at her? They must be. It was a mistake to have come; she knew all along it was a mistake. Should she go back even now?

No, too late. This was the house. It must be. A dark knot of people stood outside. Beside the gate an old, old woman with a crutch sat in a chair, watching. She had her feet on a newspaper. The voices stopped as Laura drew near. The group parted. It was as though she was expected, as though they had known she was coming here.

Laura was terribly nervous. Tossing the velvet ribbon over her shoulder, she said to a woman standing by, "Is this Mrs. Scott's house?" and the woman, smiling queerly, said, "It is, my lass."

Oh, to be away from this! She actually said, "Help me, God," as she walked up the tiny path and knocked. To be away from those staring eyes, or be covered up in anything, one of those women's shawls even. I'll just leave the basket and go, she decided. I shan't even wait for it to be emptied.

Then the door opened. A little woman in black showed in the gloom.

Laura said, "Are you Mrs. Scott?" But to her horror the woman answered, "Walk in, please, miss," and she was shut in the passage.

"No," said Laura, "I don't want to come in. I only want to leave this basket. Mother sent—"

The little woman in the gloomy passage seemed not to have heard her. "Step this way, please, miss," she said in an oily voice, and Laura followed her.

She found herself in a wretched little low kitchen, lighted by a smoky lamp. There was a woman sitting before the fire.

"Em," said the little creature who had let her in. "Em! It's a young lady." She turned to Laura. She said meaningly, "I'm 'er sister, miss. You'll excuse 'er, won't you?"

"Oh, but of course!" said Laura. "Please, please don't disturb her. I–I only want to leave—"

But at that moment the woman at the fire turned round. Her face, puffed up, red, with swollen eyes and swollen lips, looked terrible. She seemed as though she couldn't understand why Laura was there. What did it mean? Why was this stranger standing in the kitchen with a basket? What was it all about? And the poor face puckered up again.

"All right, my dear," said the other. "I'll thenk the young lady."

And again she began, "You'll excuse her, miss, I'm sure," and her face, swollen too, tried an oily smile.

Laura only wanted to get out, to get away. She was back in the passage. The door opened. She walked straight through into the bedroom where the dead man was lying.

"You'd like a look at 'im, wouldn't you?" said Em's sister, and she brushed past Laura over to the bed. "Don't be afraid, my lass,"—and now her voice sounded fond and sly, and fondly she drew down the sheet— "'e looks a picture. There's nothing to show. Come along, my dear."

Laura came.

There lay a young man, fast asleep—sleeping so soundly, so deeply, that he was far, far away from them both. Oh, so remote, so peaceful. He was dreaming. Never wake him up again. His head was sunk in the pillow, his eyes were closed; they were blind under the closed eyelids. He was given up to his dream. What did garden-parties and baskets and lace frocks matter to him? He was far from all those things. He was wonderful, beautiful. While they were laughing and while the band was playing, this marvel had come to the lane. Happy . . . happy . . . All is well, said that sleeping face. This is just as it should be. I am content.

But all the same you had to cry, and she couldn't go out of the room without saying something to him. Laura gave a loud childish sob.

"Forgive my hat," she said.

And this time she didn't wait for Em's sister. She found her way out of the door, down the path, past all those dark people. At the corner of the lane she met Laurie.

He stepped out of the shadow. "Is that you, Laura?"

"Yes."

"Mother was getting anxious. Was it all right?"

"Yes, quite. Oh, Laurie!" She took his arm, she pressed up against him.

"I say, you're not crying, are you?" asked her brother.

Laura shook her head. She was.

Laurie put his arm round her shoulder. "Don't cry," he said in his warm, loving voice. "Was it awful?"

"No," sobbed Laura. "It was simply marvellous. But Laurie—" She stopped, she looked at her brother. "Isn't life," she stammered, "isn't life—" But what life was she couldn't explain. No matter. He quite understood.

"*Isn't* it, darling?" said Laurie.

CHAPTER FIFTEEN

Lessons from Yo-Yo Ma

From: A. M. Freeman [a.m.freeman@spst.edu]

To: PRE 430 Students [lisas@spst.edu; csamir@spst.edu; joeyl@spst.edu; bparker@spst.edu; calvarez@spst.edu; ralvarez@spst.edu; aleshap@spst.edu]

Subject: This Week's Class

Colleagues,

First, I want to thank you for your patience with my being gone last week as well as your prayers. The funeral went very well, and the family appreciated my being able to minister to them in their grief.

As we look ahead to this coming Thursday, I wanted to be clear about the revised schedule and agenda. We will go ahead with the retellings as noted in the syllabus. Each of you will choose between Walker's "The Welcome Table" and O'Connor's "Revelation." The idea is to retell the story so that folks who've never heard it can enter into the experience. We've talked about this at length in class, but now we need to actually do it.

I also emailed you a copy of Katherine Mansfield's short story "The Garden Party." You should be prepared to discuss it, as well as the assigned pages in Foster's *How to Read Literature Like a Professor*. As you have no doubt already noticed, this is a very different kind of story than we've been reading. I look forward to the conversation.

Oh, and about the snack sign-up schedule. I don't have that in front of me. I don't recall who was scheduled for last week, or this one for that matter. If those of you who were affected will be in touch, you can figure it out between yourselves. Thanks so much.

Grace and peace,
A. M. Freeman

Lisa worked out the snack schedule with Brock, who would go next time. For this Thursday's goodies, she made a German chocolate sheet cake. She even went so far as to bring half a gallon of milk for those who rightly insisted chocolate cake and milk were a sacrament of sorts. We talked briefly about the funeral I'd done, happenings around campus, and the news of another terrorist leader's death in the Middle East.

For a devotional, I read the preacher Kohelet's words in Ecclesiastes 3, about a time for everything. From Nafisi's memoir I read a passage that needed some context. I said, "In her time as a professor of English literature, the Islamic fundamentalists cracked down so hard they actually had spies attending her courses. One of those persons was so offended at F. Scott Fitzgerald's *The Great Gatsby* that they actually put it on trial in the class."

Cassandra said, "They what?"

I said, "You heard me, they put a piece of literature on trial."

Cassandra said, "Literature on trial is one thing, a very weird thing; but *The Great Gatsby*? I could understand *The Catcher in the Rye* but *The Great Gatsby*?"

I said, "That's part of the issue this reading raises. Listen to what she writes:

> A good novel is one that shows the complexity of individuals, and creates enough space for all these characters to have a voice; in this way, a novel is called democratic—not that it advocates democracy but that by nature it is so.

> ———————

> A great novel heightens your senses and sensitivity to the complexities of life and of individuals, and prevents you from the self-righteousness that sees morality in fixed formulas about good and evil.

> ———————

> Just before the bell rang, Zarrin, who had been silent ever since the recess, suddenly got up. Although she spoke in a low voice, she appeared agitated. She said sometimes she wondered why people bothered to claim to be literature majors. Did it mean anything? she wondered. As for the book, she had nothing more to say in its defense. The novel was its own defense. Perhaps we had a few things to learn from it, from Mr. Fitzgerald. She had

not learned from reading it that adultery was good or that we should all become shysters. Did people all go on strike or head west after reading Steinbeck? Did they go whaling after reading Melville? Are people not a little more complex than that? And are revolutionaries devoid of personal feelings and emotions? Do they never fall in love, or enjoy beauty?

For a time of prayer, I suggested only silence, silence at the death of a Middle East tyrant in contrast with all the celebrating folks had been doing, but also silence at the death of a saint whose funeral I had done and silence for the fragile state of academic freedom in all places at all times. I ended with a simple, "Amen."

I said, "We're going to begin the hour with the retellings as assigned. I think what would be most helpful is that prior to sharing your version of the short story, you'd say a word about the biblical text you plan to pair it with and what you see as the sermon's focus. That way we can listen for the connections and the way you've shaped it. One other thing, and this is optional for now simply because you may not know yet, but can you say where in the sermon this telling might come? In other words, if you think you might open the sermon with the short story, or close with it, or, well, you get the idea. The main thing is the textual pairing and sermon focus. Any questions?"

Lisa said, "How long do we have?"

I said, "Oh, I wouldn't worry about time. Generally, these don't take but a few minutes, since they are only a portion of a sermon. By the way, what I hope to do after each person has finished is to open it up for discussion, then let you pair off and practice again using the suggestions we've made. But don't worry about how long. Well, unless it's way too long, and then I'll let you know."

I had placed a desktop podium at the head of the table. It wasn't exactly a pulpit but it would do. I draped a stole over the edge to serve as a parament. Brock, who was first, asked if he could do it sitting down. I said, "No, good storytelling requires your whole body, just like preaching." He made a joke about his body, a fairly common practice among preachers who don't really like theirs.

He chose to tackle O'Connor's "Revelation," only he got caught up in the details—all the folks in the doctor's office, some of the insignificant conversational details that take place, the whole nine yards. His attention to details was partly because there are so many to get caught up in with that story compared to the sparseness of Walker's "The Welcome Table," but also because that is Brock's tendency. During the feedback time he admitted that even with the exegesis of Scripture, he gets bogged down in details, trying to do too much. I noted how preachers have to be selective, both with short stories and biblical texts. One sermon is just that, one sermon. We can't do everything. I said, "I'm sure some of you recall my mantra from the 'Intro' course, 'Texts are about a lot of things; sermons are about one.' Well, it's the same for using short stories."

If Brock's tendency was toward too many details, Carlos had too few. He retold "The Welcome Table," but it was over in a flash and none of us felt the power of the piece. I suspected Carlos had not felt it either, although I was curious to see if Rosa had, and if so, could she communicate it.

I said, "Rosa, you're up next."

She took a deep breath and made her way to the head of the table. Rosa does not have a presence about her, not really. And yet, there had been a few times during the discussion of certain stories when I could glimpse fragments of the real Rosa wanting to break out.

She said, "I'm doing Walker's 'The Welcome Table,' and for a text I'm using a passage that we discussed at the beginning of the semester, the Samaritan woman in John 4. Jesus approaches both of these women who have been shunned, but in very different ways. So I'm preaching a word of comfort more so than a word of judgment upon those who threw her out. Anyway, here goes."

She began, "The old woman lifted up her dark eyes as she weighed what it would mean to go to church this day. It was a Sunday, shiny with promise, even if her rusty clothes were not the least bit shiny. The old woman's skin was the color of 'poor gray Georgia earth,' and she had been beaten down 'by king cotton and the extreme weather.' And she smelled of onions."

Rosa looked up from her manuscript, and then kept reading. "The old black woman walked toward the white church on the corner, its steeple shining in the sun. But the folks out front could not believe their eyes. It looked like she was coming to their church, not going to hers. The usher tried to say something but he was just a child really. The preacher said something, er, wait . . ." Rosa apologized to the class, then continued, "The preacher *should* have said something, duty required it. But whatever he managed to say, she was not to be stopped. The church folks there never did talk about this afterwards. Maybe they hoped the memory would just fade.

"The old black woman brushed past them all. Inside, she sat near the back of the plain church. It was cold inside. She noticed that right away. Very cold. She had come to worship God, so that's what she did. She hummed and rocked in place, praising Jesus.

"The church folks looked at her as they entered. The nerve of it all. They had never seen such a thing. The ladies of the church, with their fine

Sunday clothes, could not worship with her there. They insisted the right thing be done. Without warning, the men of the church picked up the old black woman, their burly fists under her smelly arms, and 'out she flew through the door, back under the cold blue sky.' And now the church was warmer, the fellowship too. They sang of God's impartial love."

Rosa paused here, not because she lost her place, but because she was clearly moved. She found her voice and said, "As the old black woman tried to gather her wits about her, something happened. Someone was coming down the road, and not just any old someone. 'She started to grin, toothlessly, with short giggles of joy, jumping about and slapping her hands on her knees.' It was Jesus. He was wearing a white robe and carrying a blue blanket over his shoulder. His eyes looked as if a candle was glowing behind them. 'Except that he was not carrying in his arms a baby sheep, he looked exactly like the picture of him that she had hanging over her bed at home.'

"Only the old black woman turned out to be that sheep. Jesus didn't carry her, but he said only two words, 'Follow me.' And she did. They walked and talked; mostly she talked. Jesus listened to her troubles, how they had tossed her out of his church. They walked and walked, until 'the ground was like clouds under their feet.'

"The church folks never knew what happened. Some said they saw her walking down the road, jabbering to herself. But she knew what had happened. The old black woman was home, home with Jesus." Rosa paused. "And I'm not sure what will come next because I'm not sure where the story will go. It seems like an ending to me, but I don't like the way I end it. Anyway, that's what I have."

Rosa was clearly nervous, worried that her retelling had somehow failed to do its work, failed to get off the ground. Her classmates assured her otherwise. Cassandra said, "I thought the attention to detail was just right. We didn't get bogged down and we didn't rush through it either. Great stuff, Rosa." Several others echoed that same sentiment, although Carlos remained silent. Then again, he remained silent during most class discussions. He did kiss her on the cheek when she sat back down.

Alesha was beaming and said, "I would agree with what others have said, but my take is this: Alice Walker would be proud." I echoed the same sentiment. Now Rosa beamed and blushed.

Cassandra went next and knocked her retelling out of the park, which was pretty amazing since it was the longer story "Revelation." Her struggle would not be with the short stories but with the preaching of them. Alesha and Lisa both tackled "The Welcome Table," as did Joey. Only Joey's retelling was something of a mess. He didn't slip in a "dude" reference, but his telling lacked presence and polish. Still, the feedback time was hilarious, Joey cracking us up with his quick wit. His humility was refreshing as always.

It was my turn to make comments, to wrap things up, so to speak. I noted how too many details could get us bogged down and too few could leave a story feeling skimpy. I said, "But those aren't the most important issues. There are two broad categories we need to consider in relation to a story's details. The first is more a technique, the second more a matter of the heart. Let's start with technique."

I had been thinking a lot about the need for a storytelling workshop of sorts in class. There are techniques that make storytelling more effective, and they can be learned with practice and feedback. I had worked up a handout a week or so earlier, but thought it would make more sense after they tried their hands at a retelling, when they had encountered firsthand some of the inherent difficulties. I said, "All right, so let's think about the skills required in retelling a short story, which are essentially the same for storytelling in general, biblical or otherwise. I have a handout that might prove helpful, especially with this balance of details."

Joey said, "What, now that we messed up, you're going to teach us how to do it? That's cruel, dude."

"Maybe a little cruel, but I thought having tried it for yourselves, you might be more open to analyzing the process. Plus, don't forget, these retellings weren't for a grade anyway." He thought those were both good points.

I said, "One of our biggest problems is time management. Only maybe not the usual way we think of 'time management.' It's true there's not enough time in a sermon to retell even the shortest of short stories in detail. But there's something else related to time management, as we shall see. Our real problem is telling a short story in such a way that the most magical moments in time, the revelatory scenes as we've been calling them, come alive. And of course we have to set the scene for those moments. Besides, we wouldn't want to retell the whole thing in detail anyway. And as we'll see in a minute, neither do these authors of short stories. More about that in a minute. Let's start, however, with one of the most common phrases among writing instructors: Show, don't tell. Have you heard that one before?"

Cassandra said, "Only about a million times during my college days."

Joey said, "I probably shouldn't admit this, but I heard it a lot in my home as well. My mom was an English teacher."

Cassandra said, "*Aha*, the truth comes out." Joey smiled sheepishly.

I said, "Okay, Cassandra, since you were the English major and Joey only the son of an English teacher, why don't you enlighten us? What exactly do they mean by *show, don't tell*?"

She said, "Glad to help. It's really rather simple. If you're writing about a character and want to point out how she or he is always responsible at work or whatever, *telling* would be when the author says, 'Gabe was always responsible at his job, always getting projects done on time . . .' We read that, and we get the idea Gabe was responsible. That's telling. The author told us that information. Showing, however, is better, better because we see the character showing up on time, frustrated with his coworkers who are behind, etc. Again, you get the idea, I think. The author showed us those scenes."

I said, "Good. Thank you. And I think that's clear enough. But as Cassandra probably knows, that advice is a bit misleading and is no longer the accepted rule of good writing. Well, it's still a good rule; it's just that there are exceptions."

Brock said, "Sounds like my Greek class. For every grammatical rule we learn, there's always an exception."

I said, "So here's the exception when it comes to showing and telling, an exception I learned only last summer when I was fortunate enough to attend an Iowa Writers Workshop with the novelist Sands Hall as instructor. In her session she repeatedly asked 'what's so good about showing and so bad about telling?' And here's why she asked that. All authors use both, and they don't have much choice. Let me flip back to an excerpt from Mansfield's 'The Garden Party' and give you an example." It took me a few moments. "Okay, here it is. This is shortly after Laura's mother suggests that the scraps could be gathered and given to the poor people in the cottages down below. Listen to this excerpt.

> "But, mother, do you really think it's a good idea?" said Laura.
> Again, how curious, she seemed to be different from them all. To take scraps from their party. Would the poor woman really like that?
> "Of course! What's the matter with you to-day? An hour or two ago you were insisting on us being sympathetic, and now—"

I said, "Notice how Mansfield uses dialogue to describe the unfolding of the scene. That's showing. But then this one line, 'Again, how curious, she seemed to be different from them all.' That's telling, not showing. How dare Mansfield, a respectable author, resort to telling. Don't tell us Laura was different; show us. Okay, so I'm kidding, but hopefully you get the point.

"If authors, even authors of short stories showed us everything and never used telling, they would run out of paper. For example, if a writer wants to describe a woman named Gloria arriving home from a hectic day of work, the writer doesn't have to write, 'Then she turned the car key to the and the engine stopped. The tachometer rested on zero, and the engine an to cool, the pistons pinging. Gloria took a deep breath, then audibly sighed.' That's too much showing, and the real point about sighing after work gets lost. Instead, the author writes, 'Gloria turned off the engine and sighed.'

"Telling is a great tool for storytelling, a way of speeding up the narrative clock, so to speak, in the interest of time. It's similar to what Hollywood calls a montage, a compressed narrative format. But here's the great thing about telling; it not only speeds up the narrative clock when necessary but allows us to slow it down when we get to an important moment in the story by switching to showing. That's the other meaning of time management in storytelling."

Brock said, "I was with you, or I think I was. But now I'm confused." Several others agreed.

I said, "I thought it might be confusing. That's why I have this handout. I think it will help." I started to pass around copies. "Look it over for a minute or two, and then I'll walk us through it."

NARRATIVE TECHNIQUES FOR STORYTELLING

What Writers Do

Telling: the narrator's commentary or summary of a character or scene in a story

> Ex. "The girl in the record store may have been eccentric, but she was always helpful to customers."

Showing: the narrator's description of a character's words, actions, and thoughts

> Ex. "The girl with the pierced tongue who worked in the record store helped the man in the suit find what he was looking for. She said, 'It's a big store. Folks get overwhelmed all the time.'"

What Preachers Do

Narrator Voice: summarizing (telling) and narrating (showing) of a story

Summarizing Examples

"Walker tells about a nameless black woman who one fine Sunday headed down the road to a white church on the corner. . . ."

"Then Luke says that Jesus joined them, only they didn't know it was him. They didn't yet believe the good news of the resurrection. . . ."

"This minister friend of mine tells a great story about when she was in seminary and one of her classmates pulled a practical joke on another student. . . ."

Narrating Examples

"The woman is still dusting herself off, when suddenly something happens. She sees Jesus coming down the highway, and he is looking at her. . . ."

"The two travelers invite Jesus to stay with them. And while at the table, Jesus breaks the bread, and suddenly, they recognize him. . . ."

"Seeing this one student asleep in class, someone taps him on the shoulder and says, 'The professor just called on you to pray.' . . ."

Preacher Voice: exposition of an exegetical, theological, or ethical insight

Exegetical Ex. "Martha's question to Jesus is even harsher in the Greek. She says, 'Lord, you really don't care, do you, that my sister has left me to do the work?' It's an accusation in which . . ."

Theological Ex. "What about the tension between divine will and human agency? Maybe you've heard the term before, prevenient grace. It stresses how . . ."

Ethical Ex. "If we measure our worth solely in terms of monetary value, we miss out. Maybe that's the measuring stick at high school reunions, but this parable challenges our value system. . ."

After the students had had awhile to read over the handout, I said, "Okay, let's start with what writers do, there at the top of the page. We were discussing this already, and it's not all that difficult once you see some examples. The author *tells* us some things about the story or character, in this case that the girl in the record store was helpful. The writer *told* us that. In the second example, the writer *shows* us what's happening, helping the customer find what he's looking for, along with some more description for texture. That's the basics of storytelling.

"Where it gets a little more confusing is when we move to the preacher. All semester we've been using the term *retelling* for when we shared our version of a short story with the class. But *retelling* is more complicated than that; when we retell a story, we employ what writers call telling *and* what they call showing. Only as you can see, I'm opting for different terms. And this could be really confusing since telling means one thing to English teachers and quite another to preachers. Most of us preachers *tell* stories. That's why I'm proposing *narrating* and *summarizing*. Forget *showing* and *telling*. Let's stick with *narrating* and *summarizing*. Look for a moment at the examples. What's the difference between the two?"

They studied the handout once again. Carlos said, "It's like in *narrating*, the preacher is actually telling us a story. But in *summarizing*, the preacher is talking about the story, not really telling it."

I said, "That's a great insight. And you do the same thing, Carlos, when you share a story. When you told that story about a family reunion, I'm guessing there were moments when you were summarizing and moments when you were narrating. That's what we do when we tell stories. Do all of you get the difference?"

Most of them shook their heads up and down, the nod of recognition. I said, "The narrative clock is crucial in storytelling, whether you're writing the next great American novel or preaching the gospel. In fact, when the author of John's gospel tells the story of Jesus—the only account of the four to tell us it was a three-year ministry—that author takes twenty-one chapters to cover three years, but five whole chapters to cover one night in the upper room. That's slowing down the narrative clock in a major way. Time management."

Lisa said, "I see another difference in your examples, although I'm not sure how important it is. In your summarizing examples, the verbs are past tense. Well, I take that back, not always past tense; but for the most part, yes. And the narrating examples are mostly present tense."

I said, "Yes, good point. That's on purpose. I'm glad you noticed. And here's the amazing thing. Listeners would likely never notice such things, at least not so they could put their finger on it. But if I have been summarizing a short story, moving the plot along, and using past tense, then suddenly switch to present, that feels different. And technically, that present tense verb is really what's called historical present. The Greek New Testament uses historical present quite frequently, even if most English translations use past tense."

I paused for a few moments. "So rather than just thinking in terms of too many and too few details, although that's helpful at times, what if we looked at the retellings you did today and thought about where you used summarizing and narrating. I think that could make a huge difference. When we break into pairs for practice time, think about these two categories. Look at the verb tenses as well.

"But we also need to think about *preacher voice*. This is probably easier to grasp since it's the voice we're accustomed to using in our sermons. It has nothing to do with your throat, your literal voice; it's a metaphor of sorts. I've named three kinds of things we do when we use preacher voice: exegetical, theological, and ethical. These things, by the way, are what preachers have done for centuries, and in all manner of preaching styles, narrative or otherwise.

"Sometimes the preacher makes an exegetical observation, the kind of thing we learned while studying the passage, and which seems relevant to the message. The second use of preacher voice is theological in nature, an insight or concept larger than this one text. It's not in the Hebrew or Greek. It's not something found in the historical background. It's an insight that arises from looking at issues addressed elsewhere in Scripture and which the church's great thinkers have wrestled with for centuries. The third voice is ethical. This is the preacher's application of the text to our modern lives. These three things are what preachers have always done, and always will. The preacher voice."

I knew all of this was overwhelming, but also realized how practicing in class would help in the coming weeks. I said, "Okay, that's the first thing, technique. The other is more a matter related to the heart. Listeners need to know you have felt the story, and this is larger than verb tenses and techniques. I think more than once I've said in here that texture is how a story feels and how it makes us feel in the hearing of it. And as we might expect, these authors are gifted in the texture department. As I noted before, narrative preaching should be storied in its texture.

"The best way I know to describe texture is with a story my daughter shared with me a few years back. I don't know if you're familiar with the musical tradition of master classes. A master class is when just a few highly accomplished musicians do a workshop of sorts with a world-class musician. While they are working together on technique and such, a select group of students get to observe. Well, my daughter, who played cello throughout high school and college, got to sit in and observe a master class with Yo-Yo

Ma, the world's leading cellist. Three cellists were selected, all of them very gifted.

"My daughter said the session started with Yo-Yo Ma asking each of them to play a piece they had selected and prepared for the day. Then he made comments on what he heard. I interrupted her story to ask how good the three cellists were, and she said they were brilliant. My daughter has a good ear, so when she says they were brilliant, they were brilliant. But what happened next was nothing like I expected. She said Yo-Yo Ma did not say one negative word. He went on and on about how talented they were, about their fingering technique, the mastery of their playing. So I asked my daughter, 'That was it? He just complimented them?' She said no, that after complimenting them he asked only one question: 'What do you think Beethoven felt when he wrote that?' She said the three of them acted like this was the strangest question they had ever heard, like he wasn't even speaking English any longer. 'What do you think Beethoven felt when he wrote that?'

"My daughter said that the three master students finally stammered out something about the mystery of the piece, and one of them something about the hints of joy underneath that. Then Yo-Yo Ma said, 'Ah, that's the only thing I didn't hear. I didn't hear that in your playing. And I'm not sure you felt it either. So I invite you to close your eyes this time, tap into that mystery and joy, and let us hear that.'

"I asked my daughter what happened next. She said it was amazing, unbelievably better." I paused for a moment, and then said to the class, "I think you get the point. What we want besides proper technique in terms of just the right amount of details and that sort of thing is attention to texture. And I think that begins with asking yourself, 'What did the author feel when she wrote that? What did she want us to feel? What do we want our listeners to experience? Have I felt that myself as preacher?' If we can tap into that, it will make a difference in our retelling of these stories, including the biblical story."

I suddenly remembered one of my favorite parts of Anna Carter Florence's work on testimony. I said, "When students ask her to look over a sermon-in-progress, knowing that something's missing, they usually ask, 'What do you think? Does it need another illustration? Maybe another story would do the trick.' Her response? 'You just need to spend more time with the text. Spend more time and you will know what to do.' She doesn't talk in terms of texture, but I think it's a related concept. Spend more time with these short stories, with these texts. You will know what to do. The story will tell you. Isn't that a lovely idea? Questions? Thoughts?"

Only silence. Several nodded their heads, while some wrote down a note or two. I said, "Let's take a break."

CHAPTER SIXTEEN

Soulful Scholarship

During the break Cassandra wanted to talk about the Yo-Yo Ma story. Turns out, she had played some violin growing up. Brock, who joined the conversation, took piano lessons growing up, and while he didn't consider himself a musician in the least, the metaphor spoke to him as well. I wasn't surprised. I've noticed over the years how many preachers have a musical background and how reclaiming it can deepen their preaching. The same for those who used to paint or do sculpture.

Since the break was nearly over, I slipped out to grab a cup of hot tea. Several enjoyed a second piece of cake, although only a sliver this time around. When everyone was settled back in their seats, I thanked them for sharing their retellings. I noted once again how personal such sharing really is, like preaching itself.

The retellings had gone longer than I expected, and I still wanted them to practice in small groups incorporating the feedback we had provided. That would take time as well. I decided we would do that as time permitted because we still needed to discuss "The Garden Party." I began, "We might as well cut to the chase when discussing the short story for this week. One of the questions for doing literary exegesis is where did you see glimpses of deity? That was relatively easy when Alice Walker has Jesus show up. But what about with a story like this one? Anybody?"

Several looked down at the tabletop, clearly confounded. Cassandra ventured, "Well, obviously it's only a 'glimpse' in this case. But I find evidence of divine presence there nonetheless. Laura experiences 'something' the others don't. I mean, there near the end when her brother, Laurie—which by the way was really confusing—agrees with her that life is 'really something,' I don't think he gets it at all. But I think Laura senses something is amiss, that God does care for all persons who live on the lane, even if at the dark bottom of the lane. I would call that a glimpse of God."

I said, "I agree. Only maybe it's not God so much as a theological issue the story raises for those of us who read through 'Christian glasses.' Maybe that's a better way of asking the question, 'Where did you catch a glimpse of a theological issue?'"

Brock said, "I'm relieved to hear you say that. This 'glimpses of God' thing seemed restrictive to me. That's very helpful." Several others agreed.

I said, "As I've said in here before, we wouldn't be reading these stories if I hadn't found some kind of theological insight, some kind of preachable facet. Trust me, there are lots of short stories out there that don't preach, at least not in my opinion. I want us to discuss the story further, along with the reading you did in Foster's *How to Read Literature Like a Professor*, but first let's think about the difference between this story and the kind we've been reading. What I mean is the glaring absence of any religious trappings per se. There is no mention of Jesus, of God, of church. Positive or negative, nothing is said about such trappings. And yet the story is preachable.

"In fact, it may be one of the most powerful kinds of preachable stories. Let me explain what I mean. A colleague of mine, Brett Younger, did his doctoral dissertation on preaching and movies. How's that for a topic?"

Joey said, "That's cool. Did he get credit for going to the movies?"

"I doubt it. But here's my point in bringing it up. Using Paul Tillich's categories for discussing paintings, Younger listed four types of movies in relation to their preachability or, more accurately, their religious content. This isn't the exact terminology, but it's close."

I listed the four categories on the board as I spoke. "These types could be applied to pretty much any art form, including short stories, even if Younger was working with movies and Tillich with paintings. The first is 'religious content, non-religious meaning.' The second is 'non-religious content, non-religious meaning.' I'll say something about these in a moment, but for now let me name the four. The third type is 'religious content, religious meaning,' and the last, 'non-religious content, religious meaning.' It sounds more complicated than it is, so let me explain. And I can probably do that best with movies since we know more movies than literature. That's a rabbit chase we might want to explore further at some point. Think about it, people watch movies but are not always aware of the transcendent themes in those movies. People don't read short stories generally speaking, and yet exposing them to these glimpses of deity might get them reading.

"Anyway, the first category would be movies that are religious only on the surface of things. They have the trappings of religion but not the true substance. Think about all those pitiful made-for-TV Easter movies the networks air around this time every year. There are movies, just as there are short stories, which are religious on the surface but not so much underneath.

"The second type is a really simple category. These are the movies that are neither religious on the surface nor underneath. Anybody want to nominate a movie for an Oscar in that category?"

Brock volunteered, "How about *Dude, Where's My Car?*"

Joey said, "It has 'dude' in the title; it can't be all bad." That cracked us all up. Then he added, "I nominate every Adam Sandler movie ever made." Now everyone was rolling, although I said there was one exception, *Reign Over Me*, which it turns out none of them had seen.

After several more nominations, I said, "Okay, so these first two categories would qualify for what the Germans call *kitsch*. Do you know that term? It means 'junk,' and is used in art criticism to label things not worth bothering about, like that Precious Moments chapel in south Missouri. But the third category is different. It has religious symbolism on the surface as well as underneath. And I nominate *Places in the Heart* for the Oscar in this category, my favorite religious movie of all time. That's your homework, rent *Places in the Heart*. It definitely preaches.

"So in terms of short stories, that's the kind we've been reading all along. 'The Welcome Table' and 'Revelation' are religious in both uses of the word, and same for 'The Pure in Heart' where a preacher hears God's voice. But not so much with 'The Garden Party,' which brings us to the fourth type. 'The Garden Party' is not religious on the surface, but it is underneath. Do you see that?"

Several of them agreed in unison. I said, "But here's what I love best about this last category. It sneaks up on us. Whether at the movies or in literature, we are in a world without any religious trappings per se, a normal kind of day-to-day world, when 'wham,' the gospel sneaks up on us. And we'll be reading a few more of those along the way. But for now, let's discuss 'The Garden Party' and Foster's chapter on it."

Joey said, "Well, I got the point of the story. Or at least I thought I did until I read Foster." Several others chimed in with similar comments.

Cassandra said, "I know what you mean, but that's what I love about Foster's book and more importantly about good literature. He shows the different levels by which readers engage certain pieces."

A debate of sorts raged for a few minutes, which I was happy to let continue for a while. This was the most animated I'd seen them over something even if it was a chapter in a book and not one of the stories we'd read or biblical texts they were using. But there was an important point to be made here. I said, "Okay, let's think about the big picture here. Foster asks his readers what the point of 'The Garden Party' is, and they get it right, the indifference of this rich family toward the lower classes around them. Simple enough. And that will preach, no doubt in my mind." Several of them agreed.

"But then he shares what might be called 'deeper readings' of this idea, the imagery of birds and flight in Mansfield's story—like the daughters floating and skimming over the lawn the way little birds might, even their very house perched on high like a nest above the cottages below. And of course Laura testing her wings, so to speak, when she leaves mother behind and ventures out into the world, even if it is the caged world of the poor down below. That's one possible insight. How many of you saw that on your own?"

No one raised their hand. "Don't worry. I didn't either. But that's okay. Or there's another set of images that Foster notes, that of a garden. As we've been reading in Foster, he's a big fan of looking for biblical imagery. Remember that chapter we read in which he says every meal is communion? Well, for him every garden is an echo of Eden. As he admits, it's not a perfect fit, but the weather was ideal, and the party, too, until the fall, so to speak. Sin has come into this idyllic world of theirs. Laura's eyes have been opened. That's another interpretation. And then there's Foster's borrowing from mythology, the whole fertility goddess dynamic. I'm guessing most of us didn't see that one at all."

Joey said, "Not in a million years, dude. I don't even see it after reading Foster."

I said, "I didn't see it either, at least not the fertility goddess part, and not the birds in flight part, as I said. I did think of the garden imagery, but that one is more biblical. Here's what I love about this exercise, though. I've felt the same way reading biblical commentaries before. Haven't you? Sometimes the meaning of a text is rather obvious, like Laura's epiphany in a poor family's cottage. Then I read the scholars and see things I never would have noticed. Some of those observations may be a bit far-fetched, but not all of them. Reading these stories—Mansfield's or some other Scriptural stories—along with the scholars can enhance our appreciation. And sometimes scholarship can hinder our appreciation.

"What I mean is there have been times when reading a commentary has nearly destroyed my appreciation for a biblical text, when the scholarship was so esoteric as to be of little or no relevance to the life of the church. That can happen. But most of the time my own initial reading of the text without scholarship isn't sufficient. I need to experience the biblical story, like the Mary and Martha story in Luke's gospel for instance. I need to sit slack-jawed as Jesus says to the woman cooking his supper, 'Martha, Martha, Martha, you are worried about too many things. Your sister Mary has chosen something better, sitting here at my feet.' What? Shouldn't Mary be helping with the meal? What is going on in a text like that? I need to sit with it.

"But I also need the help of scholars, some of whom note that this story and the Samaritan parable before it flesh out Jesus' teaching here about love of God and neighbor. Remember? That's how this section begins, a discussion between Jesus and an expert in Torah, the two greatest commandments being love of God and neighbor. So Luke pictures that for us in two stories, the Samaritan parable (love of neighbor) and the Mary/Martha story (love of God). I wouldn't get that on my own. But what I ultimately want is both, an experience of the story (Mansfield's, Luke's, etc.) and reflection upon it (the garden imagery Foster notes, Luke's composition technique)."

Several of them looked pleased, notably Cassandra, Alesha, and Lisa. With the others it was hard to tell. I said, "Questions? Comments?"

Brock scratched his head. "I think I get it. I remember hearing two well-known preachers on the radio years ago. These weren't the nut-job types either. Their shows were aired back-to-back, and both were preaching from the Beatitudes. I've always loved those verses, Jesus blessing the people. After the first guy preached, I thought I would never preach from that passage in my life. He was an expository preacher, and when he got finished, he had let all the air out of that balloon. He gave us Greek words and all sorts of technical things. Then the second one comes on the air, preaches the same text, and it was beautiful once again. Beautiful, but also more meaningful. He helped me understand it without ruining it."

Lisa added, "Scholarship with a soul."

I said, "Ooh, I like that phrase." I even wrote it on the board. "And Brock, what you said is very helpful." I could see others agreed, even Carlos, so I said, "Carlos, what are you thinking?"

He said, "I agree. I like the older styles of preaching, which is probably obvious by now. But I've also heard some traditional preachers whose sermons left me cold. I think that's the right expression, 'left me cold.'" We nodded. "I want to hear sermons that are exegetical. But I have read commentaries that were way over my head. And if they're over my head, they're probably over the heads of my listeners. What's the point of that?"

I said, "I appreciate your view. And what did you think of the short story itself? Not Foster's multiple levels of engaging it, but just the story when you read it. What did you think of it?"

Carlos shocked us all, although maybe not Rosa. He told of a similar incident in his native Guatemala, the capital Guatemala City, its modern shopping malls with marble floors just down the street from tin-roofed homes with dirt floors. He didn't use the word *juxtaposition* but the idea was plain. He said, "It was like that story in Luke's gospel, the rich man and

Lazarus. And I will never forget, as I'm sure Rosa remembers, the time she took me to buy a shirt for my birthday and then outside the gates of the mall we ran into a beggar who had nothing. Nothing. I know how Laura felt." Rosa wiped a tear from her eyes, and for a moment there was moisture in Carlos's eyes as well. I thanked Carlos for sharing.

I was tempted to stress the power of stories at this point, but Carlos had already obliged. Instead, I pressed in from the other side of narrative preaching. "So let's imagine a story like 'The Garden Party' set alongside Luke's story of the rich man and Lazarus. And let's imagine the testimony of the preacher with a story like the one Carlos shared. That would touch listeners, no doubt. Nothing wrong with that. And we've started practicing how to tell such stories so that listeners are moved. But that's not enough. We need hyphenated sermons, experience-and-exposition. So there would be *stuff*, that's the technical term, *stuff* we learned from the biblical scholars about Luke's text. But how does the preacher go about moving from one world into the other so that the sermon is seamlessly hyphenated and not disjointed? Do you understand what I'm asking?"

Alesha said, "I definitely do. I know how to do exegesis, I think. And I know how to share that in a sermon, at least in a more traditional expository one or a Bible study, but preaching, especially narrative preaching, isn't like leading a Bible study. But combining exposition and storytelling in a sermon, a narrative sermon at that, stretches my thinking. My pastor does it every week. I'm pretty sure he moves seamlessly, as you say, between the two worlds. I just don't know how he does it, if that makes sense." Several of her classmates said it made perfect sense.

I was thrilled that the class as a whole saw the value of both, experience-and-exposition. That was my main objective for the course. Now they were asking the "how" question. How do we go about that? I hadn't brought along a sample sermon, and besides, I didn't want to use another one of my own. But the stars were aligned in my favor. I remembered that in chapel the next Tuesday, at least I thought it was the next Tuesday, one of our alums was preaching, Marcus Schmeling. He had done his MDiv training in Texas, then his DMin with me at Saint Paul, during which we studied narrative preaching in some detail. I asked, "Could someone who has their computer with them check the online chapel schedule for next week? See who is preaching on Tuesday."

Joey checked. "Says here, Rev. Marcus Schmeling."

I said, "Well then, we're in luck. He is a former student who emailed me not long ago to say he was going to use a short story in his chapel sermon. If you can be there, great. If not, I'll see if we can have the library make an archived copy available. This will be a great chance for us to hear a sample sermon and look at a host of issues, theoretical as well as practical ones. And Marcus is a very good preacher. I may invite him to class next Thursday as well. We'll see.

"Meanwhile, I'd like for you to practice your retellings in small groups. Think about techniques such as narrating and summarizing. Think about attention to details. Tap into the Yo-Yo Ma texture of the stories. Listen to each other, whether that sort of dynamic is present or not. If your partner's retelling is flat, let him or her know. Retell the story a few times if time permits. And if you have time, think about the biblical text you might pair with it. What facets of exposition are you thinking need to be shared? It's good for us to be thinking in terms of experience-and-exposition. When you're done, you can go. And in peace, of course."

CHAPTER SEVENTEEN

Both/And

Marcus preached in chapel the next Tuesday morning. Turns out, he had been invited to preach on what we call "Seminary Days." Half a dozen times a year persons who are considering vocational ministry come and explore what the Saint Paul School of Theology is all about. Marcus preached from Exodus 3, when God speaks to Moses, and the short story he used was the Peggy Payne story we read earlier in the semester, about Rev. Hammond hearing God speak to him. I thought the students in my class would appreciate an example of a retelling based on something they'd actually read.

After chapel Marcus and I went to lunch, catching up on old times and each other's lives. In addition to securing permission to use his sermon in class (he was only mildly embarrassed because he was also flattered), I invited him to attend. He said he would check his schedule, then texted me later to say he'd be there. I emailed the class on Tuesday afternoon, and included a link to the podcast.

On Thursday evening I introduced Rev. Schmeling to the class, proof that people really do graduate and without too many emotional scars. There was some mild-mannered kidding between the two of us. I said we would discuss his sermon during the second half of class.

I said, "Listen once again to Nafisi. She writes, 'I discovered that the same decree that had transformed the single word *Iran* into the *Islamic Republic of Iran* had made me and all that I had been irrelevant.'" Here's her elaboration on that:

I told the Revolutionary Committee that my integrity as a teacher and a woman was being compromised by its insistence that I wear the veil under false pretenses for a few thousand tumans a month. The issue was not so much the veil itself as freedom of choice. My grandmother had refused to leave the house for three months when she was forced to unveil. I would be similarly adamant in my own refusal. Little did I know that I would soon be given the choice of either veiling or being jailed, flogged and perhaps killed if I disobeyed.

After that meeting, one of my more pragmatic colleagues, a "modern" woman, who decided to take up the veil and stayed there for another seventeen years after I was gone, told me with a hint of sarcasm in her voice, "You are fighting a losing battle. Why lose your job over an issue like this? In another couple of weeks you will be forced to wear the veil in the grocery stores."

The simplest answer, of course, was that the university was not a grocery store. But she was right. Soon we would be forced to wear it everywhere. And the morality squads, with their guns and Toyota patrols, would guard the streets to ensure our adherence. On that sunny day, however, when my colleagues and I made our protest known, these incidents did not seem to be preordained. So much of the faculty protested, we thought we might yet win.

After a word of prayer, I said, "I want us to begin with a brief review this evening. In part, it will help Marcus know where we are, and it might help some of you as well. I'll try not to repeat the same old things I've said all along, although some things bear repeating. Either way, reviews are a good thing for classes to do from time to time, especially as we head down the home stretch of the semester and start preaching our own sermons.

"The Canadian theologian Douglas John Hall says that if you flip through the pages of the New Testament, two things become readily apparent about the church: first, she is the bride of Christ, the apple of God's eye, we might say; and second, the bride has issues, serious issues. What a great insight." Several of them laughed at the metaphor. Brock started to say something about his first wife, then thought better of it.

I continued, "I think the same could be said about narrative preaching over the last forty years or so. We fell in love with narrative preaching, she was the apple of homileticians' eyes. Maybe not everyone's, but for many of us, yes. In the last few years, however, we've been noticing a few of her issues.

"Narrative preaching promised amazing things in terms of experiencing the power of the gospel story. Sometimes it came through on that promise, other times not so much. Still, experience was part of her dowry. But this bride has issues; don't we all? Narrative preaching has been weak on exposition. We've noted that before.

"So let's think about these two categories once again, exposition and experience. I like what Tom Long calls the difference between upstairs and downstairs experiences in the life of local churches. He says that when one of his colleagues is invited to speak to adult ed groups in a church, the classroom experience is heady. Folks really do want to know about apparent discrepancies between Gospel accounts or how to reconcile the realities of life with a good and loving God. They're curious about the events that led up to the Reformation and theological developments since then. In other words, the downstairs experience in the life of the church is reasonably complex. But upstairs during the sermon time, things are often much more shallow. Instead of wrestling with the hard questions regarding Scripture and life, sermons start with jokes and serve up baby food instead of substantive nourishment."

Cassandra said, "Wow, that is so true. The church I attend is a classic example. We've had professors from here come to lead Bible studies and the people eat that stuff up, even when it's a real stretch for them intellectually. Sure, the material needs to be accessible, but they crave depth. And they get it downstairs. But up in the sanctuary, that's a different story. I love both of our co-pastors, but rarely does either one of them go very deep." Several others nodded in agreement.

I said, "That's a good point, especially the qualifier you added, about the material needing to be accessible. We'll talk about that with the chapel sermon by Marcus. I think he does a great job with that aspect." He smiled sheepishly.

I continued, "Okay, so that's one dynamic, upstairs/downstairs. The other I would label inside/outside."

Joey said, "Sorry, what did you say?"

I repeated, "Inside/outside. Here's what I mean. There is a huge difference between the kinds of conversations going on in the world and those going on in the church. Outside the church's walls, people talk about topics like cancer, sexual abuse of minors, and wars that never seem to end. They talk about the stuff of their daily lives as well—forgiving an ex, coping with unemployment and the resulting lack of self-esteem. Inside the church's walls, some preachers touch on such things but not very often. During the most recent war in Iran—a war that never should have been fought in my opinion and which drug on way too long in the opinion of many—I informally surveyed preachers in workshops and the like. I asked how many had preached on the war. It was less than five. The war was constantly in the media, and rarely in the pulpit. Outside the church's walls, people talk about the critical difference between supporting the troops and protesting a war. What about inside the church's walls?"

Alesha said, "Amen to that. The 'War on Terror' resulted in a blank check for politicians to do as they please." A few smaller discussions bubbled up between some of them.

I said, "To be clear, I'm not limiting this observation to so-called political hot potatoes. The point is much larger than that. Homiletics professor Wes Allen says that preaching should be part of the church's ongoing conversation. He calls it *The Homiletic of All Believers*, borrowing from the Reformation doctrine of the priesthood of all believers."

Lisa said, "What a clever play on words, and what a needed word for the church today."

I said, "So what is the world talking about? What is the church talking about? What happens downstairs? What happens outside these walls? Why isn't the church talking about these things from the pulpit? These are items that fall under the heading of exposition, since for me exposition is existential as well as theological. That means narrative preachers have to concern themselves with justice matters, personal as well as social holiness, as John Wesley would say." The Methodist students in the room loved that.

"And as we've noted again and again, there are the theological and biblical components of preaching. Some of you know that in addition to teaching on the faculty, I also oversee the laity school we offer on six Saturdays a year. The goal is to offer something more substantive than Sunday School but less intimidating than a seminary lecture. I've taught a couple of sessions myself. The last one was on the parables of Jesus. Do you know what the battle cry is from the laity every session? At the end of the day when we are wrapping things up, almost to a person they will ask the presenter, 'Okay, so how come my pastor never shared anything like this with me before?' That's their question. How come I've been to church all my life and never heard that Matthew and Luke had a copy of Mark which they sometimes used, and apparently another document which they also shared? Or how come my pastor never noted the two creation accounts in Genesis 1 and 2?"

Joey misunderstood, "So they're upset because of the controversial nature of the topics?"

I said, "No, the folks asking these questions are upset not with the answers but the fact such information has been withheld from them for so long."

Marcus jumped in at this point. "May I?"

"Absolutely."

He said, "First, I definitely want to offer a hearty amen to the idea of preaching about issues in people's personal lives as well as the wider world. That's a given for me, regardless of sermon styles. As for the theological/biblical matters, I think there are probably lots of reasons preachers are silent. I try very hard to offer an accessible form of scholarship while also engaging people with stories and the like. But when it comes to scholarship, fear reigns supreme—all sorts of fears, too. Pastors are afraid the people won't be able to handle it. Or maybe afraid it won't be meaningful. I recall how in seminary it took me awhile to realize the information I was learning in class could not only help form me as a minister but the people who are also called to be ministers."

Several of the students appreciated Marcus's observations. One or two commented on the different kinds of fear he had mentioned. Brock said, "I don't think we respect church folks enough on these things. We think they're simpletons or something. If doctors treated patients the way we treat parishioners, most of them would think the term *funny bone* is anatomically correct." Several of us laughed aloud. He said, "No, think about it." It was obvious he felt passionately about this. He continued, "Most folks in our pews know more about medicine than theology. They know terms like *appendectomy* and *stent*. They certainly don't call them *tubey things*. How many of them know the term, I don't know, the term *theodicy*? I'm guessing not very many." Even Joey, who usually appreciates things kept simple, agreed.

Alesha said, "I think Brock's point is well-taken, and the same could be said for the legal profession. I suspect that for many people, they know more about the modern court system than the Bible. I wonder if it's because there are TV shows about law and medicine but not about theology."

I said, "It's funny you should say that. A former colleague and I used to joke about how Hollywood needs a good theological show." Several of them guffawed the suggestion. "Seriously, think about it. A show set on a seminary campus could cover a whole range of important topics, certainly the 'big three': religion, sex, and politics." Things got out of hand for a few minutes at the idea of a theological TV show, so I tried to bring us back to order. "Not to sound like a broken record, but all of this once again brings up the need for narrative preaching to be both experiential-and-expositional. And yes, that's hyphenated."

Marcus laughed. "Oh, yeah, *hyphenated*. I had forgotten that term for narrative sermons."

I said, "I'm afraid in this room I may have worn them out with it. And now I want to say it again. Here's the good news, though: while the concept of hyphenated homiletics may not be new to you, I want to look at it through some different lenses than we've considered thus far. I have three pieces in mind. The first comes from Kenneth Burke, whose theory of how stories work we explored earlier. Rhetorical scholar John O'Banion draws on Burke to name two ways of knowing—list and story." I wrote the two words on the board. "The former is logical, rooted in understanding and influenced by literacy. The latter, he says, is more experiential, rooted in participation and influenced by oral cultures."

Cassandra joked, "So if I'm a story person, do I need to make a list of what Burke says?"

I said, "Very funny." Actually, it was good to have a little humor thrown in. "O'Banion notes how in our culture people typically fall into one of these ways more than the other. At a basic level, for instance, some folks stand in checkout lines fascinated by the exploits of Hollywood's beautiful people documented in tabloids, or at a more sophisticated level, they gravitate to other kinds of storytelling, Shakespeare or opera. These are story people. But list folks cluck their tongues at such things, even at *People* magazine, preferring a subscription to the *Wall Street Journal* instead. They are list people, but if their beloved *Wall Street Journal* moves too far afield from logical and unemotional reporting, they could cancel their subscription.

"But here's O'Banion's point. Like Burke before him, O'Banion calls for dialectical tension rather than dualistic options, both/and as opposed to either/or. The reason they do so is because in the final analysis people are really both, even if they claim otherwise. Think about it, media like *The New Yorker*, dedicated to list *and* story, are harder to come by in our society as opposed to rhetoric that chooses one or the other. Unfortunately, hyphenated sermons are also harder to come by." Several of the students noted the importance of finding the right balance, or better yet, keeping these poles in tension.

I said, "This is related in some ways to the second piece I want to share, insights from George Lakoff's book *The Political Mind*, only Lakoff moves beyond rhetorical theory to actual brain research. As you might guess from the title, this really is a book about how the minds of voters work. Writing near the end of the last Bush administration, he admits up front that he's a progressive Democrat who wants to challenge Republican strategies."

Alesha said, "Amen to that." Several students smiled at this one.

Brock said, "Oh oh, here comes politics mixing with religion. I don't remember a Thanksgiving dinner in which my daddy and granddaddy didn't get into it over politics."

Alesha said, "If the eighth-century prophets are any indication, religion is supposed to speak to politics. The trouble comes when the two become indistinguishable."

I said, "Okay, there's no question there are so-called political issues that are ultimately justice issues, but Lakoff's thesis transcends politics, so try not to get distracted here. He's not interested in red and blue states, but what makes voters choose between red and blue. More specifically, what goes on in the brain to influence such decisions. His point is about how we think, and as I said, he comes at this from brain research.

"He distinguishes between what he calls *reflective* and *reflexive* thinking." I wrote the terms on the board. "The first is logical, rational, a reasoned way of being in the world; the latter is more subconscious, emotional, framed by metaphors and symbols. You can see right away how this would relate to similar concepts we've discussed. Lakoff is careful to note of course that all human beings are both, but his real point is that the Enlightenment deluded us into valuing the reflective over the reflexive. This is part of what we've discussed before.

"Lakoff says we were mistaken, that we need a New Enlightenment—which by the way, he capitalizes, like the New Homiletic—one that accounts for both ways of being in the world. His take on the political scene is that Republicans have done a better job of tapping into the reflexive and storied ways of most folks, while Democrats stubbornly hold to intellect over emotions in their various campaign strategies.

"Okay, before you react or overreact to that one, think about it this way. Regardless of party affiliation, if you and I get into a debate on some political topic, or a theological one for that matter, we will each be convinced that our position is the right one. We might have a degree of humility about it, but our position would be our position. If an observer asked each of us on what basis do you hold to such a position, we would have our reasons. Good ones, hopefully. Those reasons would be what Lakoff calls reflective; we have reflected on the matter. But his point is that reason alone is not how brains decide; the emotions and subconscious play a huge role."

I hesitated a moment to take a sip of tea, and to let them ponder for a moment. "If you buy a shirt in a department store and decide on a blue one, chances are you might have a reflective reason—'My old blue shirt is tattered'—then again maybe not: 'I don't know, I just felt like it.' Lakoff says that's fine when buying blue shirts, but not when deciding between blue and red candidates. He believes Republicans have been better at tapping into the reflexive nature of voters, telling a better story, while Democrats have relied too much on elitist reflection."

Alesha said, "I think Democrats are better storytellers than he lets on."

I said, "Maybe. Lakoff believes the one exception was Al Gore's movie, *An Inconvenient Truth*. It contained reflective thinking, no doubt, but used the storytelling techniques of Hollywood and thus, touched viewers at a deeper, more reflexive level.

"So Lakoff calls for a New Enlightenment in which we recognize that people are reflective *and* reflexive. The mistake folks make in the Old Enlightenment way of thinking is believing not just that reflective is superior but the only way of proceeding. And as I mentioned earlier, the capitalization reminds me of the New Homiletic, but also points out a key difference. The Old Homiletic was rooted in reflective modes, sermons that contained ideas. The New Homiletic has largely been reflexive, inviting listeners into an experience, touching them through stories and the like. But according to Lakoff's research, neither is sufficient by itself. This, by the way, is what biblical scholar Amos Wilder called an 'occupational cramp,' the mistaken notion that logic is superior to poetry. So maybe we need a Newer Homiletic. Or maybe we could hyphenate it, the New-Homiletic." A few other silly suggestions were made.

I continued, "The third piece I want to share comes from biblical scholar Mark Allan Powell, who names two kinds of meaning—'meaning as message' and 'meaning as effect.' He says if you ask someone what they *made* of an essay they read, their response is likely to be one of 'message,' how they understood it. But if you ask them what they *made* of a piece of art, their response is likely to be one of 'effect,' how it touched them or didn't. Same kind of thing we've been discussing, right? Only Powell goes on to tell a story about when he took an art history course in college and Jackson Pollock was all the rage. He and the other students thought that any artist who used high-powered squirt guns to shoot paint onto huge canvases was not exactly a true artist. In other words, for them, art, like science, was supposed to be 'meaning as message,' period. So Powell smarted off to the professor, 'I could splatter paint on a canvas. What's so great about that?'"

Joey said, "I'm with him. Artists with squirt guns, that's crazy."

I said, "Maybe. But listen to what his professor said in response to the challenge. He said, 'Maybe you could splatter paint on a canvas. But could you do so in such a way that people who view it know what you were *feeling* at the time and *feel* it themselves?' And Powell says the professor was right. He showed the class three slides of Pollock's paintings, asking the class to write down one word that conveyed the essence of each piece. Although folks had scribbled down different words for each, they were synonyms. Everyone felt 'hope' for one, 'despair' for another, that sort of thing. Powell writes, 'If Matthew, Mark, Luke, or John had simply wanted to convey particular messages about Christian life and faith, they could have done so more effectively by writing essays (or epistles!).' Of course, as we've noted before, the New Testament canon does both, meaning as message and meaning as effect.

"Okay, so all of that is territory we've covered during the semester, even if another way of saying the same thing. But this is crucial, experience-and-exposition." We discussed once again how hard it is for preachers to resist clinging to one of those over the other.

After a few minutes, I said, "So I'd like for us to discuss the sermon Marcus preached in chapel on Tuesday. Some of you were there, and I trust the others have listened to the podcast by now. I've brought hard copies for you to refer to so we can discuss it in more depth. In fact, why don't I pass this out and after you read through it we'll take a break and discuss it afterwards."

"A Closer Look"
Exodus 3:1–15
By Rev. Marcus Schmeling

I appreciate this invitation very much, not only to preach where I studied but on this occasion when many of you are visiting and discerning your call. Which is why I want to begin with a short story by Peggy Payne, a story Dr. Freeman shared with me not so long ago. It's the story of a Presbyterian minister by the name of Swain Hammond, whom the author describes as having received his doctorate from Yale. An Ivy League man. He's polished and rational, the kind of fellow you can only imagine as being well-read and cultured. Which is perfect, since in the story he is called to be the pastor of Westside Presbyterian in Chapel Hill, North Carolina, the home of the University of North Carolina. The atmosphere of a university town and university church suit him perfectly. That is, until the day his life is changed forever.

It's a beautiful, barefoot evening in June. He and his wife, Julie, are grilling skewers of pork and green peppers in the backyard when Swain notices a flower near the edge of their property, there where their yard ends and the woods begin. He goes out to take a look, and that's when he hears the voice, the very voice of God. Not an in-his-heart kind of voice or an impression kind of voice, but the very voice of God, the kind you hear with your ears. It sounds like a PA system suddenly switched on. "Know this. Know there is truth." Remember that scene in *Field of Dreams*? Same thing, only what the voice does to Swain it does bodily. In that moment he feels the murmuring of a million cells in his body. He is aware of the line where his two lips meet, the spears of wet grass against the soles of his feet, the half-circles of tears forming in his eyes. His own bone marrow hums like there are colonies of bees inside his hollow body.

Julie doesn't hear it. Nobody else does either, even though Swain hears it several times. Sometimes as a single word, "Son." God calls Swain "Son." Sometimes as a jumble of Bible passages, "He that heareth and doeth not . . . for there is nothing hid . . . the word is sown on stony ground." Not surprisingly, some of the folks in the church think he might be losing his marbles.

It will probably come as no surprise to you that I thought of this passage in Exodus 3. A barefoot preacher; Moses taking off his sandals. A pastor seeing a flower; Moses seeing a bush. And of course the audible voice of God that both stories have in common.

I'm sure you remember the story of Moses and the bush, of how in Exodus 2 he had seen one of the Egyptians beating a Hebrew and how when he had the chance Moses killed the Egyptian. He is found out and flees. Now, in Exodus 3, the one who had witnessed a beating witnesses a bush on fire. You know the story.

What you may not have ever noticed though is the emphasis on "seeing." More than ten variations of the verb "to see" occur in this story. Did you notice even in the verses we read? Moses sees a bush on fire, so he says, "I must turn aside to see this . . ." and when God sees him looking, that's when God speaks. In Hebrew literature, dialogue is key. Moses' words of deciding to look signal a turning point, so that God now speaks. And one of the things God says is, "I have seen." Hear it? Or maybe I should say, "Do you see it?" God declares, "I have seen the injustice done to my people." The One called "I am" is also the One who says, "I have seen . . . I have heard my people's cries . . . I know . . . I have come down."

This passage is what's called a theophany, an appearing of God. God has come down. It's a common theme in the Bible, God's appearing to people. But what is also equally common is that these appearances are accompanied by a calling. As you will learn in those required courses in Bible and theology, God takes the initiative, but always with room for human response.

Which, of course, brings us to your story, and this crazy notion of going to seminary, maybe even into vocational ministry. Anybody you know thinking maybe you've lost your marbles? Not that you've seen a bush on fire, or maybe you have. Rebecca Ann Parker, a Methodist minister, tells the story about the time she and her husband visited a fifth-century church on the shores of the Adriatic Sea. Leaving the warm sunlight, they entered the cool, damp interior, an interior adorned with mosaics on the walls. A blue sky with birds flying. Dolphins leaping out of waters. Deer scampering about. Then the one with Moses where he stands in a field of emerald green. He is young, unbearded. The bush burns gold and red with flashes of orange. He has already heard the voice about how this ground is holy. He is bent over untying his sandals. Behind him, where he cannot see, the landscape is dotted with small bushes, everywhere you look, and every one of them aflame with God.

But if every bush is on fire with God's presence (which it is) and if every parcel of ground is holy with God's presence (which it is), then how do you know? How do you know you're being called? For that Presbyterian minister, he heard a voice, in King James English, no less. I'm guessing that for most of us that is not the case. Now days, hearing voices can get you a pulpit on the AM radio, but it can also keep you out of seminary. How do you know?

I suspect Parker Palmer is right. He's the Quaker writer and speaker who in his book, *Let Your Life Speak*, claims that "vocation does not come from willfulness. It comes from listening." Not *deciding* what you're going to be but *discerning*. He encourages us to find the self we were meant to be. So maybe that love for words will have us speaking gospel to the dying patient in the hospital, or maybe it will have us drafting legislation for changes in school board policies. Maybe you'll go to seminary and end up tending the flock of God surrounded by burning bushes, or maybe you will trim folks' hedges and teach seventh graders in Sunday school.

So how do you know? I've always appreciated Frederick Buechner's advice, his description of vocation. He writes:

> By and large a good rule for finding out is this. The kind of work God usually calls you to is the kind of work (a) that you need most to do and (b) the most needs to have done. If you really get a kick out of your work, you've presumably met requirement (a), but if you work is writing TV deodorant commercials, the chances are you've missed requirement (b). On the other hand, if your work is being a doctor in a leper colony, you have probably met requirement (b), but if most of the time you're bored and depressed by it, the chances are you have not only bypassed (a) but probably aren't helping your patients much either.

Then Buechner adds, "The place God calls you to is the place where your deep gladness and the world's deep hunger meet."

"The world's deep hunger." God always hears the cries of the suffering. Do you? Is that what you hear? Maybe that's the voice of God. It's a scary thing, to be sure. Kathleen Norris, in her book, *Amazing Grace: A Vocabulary of Faith*, says when we were toddlers, you know, eighteen months or so, we were learning to talk—words like "mama," "dada," and of course, "no." "NO!" It's much later, she writes, before we're ready for the really hard word, "Yes." "Yes" is a hard word to say.

May I make a suggestion? The text says, "Come no closer." That's sage advice. I wouldn't advise you to rush in where angels fear to tread. Maybe you already know the plans God has for you. Maybe not. But some time in the near future, maybe tomorrow, maybe next week, when you can, find a quiet place and hush your racing heart long enough to take off your shoes and speak this word aloud to God, "Yes." Feel the place where your two lips meet and whisper, "Yes." It's a way of saying, "Here I am." Then wait.

In the short story, Swain Hammond hears the voice again. He no longer fights it, or worries if others hear it, or if they will believe him. He's way past that by then. He lies in bed, and just as he is waking up, it comes to him as a note of music. He is no longer frightened. What he feels is joy, pure joy.

That is our prayer for you this day, that you will know. And that when you do, it will be joy. That the bees of God will be buzzing in your bones. With pure joy. Of course, it helps to remember that the God called "I am" is not only the One who says, "I have seen . . ." but also the One who promises, "I will be with you." Amen.

CHAPTER EIGHTEEN

A Closer Look

Marcus fidgeted slightly while the class read his sermon. He's one of the more conscientious preachers I know and he had nothing to be ashamed of, but still his sermon was on display. When the students finished reading, and had returned from break, I said, "First, I want to thank Marcus for not only preaching in chapel the other day and sharing a copy of his sermon with us but being willing to discuss it with us. I don't see this discussion directed at Marcus so much as more of a lively conversation between us all about the sermon. But I do want us to take a closer look at his sermon, which seems appropriate since his sermon actually goes by that name 'A Closer Look.' And since we've been stressing the need for experience-and-exposition, maybe we should start there. Anyone want to get us started in relation to either or both of those dynamics? We could start with his use of summarizing and narrating."

Brock said he thought Marcus had done a good job of blending the different voices, but he wasn't any more specific than that even when I pressed him. So after a few moments of silence, I suggested we work through it a paragraph at a time. I said, "In the first paragraph, when he first refers to the short story, how does he do so? Is it summarizing or narrating?"

Cassandra said, "Well, the first line starts with 'It's the story of . . .' so that's obviously summarizing. We are outside the story looking in, or about to look in. And even the last line of that paragraph, 'That is, until the day his life is changed forever'—that's summarizing as well, but when we get to the second paragraph, he switches. Suddenly instead of talking *about* the story, he *tells* it, narrates it, 'It's a beautiful, barefoot evening in June. He and his wife . . .' At least that's how I see it."

194

I started to respond, but Marcus took the lead instead. "Yeah, that's how I see it, too. I begin the sermon with insights *about* the story, things like describing Swain as 'an Ivy League man' or that he's 'polished and rational.' That's what Dr. Freeman's handout calls summarizing. But you're also right, Cassandra, that once I've set up the scene, so to speak, I want to switch and tell it, or narrate it."

Several of them nodded. Joey added, "But I also noticed that in your narrating of the scene, you took some liberties. You said something about the movie *Field of Dreams*, and I'm sure that wasn't in the story. I would have remembered since it's one of my all-time favorites. So is that okay?"

I wasn't sure if he was asking me or Marcus, but I said, "Absolutely. And in a way that's a switch to yet another voice, that of the preacher. The voice of the preacher is the only voice that can interrupt the retelling of a short story or biblical text to make a comparison with a movie. And notice how it works. One moment we are in Peggy Payne's short story, and the next moment the preacher says something about a contemporary movie. From storyteller—with summarizing and narrating—to preacher, referring to a Hollywood classic."

Lisa said, "Rev. Schmeling, it seems to me you also take liberty with the description of what happens to Swain when he hears the voice. You sort of paraphrase the author about colonies of bees buzzing in his bones. Personally, I don't have a problem with it, but is that something you normally do?"

Marcus said it was fine to call him by his first name, then explained that while he used to be a manuscript preacher who would have quoted the short story in large chunks, he had become convinced that a looser paraphrase with the preacher's full presence seemed like a good trade-off. He said, "You know, the truth is what I'm trying to do more of these days in my preaching is convey the feel of the passage. And by passage, I mean the biblical one too. If a story has touched me, biblical or otherwise, I want it to touch others. So I may not get the wording exactly right, but I think listeners feel it. I do think taking too many liberties can be problematic, but perhaps that's something Dr. Freeman will want to address later." I shook my head yes.

Alesha wondered about the transitions, not just from one voice to another, but just the normal sorts of transitions that preachers have to make. She said, "I think transitions are hard enough in traditional preaching, maybe even more so when it comes to narrative preaching and all these voices. Could you say something about that?"

Marcus said, "Sure thing. The first real transition I make is when I leave the short story for a while, which we should also talk about at some point, and then move to the biblical text. Do you see it there?" He read it to them again. "This is the paragraph that starts, 'Julie doesn't hear it.' The last line reads, 'Not surprisingly, some of the folks in the church think he might be losing his marbles.' That's the end of my introduction to the story, you might say, but the very next piece, or *move* as Buttrick might say, starts with 'It will probably come as no surprise to you that I thought of this passage in Exodus 3.' I made a play on the words *surprisingly* and *surprise*. I don't know exactly when I stumbled upon this, but it's something I do quite often."

Marcus was clearly a preacher who thought intensely about his style of sermonizing. I said, "We definitely will want to come back to what Marcus said about leaving the short story behind temporarily, but for now let's keep looking at the different voices, transitions, that sort of thing. Going through a sermon in this detail is very helpful, I find. I hope that's true for all of you as well."

Several of them agreed. Carlos commented, as he had earlier on my own sermon, about the exposition and exegesis portions. He said to Marcus, "As my friends here will tell you, I'm probably more of a traditional preacher, so I was glad to see the section about the verb 'to see' and how Hebrew dialogue is important."

Marcus said, "Yes, for some reason traditional preachers—maybe all preachers, I don't know—think that narrative preaching means no more exegesis." He looked at me and asked, "Wasn't that something you mentioned to me once about teaching over in England?"

I said, "Yeah, these students probably don't know about this, but I used to teach adjunctively at Spurgeon's College in London, part of what we would call a DMin track. When I first started, I was very mindful of the British tradition of expository preaching—verse-by-verse, steeped in exegetical method and terminology. But I was also pleasantly surprised to see how excited these British preachers were by this 'new trend' called narrative preaching.

"Since the class was an intensive week together, culminating in them preaching narrative sermons before their peers, it was a grueling schedule. Okay, not so grueling that I didn't find time for visiting the British Museum, even playing an occasional round of links golf, but it was hectic."

Several of them said, "Oh, you poor thing. What a rough assignment." Several of them asked if I needed an assistant. I had been asked that many times.

I said, "Yeah, yeah, I've heard it all before. But here's my point. When it came time to preach their first narrative sermons ever, these British pastors took to it like ducks to water. They were masters at it right off."

Several of them were surprised. Brock asked, "So how did they make the switch so suddenly?"

I said, "That's the problem, actually. They weren't exactly masters, only masters in one regard. They were very quick to catch on to narrative voice and storytelling treatments of the biblical text, but they were also very quick to jettison the expositional voice. Their expository sermons that used to have them saying things like, 'In verse four, the Apostle Paul uses a Greek word that means . . .' were traded in for "My name is Simon Peter, and I'd like to tell you about the time when . . ."

Joey said, "I'd been meaning to ask you about that style of preaching, role-playing as the biblical character. Is that what it's called?" He said he knew a couple of preachers back in Oklahoma whose background in theater led them to be quite creative performers. Costumes, the whole nine yards.

Cassandra said, "I think it's called dramatic monologue, but it is a good question."

I said, "Cassandra's correct. Dramatic monologue, in which the preacher takes on the personae of a biblical character and speaks in first person, is a form of narrative preaching. But this is where I find Gene Lowry's work so helpful. In his book *How to Preach a Parable*, which by the way wasn't about preaching parables but preaching the way parables work . . ."

Joey interrupted, "Wait a minute. Why would someone name their book incorrectly?"

I assured him it wasn't the first time and that authors rarely have the final word on book titles, that they have to work with publishers. Then I got us back on track. I said, "Anyway, Lowry developed this continuum that he calls 'distance between teller and story' and it's very helpful." I wrote it on the board.

Distance Between Teller and Story

1_____2_____3_____4_____5_____

1) Inside character 2) Inside story 3) About character 4) About story 5) Away from story

I said, "There are lots of things that might be said about the continuum but here's what I want to stress. Position 1, inside the character, is where dramatic monologues occur, 'I remember going to see Jesus at night. I was a respected member of the Sanhedrin, and so I couldn't afford to be seen.' The preacher has taken on the role of Nicodemus in John 3; the preacher is inside that particular character. The great thing about position 1 is experience. What could be more experiential than listening to Nicodemus describe his encounter with Jesus in the night?

"But notice what the preacher in position 1 cannot do; and I don't mean that person can't act, although I've witnessed that before. No, she or he can't share any exposition in the truest sense of the word. If Alesha has taken on the role of Martha, Mary's sister, she can tell us how miffed she was cooking dinner for Jesus while her lazy sister neglected kitchen duty. But there is no way for her to note how Luke has constructed the tenth chapter of his Gospel. And there is no way for Alesha's 'Martha' to tell us about a short story by Alice Walker written in modern times. Trust me, I've heard some dramatic monologues in which the preacher tried such things. It was not a pretty picture.

"This is why I love Lowry's continuum, because we get to use the voice of position 1 as well as the others. 'Inside the character' is a position from which any narrative preacher might include dialogue, and by a variety of characters on stage, not just one. But because other positions are available, the preacher can tell a contemporary story, make exegetical and theological observations, the whole range of possibilities.

"Bear with me because I want to go back briefly to something I was saying about my students in London, those expository preachers learning narrative styles. And I've noticed the same thing among American preachers just learning narrative preaching as well."

Brock said, "Well, I'm glad we could keep up with the Brits in making the same kinds of mistakes."

I smiled. "So here's the common mistake. Even when the narrative voice isn't a dramatic monologue—position 1 on the continuum—preachers who take to narrative styles struggle with switching back to the preacher voice. They mysteriously seem unable to weave in traditional expositional comments with more narrative blocks. But it's not that difficult. We see that clearly in the sermon by Marcus. How did he go from narrating a short story in one paragraph, to talking about a movie in another, or switching to the preacher who shares a textual insight? The short answer is he hit the return key and started typing."

Cassandra said, "This is so cool. I always loved when my literature professors would dissect a scene from Hemingway or whomever and show us what was going on. I can still do that with literature, and now, although I hesitate to say it too confidently, it seems apparent enough with preaching." She looked like a kid in a candy store. She continued, "And I love how Rev. Schmeling, er, Marcus, switches voices so easily. One minute he's doing exegetical work with the Hebrew verbs, the next minute talking about a theology of theophanies, and then he has us touring a fifth-century church in the Mediterranean to share another illustration."

I said, "Yes, and it may well be because of television and movies that listeners are capable of such switches in our preaching. These edits, or cuts, are similar to how programs are often put together. A hundred years ago, maybe listeners more accustomed to written forms might have had troubling following us, but I don't think so today. And by the way, this is one of the things teachers of preaching noted in so much of the preaching of Craddock."

We discussed briefly whether Marcus might have used too many different pieces, especially references to books. Besides the Payne short story, there was Parker Palmer, Frederick Buechner, and Kathleen Norris. Even the Rebecca Parker story came from a book. We all agreed, Marcus included, that the sermon was slightly too literate for the oral medium of preaching. Of course, I couldn't help noting these were the kinds of authors worth reading as preachers.

Lisa said, "So you said something about coming back to how Marcus left the short story and came back to it near the conclusion. Would it be okay to discuss that now?"

I said, "Absolutely. How many of you remember the term 'Markan sandwich' from your New Testament studies? It has nothing to do with Marcus Schmeling, in case you're wondering."

Brock said, "I don't forget anything that refers to food. A 'Markan sandwich' is when in Mark's Gospel he starts telling one story, interrupts it with another, then comes back to finish the first one. The woman who tries to touch Jesus' garment is the example I seem to recall."

I said, "Yes, although her story is the one in the middle that interrupts the other story. It's in Mark 5. Remember, Jesus is on his way to heal the daughter of Jairus, when the hemorrhaging woman touches the hem of his robe. The writer leaves the first story behind for a moment. Some scholars think it's a way to build suspense. So after healing the woman, word arrives that the daughter of Jairus has died. And what would have been a healing story has now become a resurrection story since Jesus raises the little girl from the dead.

"It's a classic technique, and Mark isn't the only narrative preacher to use it. By that I'm referring to the 'gospel according to Gene Lowry.' In that same book on learning to preach like the parables, this is one of four strategies or structures he lists for narrative preaching." I erased the board and wrote the four terms there: Running the Story, Delaying the Story, Alternating the Story, and Suspending the Story.

"Now when Lowry refers to 'Story,' he means the biblical one. So a preacher might run with the biblical story, letting it pretty much be the sermon's main focus throughout. Or a preacher might start with material from our day, and not even deal with the biblical story until later. That material could even be a short story, though it wouldn't have to be. She or he would be delaying the biblical story. Alternating, as you might guess, is when the preacher goes back and forth throughout the sermon, sometimes in the biblical text, sometimes in our world. That's definitely harder to do. The last one, suspending, is what we've been talking about as a 'Markan sandwich,' even if we were referring to suspension of the short story. But all of these options are just that, options for narrative preachers. Of course, no matter the structural flow, it's important to remember that sermons should seek to bring the two worlds together. It's deadly for preaching if the sermon gets stuck in one world or the other for too long.

"I think Marcus's sermon is such a good example of how we can do so many things in narrative preaching. He invites us into the biblical story and the short story, weaving all of that together with contemporary illustrations, quotes, theological and exegetical insights, and so forth. This style of preaching, by the way, sometimes goes by the name episodic. Lowry and Craddock and others have started to embrace that term as something of an overarching term for narrative preaching. One episode is followed by another, some of it material from the Bible, some of it from our day. When preachers weave the material in that fashion, they help to collapse the distance between the two worlds. That's not to say they collapse the two worlds willy-nilly, forcing a modern world view onto an ancient one; I don't mean that. But preachers who collapse the distance in a responsible way bear witness to how God is still at work in the world. The God who spoke to Moses out of a burning bush is the one who still speaks in movies, short stories, in the everyday stories of our lives." After some measure of silence, I said, "Any last thoughts, questions?"

We all thanked Marcus for coming. I reminded them there would be no classes during Holy Week. And we departed in peace.

Chapter Nineteen

Short Easter

We had given up "Alleluias" for Lent, and now the world was filled with praise once again. In chapel services and churches everywhere, we sang of Christ being raised. Indeed! That was not the only good news this time around.

I probably sounded like Forrest Gump when I called my New Testament colleague, David; only instead of life being like a box of chocolates, it was more about life being like a short story and how you never know what you're going to get as the plot unfolds. What I meant was that I had turned the page of life and stumbled upon one of the most amazing discoveries—a small group in a church that reads a short story every week and gets together to talk about it.

David said, "What? You're kidding. How did you hear about it? What church? Details, man."

I laughed. "I know, it still amazes me. A minister friend and I met for coffee, and in passing she mentioned this small group at another church. You know the church, by the way, St. Matthew Episcopal on the south side of town."

He said he knew of the church but not any of the clergy there. He asked, "So what's the scoop on the small group?"

I said, "Well, they got started using that curriculum by Peter Hawkins, *Listening for God*, which actually uses short stories to foster religious discussion. So nothing unusual there, only here's the kicker: they've been doing this for seventeen years now."

David said, "What? I think you're cell phone cut out. Sounded like you said seventeen years."

It was obvious he was being cute. I said, "Is that amazing, or what? Every Friday morning for seventeen years they gather in the church parlor to discuss a different short story they've read that week. At least that's how my friend described it. And she said I could attend if I wanted, that she was sure it's open to everyone. She knows someone who knows someone who attends."

David said, "That's a no-brainer. You have to see what it's like."

"I know. And I am going to attend. My minister friend introduced me via email to one of the group members, an ex-lawyer, who said I was more than welcome. He told me they were presently working through *Best American Short Stories 2011*, and which story to read before Friday."

David said, "So you're going this week?"

"Yep, day after tomorrow. And it's a really interesting story, too, a kind of post-Holocaust story of Jewish life and morality. This is going to be a great adventure, I just know it."

On Friday morning I woke up at 5:30 a.m. in order to eat a quick breakfast and drive down south in time. The group meets at the ungodly hour of 6:30 on Friday mornings. During the drive, I recalled what Fred Craddock said about meetings that early in the morning, how back home in Cherry Log, Georgia, where he lives, they have a 6:30, but it's in the evening.

When I pulled up to the church, there they were, seven folks filing into the church parlor, half-asleep but clearly glad to see each other once again. And clearly glad to welcome "new blood" to the group, which seemed an appropriate metaphor for a story with substantial amounts of bloodshed. Three of them were attorneys, one still practicing and the other two retired. There was also a retired minister and a retired physician. I never did learn what the other two people did, although I didn't get the impression they were retired. The group also said something about three other regulars who were away this particular week for whatever reasons.

We sat in the church parlor, all of us thankful spring had finally sprung. After some other small talk, someone suggested we jump into the discussion of Nathan Englander's "Free Fruit for Young Widows," which I was convinced would preach. And so we did. One of the retired lawyers summarized it well, with the one word "gray." The morality of the story was in essence that life is complicated, and that even in times of war, killing is not black and white; of course, summarizing a story like that should be a misdemeanor at the very least. We all mumbled various responses, while flipping pages back and forth to see what we had underlined. Among others, this line had stood out for me: "a similar life is not a same life," a more poetic way of describing what it means to walk in another's shoes.

Some group members were clearly more interested in the particulars of this week's story, others more so in the issues the story raised for our day, including another school shooting prominent in national news. All of which is to say that sometimes we chased rabbits, and sometimes we dissected the story, but throughout it was a lively and healthy discussion. Here were church folks wrestling with life, using short stories to do so.

As we started to disband, someone thanked me again for coming, and another asked what I do for a living. I told them about my teaching at the seminary, but also the book on preaching and short stories. The retired minister cleared her throat and said, "Oh, well, then you need to meet our rector. She uses short stories in her preaching all the time."

I never play the lottery, but it felt like I had won the Powerball. I asked, "You're serious?"

She said, "Yes, not every week, but regularly throughout the year. Wouldn't y'all say Margaret uses short stories quite a bit in her preaching?" They agreed wholeheartedly.

I called David on my way back home, sharing some of the details from the morning, as well as telling him about the rector's preaching. While I was driving, he looked up the church online, and sure enough, printed manuscripts of her sermons were posted. He said her name was Margaret something or other, and added that her most recent post was her Easter sermon, with the title "Short Easter." I knew right away that that message had been inspired by a John Updike story by the same name.

When I got home I logged onto the website and read through it quickly. I couldn't believe it. Here was a preacher doing what I was proposing. What a gold mine. Personally, I wouldn't have used Updike's story the way she did, but that was beside the point. And the group had been right, this minister used short stories regularly, as I saw several as I surfed the site. I couldn't wait for next Thursday, to share this discovery with my class. Since we were still doing some practice retellings for a few weeks, and not reading other assignments, I sent them a copy of the "Short Easter" sermon, along with a note briefly explaining where I had discovered it.

"Short Easter"
Luke 24:1–11
A Sermon by
Rev. Margaret Irey

It should come as no surprise to any of you here, that this is the biggest day of the year in the church. The resurrection of Jesus is as big as it gets theologically. That being the case, you might wonder why any preacher with one shot at the good news of Easter would dare tell a story that proclaims the resurrection of Jesus only to end with the disciples not believing it. That is what Luke does. He's a preacher of course, and this is his only Gospel, his only chance to tell the resurrection story and make a good impression on folks, and what does he say? They didn't believe! You heard the story.

It begins with the women who don't believe much of anything as that Sunday dawns. Why should they? Jesus, their beloved teacher, has been dead and gone for days now. Early in the morning they bring burial spices, and while they find the stone rolled back, what they do not find is his body. Two men in dazzling apparel appear and ask them, "Why do you look for the living among the dead? He is not here, but has risen." And the women remember the words of Jesus, of how God would indeed raise him up on the third day. And remembering those words, they return and tell the others. What an amazing moment! And the response? "But these words seemed to them an idle tale, and they did not believe them." What a way to end a resurrection story. Actually, it's worse than that. That little phrase translated as "an idle tale" is *leiros* in Greek. You would be closer to translate it as a bunch of malarkey, as my parents would have said. So the good news of Christ's resurrection seemed like a lot of bull to the disciples.

So why would Luke do that, with only one chance to tell the story of Christ's resurrection, end it with disbelief on the part of the disciples? Well, maybe because like all good writers, he tells the truth. You see, writers know what TV preachers apparently don't, that the gospel doesn't always take. In fact, I'm struck by how often in literature Easter fizzles just a bit, doesn't quite live up to its billing. Do you know what I mean? Take John Updike's short story, "Short Easter."

It's the story of this fellow named Fogel. He's sixty-two and distinguished enough, only he's something of a curmudgeon. He's a cynic, easily irritated with life's annoyances. For instance, he's frustrated with folks who play the lottery instead of gambling the way he does on the stock market. And even though Easter has never been much of a holiday in his book, he's still a bit miffed when on this particular year it falls on the beginning of Daylight Savings Time. Thus, the phrase "Short Easter." The church bells ring in the dark, which is somewhat symbolic of his life. The day will be robbed of an hour, not quite complete. Fogel remembers Easter Sundays from his childhood, with chocolate bunnies and all, but mostly the starched clothes, stiff and formal. Family get-togethers in which the food was okay, but not necessarily the company. He also remembers the Easters of his adult life, including the time they were shunned by the neighbors, all because the hostess and he had broken off an affair that had gone wrong.

Fogel is looking retirement straight in the face, and perhaps mortality too, and he doesn't like what he sees. And Easter doesn't do anything to change one bit of his life. Maybe some of you feel the same way. Anyway, late in the afternoon he decides to take a nap. He falls into the world of dreams, where nothing makes much sense there either. And as he wakes, Updike describes it with the language of resurrection, or maybe almost resurrection. The last line reads, "Everything seemed still in place, yet something was immensely missing."

Everything in place, and yet something missing. You will perhaps find this hard to believe, but for many preachers this is the way we feel on Easter. You see, while this is our favorite day of the year, in many ways it is our least favorite when it comes to preaching. Part of it has to do with the mistaken notion that we must find something new to say, some new twist on a very familiar plot. When my best friend called on Monday to ask what I was up to, I said I was working on my Easter sermon. She said, "So what's it about?" I said, "Oh, I don't know, I thought I would talk about the resurrection." There's really nothing new to say.

But the main reason why I think some preachers don't like preaching on Easter is because we think it's our job to persuade folks that it's true, that Christ has been raised. And we know how impossible that seems. But here's the thing: it not only seems impossible; it *is* impossible! Preachers can't convince someone of the resurrection. I saw one of those TV preachers the other night on the religion channel on cable give it a try. He had a preacher voice and a marker board with eight bullet points on it. He called them facts, proof of the resurrection. He was convinced that by the time he got to his last bullet everyone would be Christian. I watched for a few minutes. Near as I could tell, his bullets were blanks. Think about it, these women in Luke's story had seen the empty tomb with their own eyes, heard the message with their own ears, and reported the whole thing with their own voices. And the disciples, those who had been closest to Jesus, mind you, thought the whole thing sounded like so much malarkey!

You can make someone go to church on Easter, no doubt about that. Can you hear the voice, "I don't care if you wear a tie or not, young man, but you're going. If you want to eat that ham I'm making, you better get dressed." Yeah, you can make someone go to church, but coming to faith is different. It's not a matter of coercion. All preachers can do is tell the story, tell what they've seen and what they believe.

That's what Roberta Bondi does in her book *Memories of God*. She testifies. She tells how growing up she never understood the resurrection. Not that it seemed like so much bull, but the crucifixion was something she related to better. She knew it was something she deserved. As a little child, she longed to be good, to please all of the grown-ups in her world. Her father was an especially demanding person who expected perfection, a perfection that no matter how hard she tried, she knew would never come. In school she tried to please her teachers, but her anxiety level only made learning that much harder. She struggled with the multiplication tables and most of all, her self-esteem. She would forget her money for school projects. Her father called her "an underachiever." She looked in the mirror at plain brown pigtails, glasses, and a skinny body. As a ten-year-old she once found herself looking at a rock in the yard and starting to cry as she imagined herself as that rock, alone and silent. Jesus' death seemed to make sense. It gave her a reason to be depressed.

Her parents eventually divorced, something she considered her fault. After graduating from high school, she married and soon discovered that not only was she a miserable daughter, but a poor excuse for a wife. She became a seminary professor and tried to be good at that, while also trying to be a good mother to the two children she had birthed. Later, she divorced and remarried. By the time she was forty-seven her depression became severe. She hit bottom on the Friday afternoon before the Saturday night party to celebrate her tenth wedding anniversary. They had been married ten years earlier on Easter Sunday, a beautiful spring day smelling of dogwoods and azaleas.

Here she was, ten years later, trying desperately to celebrate their anniversary, but terribly depressed. She sank down into a tall red chair and cried to God of how she had failed at everything. Then something happened. How long she sat there she had no idea. But she fell asleep, then suddenly awoke with words from the Roman Catholic mass going through her head: "The joy of the Resurrection renews the whole world." She had heard the words before, but for the first time every cell in her body knew they were true, true for her. It wasn't that she never battled depression again, but these words brought new life, "The joy of the Resurrection renews the whole world." She felt drunk with joy. "The joy of the Resurrection renews the whole world," she kept repeating.

That's how the Easter message works, or doesn't—someone believes, or they don't. So here's what I believe: that Christ has been raised from the dead and that he is only the first of many whose lives have also been resurrected. I believe that. And if it seems like an idle tale, I understand completely. Really. But if that sounds like maybe the truest thing you've ever heard in your life, well that's called Easter faith. And the only thing I can say is that "the joy of the Resurrection renews the whole world!" May it be so, and may your Easter be anything but short. Amen.

When Thursday rolled around, the evening's devotional was yet another excerpt from Nafisi's memoir:

> My constant obsession with the veil had made me buy a very wide black robe that covered me down to my ankles, with ki-monolike sleeves, wide and long. I had gotten into the habit of withdrawing my hands into the sleeves and pretending that I had no hands. Gradually, I pretended that when I wore the robe, my whole body disappeared: my arms, breasts, stomach and legs melted and disappeared and what was left was a piece of cloth the shape of my body that moved here and there, guided by some invisible force.
>
> The beginning of this game I can track back quite specifically to the day I went to the Ministry of Higher Education with a friend who wanted to have her diploma validated. They searched us from head to foot and of the many sexual molestations I have had to suffer in my life, this was among the worst. The female guard told me to hold my hands up, up and up, she said, as she started to search me meticulously, going over every part of my body. She objected to the fact that I seemed to be wearing almost nothing under the robe. I explained to her that what I wore under my robe was none of her business. She took a tissue and told me to rub my cheeks clean of the muck I was wearing. I explained that I wore no muck. Then she took the tissue herself and rubbed it against my cheeks, and since she did not achieve the desired results, because I had not worn any makeup, as I had told her, she rubbed it even harder, until I thought she might be trying to rub my skin off.

We had a time of prayer, after which Brock supplied the snack for the evening, homemade pretzels, soft and with salt. Someone remembered that the shape of pretzels were intended to resemble a monk at prayer, with arms folded across the chest, and how pretzels are a common snack in Lent. Brock's pretzels hardly compared to a hair shirt; they seemed luxurious and indulgent, a good Eastertide snack.

Besides letting the students practice their retellings and help each other with sermons that should have been in progress by now, I had two previously unplanned agendas for the evening: discussion of the "Short Easter" sermon and what it means to preach these stories to people who haven't read them before.

I started by filling in the details about the short story group at St. Matthew, including the part about a tradition seventeen years old and counting. Cassandra said, "I thought you were kidding about the small group thing. It almost sounds too good to be true."

Several of them debated whether that sort of thing could ever happen in their churches. Alesha weighed in, "I can see how a pastor could be pessimistic about this, but I also know that small groups everywhere are hungry for material to study and discuss. And most pastors I know are always looking for curriculum materials. This could be the next hot thing in small groups."

Brock said, "Yeah, that's true, but in rural churches I don't think what they're looking for is stories from *The New Yorker*."

I said something about how maybe we've sold rural folks short, when nowadays farmers in remote locations are linked to weather reports and agricultural blogs out of Washington, D.C. I wondered if we might be surprised at their reading habits. And even if that wasn't the case, it was hard to imagine a story like O'Connor's not resonating with country folks.

After some further discussion—pros and cons—I said, "I want to spend the last half of class this evening working in pairs, partners helping each other with your sermons as well as retellings. I also want you to practice retelling the biblical story you are using for your sermons. But I want to start with a discussion of the 'Short Easter' sermon I emailed you. I think it raises an important issue for us to ponder.

"If you have it in front of you, let's talk about it. What does Rev. Irey do well? What suggestions or critiques might we offer?" Several of them scrolled through the pages on screens, others flipping stapled pages. No one said a thing. I said, "Anyone? What about the 'hyphenation' of the sermon, her exposition-and-experience?"

That struck a chord. Joey said, "Seems to me she does a good job with both. I mean there's obviously an emphasis on experience with all the storytelling. And I think there's a good amount of exposition."

Carlos said, "I don't see much exposition at all. She mentions an important Greek word, and says a few things about the text. But I need more exposition than this."

Lisa said, "I think this sermon is different in terms of exposition. Rather than it being textual, it's more theological. She wrestles with the larger meaning of resurrection, not so much the textual details."

We debated the merits of that observation. We also noted how exposition is in the eye of the beholder, that there's always one more textual or theological insight that could be added to sermons. As a class we were trying to describe the perfect balance, the formula for hyphenated sermons. We agreed that formulas probably weren't helpful.

I said, "Speaking of formulas, one of the things we discussed earlier this semester was how much of an appearance the short stories should make in our sermons. Remember, I said I prefer not to think in terms of formulas, but that the short story should make more than a cameo appearance, that these are more substantive than illustrations. But in this case, Rev. Irey has used 'Short Easter' as more of an illustration. Do you see that? How does the story function in the sermon? What role does it play?"

Cassandra raised her hand, even if the class ritual was usually less formal. I said, "Cassandra?"

She said, "It seems to me it really is a different kind of usage. She doesn't invite us into the story's plot and all. It's briefer in some ways than we've discussed. And I think her point in using it is to talk about how folks sometimes find 'something missing' [she used air quotes] when it comes to Easter."

Alesha said, "I agree. It works, but it does feel more like an illustration."

I said, "I think so too. But I'm questioning my own teaching here."

Joey said, "I question my own learning all the time, dude. Welcome to the club."

I laughed. "I think we do an injustice to the multi-faceted and rich stories we've been reading if all we do is summarize them too quickly and use them as yet another way to make our points. But now I'm thinking that using them like that from time to time makes good sense. Did you think it worked well as an illustration of 'something missing' when it comes to Easter?"

Everyone seemed to agree, except Lisa. She said, "I'm not so sure. I do think it's a good illustration, and that it's used as an illustration. But what I mean is, I didn't really get it. Wait, that's not right. I guess what I really mean is that this is the first sermon we read using a short story we haven't read. So I don't know if it's because of that or because she only used it as a brief illustration, but it didn't touch me as deeply."

I said, "I appreciate that observation. Illustrations, in the traditional sense of the word, typically aren't about feeling something, having an experience. More often they are used to help listeners understand something. And looking at this use of 'Short Easter,' that's okay. But there's something else this raises for me. Now we all know that seminary classes are not always fair representations of real-life experiences."

Cassandra interrupted, "No. Tell me it's not so."

Slightly flustered, I said, "Yeah, it's true. Sometimes. But in this case, what I have in mind is how we've been judging each other's sermons and retellings knowing the stories intimately. And this could also be applied to the biblical texts. Maybe we've assumed too much when it comes to the biblical narratives, as if everyone in the pews knows who Samaritans were or what have you. And if that's the case with the biblical stories, which they've probably at least heard before, what does that say about our retellings of a short story they've likely never read?

"So here's what I'm thinking, and I will let you decide. I'm wondering if we wouldn't be better off inviting guests to our retellings and especially when we start preaching. I mean, fellow-seminarians who don't have a Thursday evening class could come and listen in. Then we could ask them whether it made sense—the short story they heard retold, the telling of the biblical story, and the connections. What do y'all think?"

Brock said, "Well, I was hoping no one would ever hear the sermon I'm working on, so I hate to admit it, but it's a good idea." Several others chimed in with similar comments. So we agreed, starting next week, they would round up whomever they could—colleagues with an evening free, staff persons who might be working late, maybe even friends from church—and invite them to class. We would go into the highways and byways. We were going to have "church" as they started preaching. We even decided the preaching, unlike the retellings, should happen in the chapel.

We took a break, two or three of us here and there discussing what having guests would mean. Afterwards, we spent the rest of the evening practicing our retellings, wondering what we who were familiar with these stories had been taking for granted. I also encouraged them to bounce sermon ideas off each other. As usual, we departed in peace.

CHAPTER TWENTY

The Most Important Word

I received an alarming email from my homiletics colleague, Andy. The term "alarming" might seem over the top to some folks at the death of a dog, but Ashley, their gorgeous Golden Retriever, had been hit by a car and killed. To make matters worse, she had given birth to eight of the cutest puppies ever just two weeks earlier. Andy and I visited by phone; it was terribly sad. The death not only left me feeling melancholy for the better part of the next month or so, but it made me think more intently about preaching in general.

What kinds of sermons does it take to speak to such pain? And what kind of preaching does it take to address unspeakable joy, like when our daughter became engaged at roughly the same time and our son and his wife shared the news they were expecting their first child, our first grandchild? Was a narrative sermon up to moments like that? I couldn't help but think that "three points and a poem" would never do. And I was amazed at how many such sermons I had heard lately.

Of course, I'm only one observer and I only get around to so many churches when not preaching myself. But it felt to me like the state of preaching was in flux. Again! My wife and I had just celebrated our fortieth anniversary, and I realized so had the New Homiletic a couple years earlier. When ministers the age of Brock had started out years ago, sermons were dry, tedious, and let's face it, boring. Biblically boring at that. They stuck with the text, which was great in a way; but they stuck with it so thoroughly as to lose touch with folks who lived here and now, not back then and there. "There are three things you should know about Paul's missionary journeys in the latter part of the book of Acts . . ." I think it was Krister Stendahl who warned about "playing Bibleland" in our preaching. When Craddock released *As One without Authority* back in the early '70s, it was like Elvis gyrating on Ed Sullivan's stage, shocking to some but liberating for others.

For the past twenty years of those forty, I had invited my students who cut their teeth on expository sermons to try something new, something old really, as old as Jesus spinning yarns about the reign of God in the form of parables. Not everyone took to the New Homiletic, of course not. But many did. Forty years later, however, many of them were Joey's age. They didn't know the history, or hadn't lived it anyway. For them the New Homiletic was old stuff, maybe the only stuff they had ever known in terms of preaching styles.

Lately, however, I had noticed an old wind blowing, the Old Homiletic, alive and well. It was Tom Long, I think, who said something about homileticians dancing on the grave of those older styles, only to hear a voice calling it forth from a tomb. I don't know if the voice was that of Jesus or some other voice altogether. Either way, in the last two months alone, I heard a sermon in the seminary's chapel that not only was built on three points but had three subpoints under each of those. And the text was Jesus turning water into wine! A narrative text! As good as the content was, it felt like the preacher had turned wine back into water.

And then I went to lunch with the pastor of a fairly large church here in Kansas City. Surely the pastor has to be doing something right in his preaching. Only he told me his sermons are forty-five minutes of pure exposition. Stories are an endangered species at his church. He even ends his sermons every week by saying, "So what have we learned this morning? Let's review." And the people eat this up by the thousands. I followed up that lunch meeting with an email, and we had a good exchange on the subject for awhile. He prided himself in preaching to head and heart, whereas I thought he privileged head over heart. He asked what I thought about the one illustration he had used, the story (and slides to go with it) about a man who restores old guitars. I thought it was a good analogy, but not the sort of thing that touches people. In fact, I wrote, the people seated around me oohed and aahed when the new guitar was shown, but I doubt seriously they were touched deep in their hearts in a religious sort of way. The email exchange ended with no resolution.

I'm not sure some pastors truly value the power of story and emotions. That same minister told me he had no interest in the movie *12 Years a Slave* because he already knew about slavery, and it seemed depressing on top of that. To me, that's the thing about good movies, they take us beyond intellectual knowing and touch us in deep places. It's a different kind of knowing. When I first started teaching, I used to say that church folks raised on the

Old Homiletic may have had their notebooks full, but perhaps their lives felt empty. Notes can only take you so far in life. Stories, I used to say, that's the real deal.

As I thought about the death of a dog and the birth of puppies, the engagement of lovers, the birth of a child—not to mention the threat of chemical weapons in the Middle East and other world events too numerous to name—the way I figured it, some thoughtful reflection called exposition was in short supply, and sure, the preacher was obligated to say something meaningful. But did exposition have to be the lone voice? Why were we hardwired to choose between exposition and experience, when hyphenated likely held the key? Was it too much to ask that I go to church in my grief and joy to hear a message that both spoke to my intellect and touched me in the deepest recesses of my being?

The former college basketball coach Jimmy Valvano, who died tragically young from cancer, offered some advice shortly before his death. He said there are three things we should do each day: laugh, think, and cry. Laughing and crying are some of the ways we experience life. And he said we should find something deep to ponder. This seemed like good advice for preachers.

On Easter Sunday that year, the same Sunday when Margaret Irey used Updike's short story, I worshiped at the nursing home with my mother, whose absent-mindedness had recently surrendered to full-blown dementia. What a cruel disease! Surrounded by twenty or so persons in wheelchairs and various states of mind and spirit, I waited for the preacher to bring a word of hope, a word of resurrection that might make a difference, to the residents and to us guests. Never have I been more disappointed. Instead, he bored us stiff with words. He declared why the resurrection is true, and how he could prove it. He derided anyone with doubts. He talked about all four Gospel accounts, putting them in a blender and making a Gospel smoothie out of them as far as I was concerned. True, this was poor exposition; but it wasn't just his faulty exegesis that got to me. It was the exclusively heady approach. To make matters worse, the sermon went on and on. What a Bozo, I thought. But having been taught well by my mom, I held my tongue as people do in polite company. People with dementia, however, often lose control over such filters. Twenty-five minutes into his message, my mom said, "Are you ever going to shut up and sit down?" I had to bite my cheeks to keep from laughing out loud.

What kind of preaching can play in the nursing home? Maybe that's the Peoria for preachers. In show business they say, "If it plays in Peoria, it can play anywhere." What kind of preaching plays in the nursing home? Or in children's church? Or in big church, as it's sometimes called? What kind of preaching does the church need? These were the things I pondered as we headed into the home stretch of the semester.

I had decided we would only listen to two sermons per week, even if we did have three hours of class time each session. It wasn't a matter of having enough time for the preaching itself, since most of the sermons typically lasted less than twenty minutes; it was more a matter of having enough time for discussion. As with most preaching classes, after each person preached there would be a few minutes for the preacher to catch her/his breath while the others filled out critique sheets. Then there would be a time of discussion: initial affirmations of where we heard the gospel, suggestions for improvement, and finally recognition of the sermon's strengths. I just didn't want that time to be rushed. Sometimes in the introductory course we hardly have time to reflect before it's time for the next preacher. Electives are smaller, so taking our time seemed important.

Over the next few weeks we started preaching, with Carlos and Alesha the first night, Brock and Joey the next week, Cassandra and Rosa the third week, which left Lisa alone the last night of the semester. Here are some of my recollections about their preaching those last few weeks. At the beginning of the semester Carlos had made a point of wanting to go first, something common among those who not only want to "get it over with" (which doesn't sound like a positive disposition toward preaching), but who are worried that compared to their colleagues, their sermons won't measure up. Carlos clearly gave his all the evening he preached, so there were no hints of disdain, but his sermon was less than stellar, to say the least. Not surprisingly, it was strong on exposition, only those pieces of exposition weren't worked into the message very fluidly. Kicking and screaming is another way of saying it. "The Welcome Table," which we had heard him retell or practice many times, didn't seem to exert much presence in the sermon overall. Everyone knew it, Carlos included, although the discussion time was more upbeat than I expected. He would not become a lover of literature it seemed, but he had come a long way from where he started. Personally, I thought if he could tap into the passion of that time he went shopping in Guatemala City and encountered a homeless person, those kinds of things might enliven his preaching, combined with his love of teaching.

Alesha, on the other hand, set the chapel on fire with her rendition of "The Welcome Table." We may not have been a lively black congregation offering vocal support ("Amen. Preach it, sister."), although one of the guests from her church did speak out a time or two. But all of us, the class and guests, felt everything she said. She even hummed the tune to a Negro spiritual at one point, almost breaking into song. Our critique consisted mostly of affirming the sermon's affect while longing for more exposition. In a way, what most of us wanted was something in between Carlos's purely heady sermon and Alesha's mostly heart message.

Brock and Joey struck something of a balance between head and heart. Both sermons were episodic, although Joey's was more a series of unrelated episodes. The focus of his message was hard to discern. Having guests the previous week, we decided this time to invite them into the discussion more intentionally. Paula, who works at the seminary in student recruitment, had stayed after work to participate because Joey had invited her, the two of them always kidding each other about his Sooners and her Crimson Tide. She was gracious in her comments, but noted that with both sermons it wasn't always clear what to make of the focus overall or the different short stories they had summarized. She sounded sorry for having to say it.

Cassandra and Rosa both nailed it, only in different ways. Cassandra's background in literature was obvious, since she could not only talk about the story she shared, but understood at a deep level how to communicate that to us and to our guests. Flannery O'Connor would have been pleased. Rosa nailed everything, as far as I was concerned. Her exegesis was spot on, as was the telling of the Alice Walker short story we'd heard her do before, and how she put it all together. Sure, her embodiment still lacked presence, partly because of language difficulties but also the overreliance on her manuscript. Still, both sermons were outstanding.

At the end of the evening that next-to-last session, I said that we would begin with Lisa's preaching next time and then spend the remainder of the three hours critiquing her work. She said, "Uh, huh, thanks a lot." She knew I was kidding.

I said, "No, after Lisa's sermon, we will conclude with a wrap-up of the semester."

Even with time being important, we began each of the preaching weeks with a devotional, including a prayer for that night's preachers. The prayer of illumination I offered each time was one of my favorites prior to preaching, something I borrowed from a former colleague years earlier. We read it in unison: "Most gracious God, bless your word this day, wherever it is read, wherever it is heard; wherever it is preached, and especially wherever it is lived. Amen."

On the last night of the semester I selected one final reading from Nafisi's *Reading Lolita in Tehran*, a book that seemed even more important as the Arab Spring had resulted in clashes throughout the Middle East, especially Egypt of late, which deeply concerned Cassandra.

It was during this period that I joined a small group who came together to read and study classical Persian literature. Once a week, on Sunday nights, we gathered at one of the participants' houses and for hours we studied text after text. Sunday nights— sometimes during the blackouts by candlelight—in different houses, belonging to the different members of the groups, we would gather year after year. Even when our personal and political differences alienated us from one another, the magical texts held us together. Like a group of conspirators, we would gather around the dining room table and read poetry and prose from Rumi, Hafez, Sa'adi, Khayyam, Nezami, Ferdowsi, Attar, Beyhaghi.

We would take turns reading passages aloud, and words literally rose up in the air and descended upon us like a fine mist, touching all five senses. There was such a teasing, playful quality to their words, such joy in the power of language to delight and astonish. I kept wondering: when did we lose that quality, that ability to tease and make light of life through our poetry? At what precise moment was this lost? What we had now, this saccharine rhetoric, putrid and deceptive hyperbole, reeked of too much cheap rosewater.

I was reminded of a story I had heard and reheard about the Arab conquest of Persia, a conquest that brought Islam into Iran. By this account, when the Arabs attacked Iran, they won because the Persians themselves, perhaps too tired of tyranny, had betrayed their king and opened the doors to their enemies. But after the invasion, when their books were burned, their places of worship destroyed and their language overtaken, the Persians took revenge by re-creating their burned and plundered history through myth and language. Our great epic poet Ferdowsi had rewritten the confiscated myths of Persian kings and heroes in a pure and sacred language. My father, who all through my childhood would read me Ferdowsi and Rumi, sometimes used to say that our true home, our true history, was in our poetry. The story came back to me then because, in a sense, we had done it again. This time we had opened the gates not to foreign invaders but to domestic ones, to those who had come to us in the name of our own past but who had now distorted every inch of it and robbed us of Ferdowsi and Hafez.

For their sermons I had assumed everyone would use the short stories they had been practicing all along; that made good sense, and that's what most of them did. But I also didn't want to rule out that someone might stumble across a different story later in the semester, one that begged to be preached, so I did offer that option. Lisa was the only one who took me up on it, which was refreshing after so many sermons using "The Welcome Table" or "Revelation." She chose Raymond Carver's "Cathedral." I think partly she made that choice because going last meant she had more preparation time, but also because the story had blown her away. Those were her words, "blown me away," in the email she sent making sure she could use it. I thought the phrase "blown me away" might be the vernacular for epiphany. Here's the printed version of her message she emailed me, although the preached sermon was even more powerful.

"Cathedral"
Acts 10:1–48

This semester at the seminary I'm taking a course called "The Sermon and the Short Story." I know, it's a graduate theological school, and students are supposed to be reading dry, dusty volumes of theology. Well, in this class we are getting credit for reading literature. But don't let the process fool you. On the surface these stories don't seem all that religious, but underneath they are brimming with the stuff of real life, which is what religion is really about. Some of the authors we've read thus far include Alice Walker, John Updike, Flannery O'Connor, even Stephen King if you can believe that. We look at these stories with a microscope, or maybe better yet, a stethoscope. We're trying to hear their heartbeats.

One of the things we look at is plot. Not, "What is the story about?" so much as, "How does it go?" In recent years biblical scholars have suggested that we read our Bibles that way, using the techniques of literary criticism. What's the plot? In Acts 10, the plot is not all that complicated, even if it's longer than most passages read in churches on any Sunday. One scholar finds in this passage a seven-act drama. But no matter how you slice it, it's not that hard to follow. You heard it:

It begins with Cornelius who has this angelic vision that he should send for a fellow named Simon Peter. So Cornelius dispatches a party to the place where Peter's staying. And as so often happens in stories, we cut to where Peter's staying to find something going on there as well. As the people sent from Cornelius are approaching, Peter has his own vision. In a dream he's told to eat animals that Jews would have considered unclean, off-limits. Three times this happens, with Peter finally being told that what God considers clean he should not call profane.

Then the doorbell rings, so to speak. Peter is told by God that they have come for him. The people sent by Cornelius tell him God has sent them. Two lives intersecting. The next day Peter and some other believers return with Cornelius's people. Peter the Jewish believer and Cornelius the Gentile soldier, they each tell their stories, of the visions they've had. Peter preaches a sermon of sorts, and while he's preaching the Spirit of God comes upon the Gentiles gathered there.

And that's the basic plot, that's what happens. And you're not terribly excited, are you? Of course, plot can only take you so far in looking at a story. There's what happens, and then *there's what happens* if you know what I mean. It's like saying the new James Bond movie is about good versus evil. Well, okay, but I think there's more. Or it's like dissecting a frog; once you finish, you understand it better, but it's also dead.

Among the many other things worth looking at in a story, one of the most crucial is its texture. The texture of a story is how it feels, not so much between your fingers but in your gut. Or maybe it's not so much how the story feels, but how it makes you feel when you read it. A story's texture can be haunting, airy, mysterious, dark. The list goes on. If I had to pick one word for this passage it would be *dirty*. It's a dirty story. Not dirty as in pornographic but definitely dirty. Stained. Soiled. It's like reading the newspaper, when you're finished you have to wash your hands. Or maybe it's like handling raw chicken. Dirty.

Cornelius is a Gentile, an Italian military man. He is living in Caesarea, a Gentile city named after one of Rome's many Caesars. Peter is staying with a tanner, one who works with animal hides. If you've ever been near a slaughterhouse, you get the idea. When Peter has a vision, it's about animals the Jews consider unclean. It's a dirty story. Picture an episode of *Law and Order* where the case takes them into the seedier side of the city, brothels and tenements with drug dealers. Dirty.

But as we've been noting in the short story class, stories often move from one texture into another. In this case, the dirty becomes clean. Cornelius the far-off Gentile receives the Spirit of God. That's mission right, changed lives and all. And we could have testimonies right about now, because my hunch is that while the particulars would be different, most of us have seen the dark and dirty side of life. And then we found God, or God found us. That's why we send folks on mission trips. That's why someone stands here and announces a trip to an orphanage in Costa Rica or wherever. It's why we announce mission trips to Thailand where some group is helping prostitutes leave that life behind. What else could mission be than going where life is dirty and announcing the cleansing power of God to change lives?

Only as it turns out, that's only one side of the equation. Don't forget Peter. Cornelius isn't the only who's changed by this encounter. God was working in both of them. Peter learns there's no such thing as dirty. Not that the dirty can be made clean, but that there's no such thing as dirty. After all, Cornelius is described as a man who feared God. Maybe mission is not so much about what we do for others, but what God does in us until we no longer see them as an "other." Did you ever go on a mission trip?

A couple of weeks ago on a beautiful Saturday afternoon, I took my dog for a walk in the park near our house. I met this couple there, and we started chatting. I told them I was in seminary and serving this church. They told me they ran a small business, but that they considered themselves to be missionaries of a sort. They said they had been vacationing in South Africa when they became aware of the AIDS orphan crisis, all these millions of children whose fathers had fled and whose mothers died from AIDS. The husband said that what they saw changed their lives. Maybe that's the bigger picture of missions, how it changes us.

Peter had a notion of clean and unclean. He got it from reading his Bible; it's in Leviticus. Clean and unclean. You know, two kinds of people in the world. You've heard that before, right? In his culture, Jew and Gentile. In our day, lots of versions. American and Iraqi. Shia and Sunni. Black and white. Gay and straight. Red states, blue states. Good and bad. People are always dividing the world into two kinds of people. Some church folks use the terms lost and saved. Two kinds of people. Convenient, isn't it, that one group always gets to decide who's clean, who's not. Only mission blurs the line.

In the short story class, we read a Raymond Carver piece the week before last. It's called "Cathedral." It's about this fellow nicknamed Bub, who's not all that happy when his wife informs him that Robert, an old friend of hers, is coming to stay with them for a few days. Turns out, Robert is blind. She used to work for him years ago, reading books onto tape, that sort of thing. Bub is not impressed. He's not your sensitive sort of guy. He's heard his wife's stories about how Robert let her touch his face and how powerful it was. He's heard how she started writing poetry as a result of her experience with Robert. There's nothing between his wife and blind Robert, not now and not back then. But Bub is not into poetry and touching and all that kind of sensitive stuff.

Bub's the kind of guy that likes to drink some Scotch, kick back on the sofa at night and watch television late into the night after his wife's gone to bed. He's the kind of guy who jokingly suggests maybe blind Robert would want to go bowling while he's in town. Bub's the kind of guy who can't figure out why a blind man would wear a beard. What does he care how he looks? He's blind. Bub's the kind of guy who when his wife reminds him that Robert's wife Beulah had just died, all Bub can say is, "Beulah? What kind of name is that? Was she black?" Bub's a jerk.

Well, Robert arrives from the train station and the three of them make small talk until dinner time. They drink Scotch and during dinner, Bub listens as the two of them catch up on old times. After dinner, it's more Scotch, and when his wife goes upstairs to prepare the spare bedroom, that's when Bub turns on the television. It's hard to tell if it's Bub's practical joke on a blind man, or he's just that insensitive. It never occurs to him that the blind man has a television, too. So the two of them watch television together. They watch late into the night, drinking Scotch, even smoking a joint at one point. Bub even admits he enjoys the company. That's a big thing for Bub.

As they're flipping through the channels, Bub comes upon a documentary about cathedrals from the Middle Ages. Robert says whatever he wants is fine with him. "I'm always learning, always learning something. I've got ears. I'm always learning." So they watch this special on cathedrals. Images of these great edifices in Spain, and England, and even Notre Dame in Paris. Images of gargoyles and intricate patterns in the stonework. Beautiful cathedrals.

Bub suddenly asks, "Do you know what a cathedral is? I mean, do you have any idea of the difference between a cathedral and, say, a Baptist church?" Robert says he knows what he's heard so far, that they're huge and that they took more than a hundred years to build, that workers could be there their whole life and it still wasn't completed. "Kind of like us, right?" says Robert. They watch on in silence, until Robert says, "Maybe you could describe a cathedral to me." Bub tries, he really does. And something is happening between them, but he can't describe a cathedral, not really. Then Robert get this brilliant idea. "We could draw one, me and you. Get some big pieces of sturdy paper."

He fetches some ballpoint pens and a grocery bag from the pantry. They sit on the carpet hunched over the coffee table, Robert's hand on Bub's. That's a big thing for Bub, too. "Go ahead and draw," Robert says. "You can do it." And Bub, who's not the least bit of an artist, starts to draw. He sketches this large rectangle, with a roof. And then spires. And before long, it starts to look like a cathedral. Robert says, "I bet you never thought anything like this could happen in your lifetime, did you? Well, it's a strange life. We all know that." And it is, because their joined hands keep on drawing. Flying buttresses, windows with arches, great doors. The program goes off the air, and still they keep drawing. Robert says, "Be sure and put some people in there. What's a cathedral without people?"

And near the end Robert says, "Now close your eyes. Close your eyes and keep drawing." And Bub does it. It was like nothing either had ever experienced. Finally, they are finished. Robert says, "Now open your eyes and tell me what you think." But Bub is not the same man he was before. He keeps them closed. He realizes he's still in his own house, that nothing has changed, and yet everything has changed. And with his eyes closed, Bub says, "It's really something. It's really something."

When I read this story for class, I sat there mesmerized by its magic. I thought about a blind man teaching a sighted person how to see. Both of them changed. I thought about Peter and Cornelius. Nothing like a god-fearing Gentile soldier to teach Peter about clean and unclean. I don't know if you noticed, but during Peter's little sermon he says the most amazing thing. He says, "I truly understand God shows no partiality." It's that little word *truly*. He finally gets it. He'd preached on that very thing before, but he finally gets it.

As it turns out, there really are two kinds of people in the world. Not clean and unclean. Not saved and lost. No, there are those who divide the world into two kinds of people and those who don't.

If the short story "Cathedral" had blown Lisa away, her sermon by the same name blew us away. This was one of those moments professors live for, why classes are even offered. Not only was the exposition solid—the insight about Peter's use of the word "truly," for example—but every element of the message was worked in naturally. And the raw emotion of hearing her message impressed all of us. We felt Carver's story, and I think we felt the Acts story as well. Lisa told us that even though she had been working with another story all along, when she read this one she had no choice.

I said, "I know exactly what you mean. A friend of mine recently told me about Muriel Barbery's amazing novel, *The Elegance of the Hedgehog*."

Cassandra said, "Oh, my God. I haven't read the novel, but the movie is amazing."

I said, "Yeah, that's what I've heard. Anyway, there is this one passage in which the main character describes how to judge a piece of literature. She calls it the 'cherry plum test.' You get a bowl of ripe cherry plums out and set them on the counter next to the book you're reading. If one of those is more succulent than the other, something's terribly wrong. Is that great?" I added, "Oh, and she says if you don't have cherry plums, dark chocolate will do as well."

Cassandra said, "Amen."

Then Lisa blew us away even more, right there during the discussion time. After the affirmations and critiques, she reached into her backpack and fetched a rolled-up piece of paper, a grocery bag that had been cut open and converted into an artist's canvas. She unrolled it and there was a sketch of a cathedral much like Bub and Robert had drawn. Lisa's skills from her art major days were fully on display, even though she claimed to have drawn it in a matter of minutes. But taking in that paper bag cathedral after hearing her sermon was an experience beyond words. I could have sat in silence for a long time, sucking on a cherry plum or savoring dark chocolate. Lisa later gave me a copy of that cathedral, and I have displayed it on my office door at the seminary ever since.

We celebrated how she had combined experience and exposition. Clearly, this shy young lady had found her preaching voice. This was a message of maturity and depth. A couple of the things I had planned to say fit well after hearing Lisa preach, especially as a kind of wrap-up of the semester. One of them was a recent find. I said, "I've just discovered an amazing book, one that I wish I had known about earlier in the semester. Not that I would have adopted it for the class, since the first half requires a degree in the anatomy of the brain; but it's a fascinating book nonetheless."

Joey said, "What, I didn't tell you I used to be a brain surgeon?"

I ignored his comment. "Thankfully, though, the second half of the book, weighing in at ten pounds by itself, is quite accessible." I held up a copy of Iaian McGilchrist's tome, *The Master and His Emissary*. "The title is a reference to a parable Nietzsche told, about a master whose domain became so large he had to enlist emissaries to represent him. Unfortunately, his most clever emissary resented the master and began to sow discord throughout the kingdom. McGilchrist believes this is the best metaphor for understanding the right brain/left brain divide that most of us have heard about before. Thus, the subtitle, *The Divided Brain and the Making of the Western World*."

Cassandra said, "That's the right side is creative, left side is more for theory, right?"

Brock replied, "Actually, it's the theory that the women in here are right-brained and the rest of us left-brained." Several of us laughed, and although he exaggerated, it was true that the female students had exhibited more creativity. The women in the class just smiled.

I said, "I'm not going there, but here's what I wanted to say. The author contends that the issue is a lot more complicated than we've been led to believe. McGilchrist says it's true that creativity resides primarily in the right side of the brain, but not exclusively. And the same for analytical impulses being found on both sides, even if primarily on the left side. But there's more to it. He says that information gets sent back and forth between the two sides as we process thoughts. Only it turns out, the left side, the rational side, is not nearly so flexible as the right. And not very trusting either.

"In other words, the left side is a paranoid master worried that his emissaries are going to betray him, overthrow his kingdom. And so McGilchrist traces this epic battle throughout history. The Protestant Reformers, for example, in their haste to ban works of art, to attack music, valued the left side of the brain over the right. As he notes, 'the cardinal tenet of Christianity—the Word is made Flesh' was reversed, 'the Flesh is made Word.' Now that is a sad indictment. And he traces the influence of such thinking through the left-brained Enlightenment over against right-brained Romanticism, or later the left-brained Industrial Revolution. In essence, what he traces historically is that while the brain functions best when both sides work together, cooperation has rarely been achieved."

We discussed all sorts of evidence anecdotally, including some preachers we know and what this means for a kind of narrative style that seeks to embrace both exposition-and-experience. I said, "And this reminds me of one last thing I wanted to share with you this evening. Some of you may know the name Elton Trueblood, the Quaker writer." No one showed any signs of recognition. "There's a great story about a time when a pastor went to spend some time with Trueblood, to pick his brain on a variety of topics related to church life. Only Trueblood quizzed the pastor. He asked, 'What do you think is the most important word in the Bible?' We don't have the details of how the conversation unfolded, but Trueblood's answer is brilliant. He said the most important word is *and*. And—as in love of God *and* love of neighbor. Law *and* gospel. Personal *and* social holiness. Monastic *and* active forms of spirituality. This *and* that. The most important word is *and*." I let the insight sink in a few moments.

"*And* since that's true of Scripture and theology in general, I should add, I think it's true of preaching as well. Experience *and* exposition."

We talked about the simplicity and profound nature of that insight. I did remind them to look on Moodle when they got a chance, that I had finally posted the promised list of "preachable" short stories, over a hundred, although I hadn't counted in some time. I also shared one last reading from Nafisi, near the end of the book:

> I have a recurring fantasy that one more article has been added to the Bill of Rights: the right to free access to imagination. I have come to believe that genuine democracy cannot exist without the freedom to imagine and the right to use imaginative works without any restrictions. To have a whole life, one must have the possibility of publicly shaping and expressing private worlds, dreams, thoughts, and desires, of constantly having access to a dialogue between the public and private worlds. How else do we know that we have existed, felt, desired, hated, feared?
>
> We speak of facts, yet facts exist only partially to us if they are not repeated and re-created through emotions, thoughts and feelings. To me it seemed as if we had not really existed, or only half-existed, because we could not imaginatively realize ourselves and communicate to the world, because we had used works of imagination to serve as handmaidens to some political ploy.

I closed the book, laid it down, and said, "Go in peace." A few of them thanked me for the class. All of them said their good-byes to each other, filed out of the chapel and headed home. The semester was over. Summer was upon us.

I started putting away my books, and then looked up, surprised to see that Lisa and Cassandra had stayed after. Cassandra delicately traced her fingers along the paper-bag cathedral, and shared more of her enthusiasm for Lisa's really fine sermon. Both questioned the open-ended nature of Carver's story. A lot of people I know can't even get Carver's story. I thought Lisa got it for sure.

As I got in my car to drive home on this beautiful spring evening, I thought, *That's the thing about narratives. People either get them or they don't. Or maybe they do.*

List of "Preachable" Short Stories

Saint Paul School of Theology

A. M. Freeman, PhD

Note: If readers discover "preachable" short stories not listed here, feel free to message me on my Facebook page at www.facebook.com/Dr.MikeGraves. I'll be sure to get them to Dr. Freeman and post an updated version of the list from time to time.

Allison, Dorothy. "River of Names." In *The Vintage Book of Contemporary American Short Stories*, edited by Tobias Wolff, 3–12. New York: Vintage, 1994.

Anderson, Sherwood. "I Want to Know Why." In *The Norton Anthology of Short Fiction*, 6th ed., edited by R. V. Cassill and Richard Bausch, 1–7. New York: Norton, 2000.

Baldwin, James. "Exodus." In *God: Stories*, edited by C. Michael Curtis, 1–7. Boston: Houghton Mifflin, 1998.

———. "Sonny's Blues." In *You've Got to Read This*, edited by Ron Hansen and Jim Shepard, 32–56. New York: HarperCollins, 1994.

Barthelme, Donald. "A City of Churches." In *The Best American Short Stories of the Century*, edited by John Updike, 503–6. Boston: Houghton Mifflin, 1999.

Bausch, Richard. "Design." In *God: Stories*, edited by C. Michael Curtis, 8–21. Boston: Houghton Mifflin, 1998.

Berry, Wendell. "A Burden." In *A Place in Time: Twenty Stories of the Port William Membership*, 37–47. Berkeley, CA: Counterpoint, 2012.

———. "A Desirable Woman." In *A Place in Time: Twenty Stories of the Port William Membership*, 48–68. Berkeley, CA: Counterpoint, 2012.

———. "An Empty Jacket." In *A Place in Time: Twenty Stories of the Port William Membership*, 182–87. Berkeley, CA: Counterpoint, 2012.

———. "The Girl in the Window." In *A Place in Time: Twenty Stories of the Port William Membership*, 3–13. Berkeley, CA: Counterpoint, 2012.

Bissell, Tom. "A Bridge Under Water." In *The Best American Short Stories: 2011*, edited by Geraldine Brooks, 32–55. New York: Houghton Mifflin, 2011.

Bloom, Amy. "Silver Water." In *The Norton Anthology of Short Fiction*, 6th ed., edited by R. V. Cassill and Richard Bausch, 121–27. New York: Norton, 2000.

Bly, Carol. "After the Baptism." In *Listening for God: Contemporary Literature and the Life of Faith*, vol. 2, edited by Paula J. Carson and Peter S. Hawkins, 87–104. Minneapolis: Augsburg Fortress, 1996.

———. "Talk of Heroes." In *The Vintage Book of Contemporary American Short Stories*, edited by Tobias Wolff, 48–68. New York: Vintage, 1994.

Böll, Heinrich. "Candles for the Madonna." In *The Substance of Things Hoped For: Short Fiction by Modern Catholic Authors*, edited by John B. Breslin, SJ, 197–207. Garden City, NY: Doubleday, 1987.

Boyle, T. Coraghessan. "The Devil and Irv Cherniske." In *The Best American Catholic Short Stories*, edited by Daniel McVeigh and Patricia Schnapp, 239–51. Lanham, MD: Rowman and Littlefield, 2007.

Brown, Mary Ward. "A New Life." In *God: Stories*, edited by C. Michael Curtis, 22–34. Boston: Houghton Mifflin, 1998.

Butler, Robert Olen. "Mr. Green." In *A Celestial Omnibus*, edited by J. P. Maney and Tom Hazuka, 40–48. Boston: Beacon, 1997.

Callaghan, Morley. "Absolution." In *The Substance of Things Hoped For: Short Fiction by Modern Catholic Authors*, edited by John B. Breslin, SJ, 293–97. Garden City, NY: Doubleday, 1987.

Carver, Raymond. "Cathedral." In *You've Got to Read This*, edited by Ron Hansen and Jim Shepard, 138–49. New York: HarperCollins, 1994.

———. "A Small, Good Thing." In *Cathedral: Stories*, 59–89. New York: Vintage, 1984.

———. "Where I'm Calling From." In *The Best American Short Stories of the Century*, edited by John Updike, 581–94. Boston: Houghton Mifflin, 1999.

Cheever, John. "The Lowboy." In *The Stories of John Cheever*, 404–12. New York: Vintage, 2000.

———. "The Sutton Place Story." In *The Stories of John Cheever*, 65–78. New York: Vintage, 2000.

———. "The Swimmer." In *The Stories of John Cheever*, 603–12. New York: Vintage, 2000.

Dark, Alice Elliott. "In the Gloaming." In *The Best American Short Stories of the Century*, edited by John Updike, 688–704. Boston: Houghton Mifflin, 1999.

Dinesen, Isak. "Babette's Feast." In *Babette's Feast and Other Anecdotes of Destiny*, 3–48. New York: Vintage, 1988.

Drury, David. "Things We Knew When the House Caught Fire." In *The Best Christian Short Stories*, edited by Bret Lott, 49–73. Nashville: WestBow, 2006.

Dubus, Andre. "A Father's Story." In *God: Stories*, edited by C. Michael Curtis, 35–54. Boston: Houghton Mifflin, 1998.

Englander, Nathan. "Free Fruit for Young Widows." In *The Best American Short Stories: 2011*, edited by Geraldine Brooks, 74–86. New York: Houghton Mifflin, 2011.

Gautreaux, Tim. "Deputy Sid's Gift." In *Same Place, Same Things*, 195–208. New York: Picador, 1996.

———. "Good for the Soul." In *Welding with Children*, 39–59. New York: Picador, 1999.

———. "People on the Empty Road." In *Same Place, Same Things*, 87–108. New York: Picador, 1996.

———. "The Piano Tuner." In *Welding with Children*, 79–102. New York: Picador, 1999.

———. "Returnings." In *Same Place, Same Things*, 183–94. New York: Picador, 1996.

———. "Waiting for the Evening News." In *Same Place, Same Things*, 19–36. New York: Picador, 1996.

———. "Welding with Children." In *Welding with Children*, 1–19. New York: Picador, 1999.

Godin, Alexander. "My Dead Brother Comes to America." In *The Best American Short Stories of the Century*, edited by John Updike, 153–58. Boston: Houghton Mifflin, 1999.

Godwin, Gail. "An Intermediate Stop." In *Listening for God: Contemporary Literature and the Life of Faith*, vol. 2, edited by Paula J. Carson and Peter S. Hawkins, 105–19. Minneapolis: Augsburg Fortress, 1996.

Greene, Graham. "The Second Death." In *Christian Short Stories: An Anthology*, edited by Mark Booth, 168–72. New York: Crossroad, 1984.

Hawthorne, Nathaniel. "The Minister's Black Veil." In *50 Great Stories*, edited by Milton Crane, 486–500. New York: Bantam Dell, 1952.

———. "Young Goodman Brown." In *Faith: Stories*, edited by C. Michael Curtis, 38–50. Boston: Houghton Mifflin, 2003.

Helprin, Mark. "The Pacific." In *The Pacific and Other Stories*, 353–66. New York: Penguin, 1982.

———. "Vandevere's House." In *The Pacific and Other Stories*, 103–14. New York: Penguin, 1982.

Henry, O. "The Gift of the Magi." In *Great American Short Stories*, edited by Corinne Demas, 331–36. New York: Barnes and Noble, 2004.

Hoffman, William. "The Question of Rain." In *God: Stories*, edited by C. Michael Curtis, 95–107. Boston: Houghton Mifflin, 1998.

Horrocks, Caitlin. "The Sleep." In *The Best American Short Stories: 2011*, edited by Geraldine Brooks, 104–18. New York: Houghton Mifflin, 2011.

Jackson, Shirley. "The Lottery." In *The Art of the Short Story*, edited by Dana Gioia and R. S. Gwynn, 390–96. New York: Pearson, 2006.

Jones, Thom. "The Pugilist at Rest." In *The New Granta Book of the American Short Story*, edited by Richard Ford, 285–302. London: Granta, 2007.

Kemper, Marjorie. "God's Goodness." In *Faith: Stories*, edited by C. Michael Curtis, 51–66. Boston: Houghton Mifflin, 2003.

Kincaid, Jamaica. "Girl." In *You've Got to Read This*, edited by Ron Hansen and Jim Shepard, 346–47. New York: HarperCollins, 1994.

King, Stephen. "The Man in the Black Suit." In *A Celestial Omnibus*, edited by J. P. Maney and Tom Hazuka, 251–71. Boston: Beacon, 1997.

Kunkel, Jeff. "Doing Sixty." *Christian Century*, October 21, 1998, 971–74.

Le Guin, Ursula K. "The Ones Who Walk Away from Omelas." In *The Norton Anthology of Short Fiction*, 6th ed., edited by R. V. Cassill and Richard Bausch, 996–1000. New York: Norton, 2000.

L'Heureux, John. "The Expert on God." In *A Celestial Omnibus*, edited by J. P. Maney and Tom Hazuka, 57–60. Boston: Beacon, 1997.

López y Fuentes, Gregorio. "A Letter to God." In *Great Short Stories of the World*, edited by Reader's Digest, 188–91. Pleasantville, NY: Reader's Digest, 2000.

McGraw, Erin. "Daily Affirmations." In *The Good Life*, 101–19. Boston: Houghton Mifflin, 2004.

———. "The Penance Practicum." In *The Good Life*, 154–72. Boston: Houghton Mifflin, 2004.

———. "A Suburban Story." In *Lies of the Saints*, 22–42. San Francisco: Chronicle, 1996.

MacLaverty, Bernard. "The Beginnings of a Sin." In *The Substance of Things Hoped For: Short Fiction by Modern Catholic Authors*, edited by John B. Breslin, SJ, 3–12. Garden City, NY: Doubleday, 1987.

Malamud, Bernard. "Angel Levine." In *The Norton Anthology of Short Fiction*, 6th ed., edited by R. V. Cassill and Richard Bausch, 1056–64. New York: Norton, 2000.

Mansfield, Katherine. "The Garden Party." In *50 Great Short Stories*, edited by Milton Crane, 1–16. New York: Bantam Dell, 1952.

Márquez, Gabriel García. "A Very Old Man with Enormous Wings." In *The Art of the Short Story*, edited by Dana Gioia and R. S. Gwynn, 289–93. New York: Pearson, 2006.

Maupassant, Guy de. "The Diamond Necklace." In *Great Short Works of Guy de Maupassant*, 233–43. New York: Barnes and Noble, 1993.

Mauriac, François. "A Christmas Tale." In *The Substance of Things Hoped For: Short Fiction by Modern Catholic Authors*, edited by John B. Breslin, SJ, 20–29. Garden City, NY: Doubleday, 1987.

Maxwell, William. "What He Was Like." In *All the Days and Nights: The Collected Stories*, 309–12. London: Harvill, 1965.

Moore, Lorrie. "People Like That Are the Only People Here: Canonical Babbling in Peed Onk." In *Children Playing Before a Statue of Hercules*, edited by David Sedaris, 213–50. New York: Simon and Schuster, 2005.

Mukherjee, Bharati. "The Management of Grief." In *The New Granta Book of the American Short Story*, edited by Richard Ford, 201–16. London: Granta, 2007.

Munro, Alice. "The Bear Came Over the Mountain." In *Hateship, Friendship, Courtship, Loveship, Marriage: Stories*, 275–91. New York: Vintage, 2001.

Mysko, Madeleine. "Sisters of the Prodigal." *Christian Century*, June 1–8, 1994, 576–78.

Oates, Joyce Carol. "Where Are You Going, Where Have You Been?" In *The Vintage Book of Contemporary American Short Stories*, edited by Tobias Wolff, 347–65. New York: Vintage, 1994.

O'Brien, Tim. "The Things They Carried." In *The Best American Short Stories of the Century*, edited by John Updike, 616–32. Boston: Houghton Mifflin, 1999.

O'Connor, Flannery. "The Displaced Person." In *The Complete Stories*, 194–235. New York: Noonday, 1946.

———. "Good Country People." In *The Complete Stories*, 271–91. New York: Noonday, 1946.

———. "A Good Man Is Hard to Find." In *The Complete Stories*, 117–33. New York: Noonday, 1946.

———. "Revelation." In *The Complete Stories*, 488–509. New York: Noonday, 1946.

———. "The River." In *The Complete Stories*, 157–74. New York: Noonday, 1946.

———. "A Temple of the Holy Ghost." In *The Complete Stories*, 236–48. New York: Noonday, 1946.

Payne, Peggy. "The Pure in Heart." In *God: Stories*, edited by C. Michael Curtis, 222–35. Boston: Houghton Mifflin, 1998.

Powers, J. F. "The Warm Sand." In *The Substance of Things Hoped For: Short Fiction by Modern Catholic Authors*, edited by John B. Breslin, SJ, 208–18. Garden City, NY: Doubleday, 1987.

Pritchett, V. S. "The Saint." In *50 Great Short Stories*, edited by Milton Crane, 33–46. New York: Bantam Dell, 1952.

Rash, Ron. "Burning Bright." In *Burning Bright*, 107–23. New York: HarperCollins, 2010.

Roth, Philip. "The Conversion of the Jews." In *A Celestial Omnibus*, edited by J. P. Maney and Tom Hazuka, 61–74. Boston: Beacon, 1997.

Ruffin, Paul. "Time of the Panther." In *Jesus in the Mist: Stories*, 115–31. Columbia, SC: University of South Carolina Press, 2007.

———. "When Momma Came Home for Christmas and Talmidge Quoted Frost." In *Jesus in the Mist: Stories*, 3–13. Columbia, SC: University of South Carolina Press, 2007.

Russo, Richard. "The Whore's Child." In *The Best American Catholic Short Stories*, edited by Daniel McVeigh and Patricia Schnapp, 277–90. Lanham, MD: Rowman and Littlefield, 2007.

Salinger, J. D. "De Daumier-Smith's Blue Period." In *Nine Stories*, 198–252. Boston: Little, Brown, 1948.

Saroyan, William. "Resurrection of a Life." In *The Best American Short Stories of the Century*, edited by John Updike, 159–68. Boston: Houghton Mifflin, 1999.

Silone, Ignazio. "Polikushka." In *The Substance of Things Hoped For: Short Fiction by Modern Catholic Authors*, edited by John B. Breslin, SJ, 126–34. Garden City, NY: Doubleday, 1987.

Singer, Isaac Bashevis. "Gimpel the Fool." In *A Celestial Omnibus*, edited by J. P. Maney and Tom Hazuka, 304–16. Boston: Beacon, 1997.

Smith, Lee. "Intensive Care." In *The Norton Anthology of Short Fiction*, 6th ed., edited by R. V. Cassill and Richard Bausch, 1427–45. New York: Norton, 2000.

———. "Tongues of Fire" In *The Christ-Haunted Landscape: Faith and Doubt in Southern Fiction*, edited by Susan Ketchin, 5–43. Jackson, MS: University Press of Mississippi, 1994.

Taylor, Peter. "The Decline and Fall of the Episcopal Church." In *The Oracle at Stoneleigh Court*, 223–48. New York: Alfred A. Knopf, 1993.

Tolstaya, Tatyana. "See the Other Side." In *White Walls: Collected Stories*, 397–404. New York: New York Review of Books, 2007.

Tolstoy, Leo. "How Much Land Does a Man Need?" The Literature Network. http://online-literature.com/tolstoy/2738/.

Tyler, Anne. "People Who Don't Know the Answers." In *Listening for God: Contemporary Literature and the Life of Faith*, vol. 2, edited by Paula J. Carlson and Peter S. Hawkins, 21–44. Minneapolis: Augsburg Fortress, 1996.

Updike, John. "The Astronomer." In *The Early Stories: 1953–1975*, 656–60. New York: Ballantine, 2003.

———. "Pigeon Feathers." In *A Celestial Omnibus*, edited by J. P. Maney and Tom Hazuka, 75–95. Boston: Beacon, 1997.

———. "Short Easter." In *The Afterlife and Other Stories*, 92–102. New York: Fawcett Columbine, 1994.

Walker, Alice. "Everyday Use." In *In Love and Trouble*, 47–59. Orlando: Harcourt, 1973.

———. "The Flowers." In *In Love and Trouble*, 119–20. Orlando: Harcourt, 1973.

———. "The Welcome Table." In *In Love and Trouble*, 81–87. Orlando: Harcourt, 1973.

Warren, Robert Penn. "The Circus in the Attic." In *The Circus in the Attic and Other Stories*, 3–62. New York: Harcourt, Brace and Co., 1931.

———. "A Christian Education." In *The Circus in the Attic and Other Stories*, 134–42. New York: Harcourt, Brace and Co., 1931.

————. "The Confession of Brother Grimes." In *The Circus in the Attic and Other Stories*, 170–74. New York: Harcourt, Brace and Co., 1931.

White, E. B. "The Door." In *50 Great Short Stories*, edited by Milton Crane, 348–53. New York: Bantam Dell, 1952.

————. "The Second Tree from the Corner." In *The Best American Short Stories of the Century*, edited by John Updike, 281–85. Boston: Houghton Mifflin, 1999.

Williams, Lynna. "Personal Testimony." In *Texas Bound: 19 Texas Stories*, edited by Kay Cattarulla, 191–204. Dallas: Southern Methodist University Press, 1994.

Wolff, Tobias "Bullet in the Brain." In *Our Story Begins: New and Selected Stories*, 263–70. New York: Alfred A. Knopf, 2008.

————. "In the Garden of the North American Martyrs." In *Our Story Begins: New and Selected Stories*, 3–14. New York: Alfred A. Knopf, 2008.

————. "The Rich Brother." In *Our Story Begins: New and Selected Stories*, 73–90. New York: Alfred A. Knopf, 2008.

————. "A White Bible." In *Our Story Begins: New and Selected Stories*, 287–300. New York: Alfred A. Knopf, 2008.

Yates, Richard. "Bells in the Morning." In *The Collected Stories of Richard Yates*, 399–402. New York: Picador, 2002.

Sources Consulted

Allen, O. Wesley, Jr. *The Homiletic of All Believers: A Conversational Approach.* Louisville: Westminster John Knox, 2005.

———. ed. *The Renewed Homiletic.* Minneapolis: Fortress, 2010.

Augustine, Aurelius. *On Christian Teaching.* Translated by R. P. H. Green. New York: Oxford University Press, 1997.

Balthasar, Hans Urs von. *The Scandal of the Incarnation: Irenaeus Against the Heresies.* Translated by John Saward. San Francisco: Ignatius, 1981.

Barbery, Muriel. *The Elegance of the Hedgehog.* Translated by Alison Anderson. New York: Europa Editions, 2008.

Barth, Karl. *Homiletics.* Translated by Geoffrey W. Bromiley and Donald E. Daniels. Louisville: Westminster John Knox, 1991.

Bartlett, David L. "Story and History: Narratives and Claims." *Interpretation* 45 (July 1991) 229–40.

Bass, Diana Butler. *Christianity after Religion: The End of Church and the Birth of a New Spiritual Awakening.* New York: HarperOne, 2013.

Beck, Robert R. *Nonviolent Story: Narrative Conflict Resolution in the Gospel of Mark.* Eugene, OR: Wipf and Stock, 2009.

Brueggemann, Walter. *An Introduction to the Old Testament: The Canon and Christian Imagination.* Louisville: Westminster John Knox, 2003.

Brooks, Cleanth. *The Well Wrought Urn: Studies in the Structure of Poetry.* New York: Harvest, 1947.

Burke, Kenneth. *A Rhetoric of Motives.* 2nd ed. Berkeley, CA: University of California Press, 1969.

Burroway, Janet. *Imaginative Writing: The Elements of Craft.* 3rd ed. Boston: Longman, 2010.

Buttrick, David. *Homiletic: Moves and Structures.* Philadelphia: Fortress, 1987.

Campbell, Charles L. "A Not-So-Distant Mirror: Nineteenth Century Popular Fiction and Pulpit Storytelling." *Theology Today* 51 (January 1995) 574–82.

———. *Preaching Jesus: New Directions for Homiletics in Hans Frei's Postliberal Theology.* Grand Rapids: Eerdmans, 1997.

Chekhov, Anton. In *The Art of the Short Story,* edited by Dana Gioia and R. S. Gwynn. New York: Pearson, 2006.

Craddock, Fred B. *As One without Authority.* Rev. ed. St. Louis: Chalice, 2001.

———. *Overhearing the Gospel: Preaching and Teaching the Faith to Persons Who Have Heard It All Before.* Nashville: Abingdon, 1978.

————. *Preaching.* Twenty-fifth anniversary ed. Nashville: Abingdon, 2010.

Davis, H. Grady. *Design for Preaching.* Philadelphia: Fortress, 1958.

Dillard, Annie. *The Writing Life.* New York: Harper Perennial, 1989.

Dodd, C. H. *The Parables of the Kingdom.* New York: Charles Scribner's Sons, 1961.

Dubus, Andre. "Sacraments." In *Meditations from a Movable Chair,* 85–99. New York: Alfred A. Knopf, 1998.

Florence, Anna Carter. *Preaching as Testimony.* Louisville: Westminster John Knox, 2007.

————. "Put Away Your Sword! Taking the Torture Out of the Sermon." In *What's the Matter with Preaching Today?,* edited by Mike Graves, 93–108. Louisville: Westminster John Knox, 2004.

Foster, Thomas C. *How to Read Literature Like a Professor: A Lively and Entertaining Guide to Reading between the Lines.* New York: Quill, 2003.

Gordon, T. David. *Why Johnny Can't Preach: The Media Have Shaped the Messengers.* Phillipsburg, NJ: P&R Publishing, 2009.

Graves, Mike, ed. *What's the Matter with Preaching Today?* Louisville: Westminster John Knox, 2004.

Greeley, Andrew. *The Catholic Imagination.* Berkeley: University of California Press, 2000.

Hall, Douglas John. *Confessing the Faith: Christian Theology in a North American Context.* Minneapolis: Augsburg Fortress, 1998.

Hall, Sands. *Tools of the Writer's Craft.* 2nd ed. San Francisco: Moving Fingers, 2007.

Hauerwas, Stanley. *With the Grain of the Universe.* Grand Rapids: Brazos, 2001.

Hilkert, Mary Catherine. *Naming Grace: Preaching and the Sacramental Imagination.* New York: Continuum, 1997.

Hogan, Patrick Colm. *The Mind and Its Stories: Narrative Universals and Human Emotion.* Cambridge: Cambridge University Press, 2003.

Holbert, John. "Revelation According to Jacob and Mrs. Turpin: Early Reflections on Preaching and Contemporary Literature." *Journal for Preachers* 17 (Advent 1993)11–21.

Holland, Scott. *How Do Stories Save Us? An Essay on the Question with the Theological Hermeneutics of David Tracy in View.* Louvain: Peeters, 2006.

Jensen, Richard A. *Telling the Story: Variety and Imagination in Preaching.* Minneapolis: Augsburg, 1980.

————. *Thinking in Story: Preaching in a Post-Literate Age.* Lima, OH: CSS, 1993.

Kennedy, George A. *Classical Rhetoric and Its Christian and Secular Tradition: From Ancient to Modern Times.* 2nd ed. Chapel Hill, NC: University Of North Carolina Press, 1999.

Lakoff, George. *Why You Can't Understand 21st Century Politics with an 18th Century Mind.* New York: Viking, 2008.

Lathrop, Gordon W. *Holy Things: A Liturgical Theology.* Minneapolis: Fortress, 1993.

Leitch, Thomas M. *What Stories Are: Narrative Theory and Interpretation.* University Park, PA: Pennsylvania State University Press, 1986.

Lischer, Richard. "The Limits of Story." *Interpretation* 38 (January 1984) 26–38.

Long, Thomas G. "And How Shall They Hear? The Listener in Contemporary Preaching." In *Listening to the Word: Studies in Honor of Fred B. Craddock,* edited by Gail R. O'Day and Thomas G. Long, 167–88. Nashville: Abingdon, 1993.

————. *Preaching from Memory to Hope.* Louisville: Westminster John Knox, 2009.

————. "When the Preacher Is a Teacher." *Journal for Preachers* 16 (1992) 21–27.

————. *The Witness of Preaching.* 2nd ed. Louisville: Westminster John Knox, 2005.

Lowry, Eugene L. *The Homiletical Plot: The Sermon as Narrative Art Form.* Expanded ed. Louisville: Westminster John Knox, 2001.

————. *How to Preach a Parable: Designs for Narrative Sermons.* Nashville: Abingdon, 1989.

————. "The Revolution of Sermonic Shape." In *Listening to the Word: Studies in Honor of Fred B. Craddock,* edited by Gail R. O'Day and Thomas G. Long, 93–112. Nashville: Abingdon, 1993.

McGilchrist, Iaian. *The Master and His Emissary: The Divided Brain and the Making of the Western World.* New Haven: Yale University Press, 2009.

McGill, Arthur C. *The Celebration of Flesh: Poetry in Christian Life.* Eugene, OR: Wipf and Stock, 1964.

McKenzie, Alyce M. *Novel Preaching: Tips from Top Writers on Crafting Creative Sermons.* Louisville: Westminster John Knox, 2010.

McLuhan, Marshall and Quenin Fiore. *The Medium Is the Massage.* New York: Random House, 1967.

Mitchell, Henry H. *Celebration and Experience in Preaching.* Nashville: Abingdon, 1990.

Murch, Walter. *In the Blink of an Eye: A Perspective on Film Editing.* 2nd ed. Los Angeles: Silman-James, 2001.

Nafisi, Azar. *Reading Lolita in Tehran: A Memoir in Books.* New York: Random House, 2003.

O'Banion, John D. *Reorienting Rhetoric: The Dialectic of List and Story.* University Park, PA: Pennsylvania State University, 1992.

O'Connor, Flannery. *Mystery and Manners: Occasional Prose.* London: Faber and Faber, 1972.

Oden, Thomas C., ed. *Parables of Kierkegaard.* Princeton, NJ: Princeton University Press, 1978.

Ozick, Cynthia. "And God Saw Literature, That It Was Good: Robert Alter's Vision." In *The Din in the Head,* 157–62. Boston: Houghton Mifflin, 2006.

Pagels, Elaine. *Beyond Belief: The Secret Gospel of Thomas.* New York: Random House, 2003.

Phelps, Teresa Godwin. *Shattered Voices: Language, Violence, and the Work of Truth.* Philadelphia: University of Pennsylvania Press, 2004.

Poe, Edgar Allan. "Review of 'Twice-Told Tales.'" In *Great American Short Stories: From Hawthorne to Hemingway,* edited by Corinne Demas, vii. New York: Barnes and Noble Classics, 2004.

Postman, Neil. *Amusing Ourselves to Death: Public Discourse in the Age of Show Business.* New York: Penguin, 1985.

Powell, Mark Allan. *Chasing the Eastern Star: Adventures in Biblical Reader-Response Criticism.* Louisville: Westminster John Knox, 2001.

Prothero, Stephen. *Religious Literacy: What Every American Needs to Know and Doesn't.* New York: HarperOne, 2007.

Ramsey, G. Lee, Jr. *Preachers and Misfits, Prophets and Thieves: The Minister in Southern Fiction.* Louisville: Westminster John Knox, 2008.

Resner, André, Jr. *Preacher and Cross: Person and Message in Theology and Rhetoric.* Grand Rapids: Eerdmans, 1999.

Reynolds, David S. "From Doctrine to Narrative: The Rise of Pulpit Storytelling in America." *American Quarterly* 32 (Winter 1980) 479–98.

Rice, Charles L. *Interpretation and Imagination: The Preacher and Contemporary Literature.* Philadelphia: Fortress, 1970.

Robinson, Wayne Bradley, ed. *Journeys toward Narrative Preaching.* New York: Pilgrim, 1990.

Rosenblatt, Roger. *Unless It Moves the Human Heart: The Craft and Art of Writing.* New York: HarperCollins, 2011.

Runia, Klaas. "What Is Preaching according to the New Testament?" *Tyndale Bulletin* 29 (1978) 3–48.

Scott, A. O. "Brevity's Pull: In Praise of the American Short Story." *New York Times,* April 5, 2009.

Shoop, Marcia W. Mount. *Let the Bones Dance: Embodiment and the Body of Christ.* Louisville: Westminster John Knox, 2010.

Smith, James K. A. *Desiring the Kingdom: Worship, Worldview, and Cultural Formation.* Grand Rapids: Baker Academic, 2009.

Stendahl, Krister. *Meanings: The Bible as Document and as Guide.* 2nd ed. Minneapolis: Fortress, 2008.

Steimle, Edmund A., Morris J. Niedenthal, and Charles L. Rice. *Preaching the Story.* Philadelphia: Fortress, 1980.

Strawson, Galen. "Against Narrativity." *Ratio* 17 (December 2004) 428–52.

Taylor, Barbara Brown. *An Altar in the World: A Geography of Faith.* New York: HarperOne, 2009.

Thomas, Frank A. *They Like to Never Quit Praisin' God: The Role of Celebration in Preaching.* Cleveland: Pilgrim, 1997.

Tillich, Paul. *The Protestant Era.* Chicago: University of Chicago Press, 1948.

———. *The Shaking of the Foundations.* New York: Scribner's, 1948.

———. *Theology of Culture.* New York: Oxford University Press, 1959.

Troeger, Thomas H. *Imagining a Sermon.* Nashville: Abingdon, 1990.

Turner, Mark. *The Literary Mind: The Origins of Thought and Language.* New York: Oxford University Press, 1995.

Wilder, Amos N. *Early Christian Rhetoric: The Language of the Gospel.* Cambridge, MA: Harvard University Press, 1971.

Willimon, William H. *Conversations with Barth on Preaching.* Nashville: Abingdon, 2006.

———. "Preaching: Entertainment or Exposition?" *Christian Century,* February 28, 1990, 204–6.

Wilson, Paul Scott. *The Four Pages of the Sermon: A Guide to Biblical Preaching.* Nashville: Abingdon, 1999.

———. *Imagination of the Heart: New Understandings in Preaching.* Nashville: Abingdon, 1988.

Made in the USA
Lexington, KY
17 March 2015